Contributions to Political Science

The series Contributions to Political Science contains publications in all areas of political science, such as public policy and administration, political economy, comparative politics, European politics and European integration, electoral systems and voting behavior, international relations and others. Publications are primarily monographs and multiple author works containing new research results, but conference and congress reports are also considered. The series covers both theoretical and empirical aspects and is addressed to researchers and policy makers.

More information about this series at https://link.springer.com/bookseries/11829

Dimitrios Souliotis

The European Parliament in the News

A Critical Analysis of the Coverage in the United Kingdom and Greece

 Springer

Dimitrios Souliotis
Journalism Studies and Communication Applications Lab,
Department of Communication and Media Studies,
The National and Kapodistrian University
of Athens
Athens, Greece

ISSN 2198-7289   ISSN 2198-7297 (electronic)
Contributions to Political Science
ISBN 978-3-030-93811-6   ISBN 978-3-030-93809-3 (eBook)
https://doi.org/10.1007/978-3-030-93809-3

© The Editor(s) (if applicable) and The Author(s), under exclusive license to Springer Nature Switzerland AG 2022

This work is subject to copyright. All rights are solely and exclusively licensed by the Publisher, whether the whole or part of the material is concerned, specifically the rights of translation, reprinting, reuse of illustrations, recitation, broadcasting, reproduction on microfilms or in any other physical way, and transmission or information storage and retrieval, electronic adaptation, computer software, or by similar or dissimilar methodology now known or hereafter developed.

The use of general descriptive names, registered names, trademarks, service marks, etc. in this publication does not imply, even in the absence of a specific statement, that such names are exempt from the relevant protective laws and regulations and therefore free for general use.

The publisher, the authors and the editors are safe to assume that the advice and information in this book are believed to be true and accurate at the date of publication. Neither the publisher nor the authors or the editors give a warranty, expressed or implied, with respect to the material contained herein or for any errors or omissions that may have been made. The publisher remains neutral with regard to jurisdictional claims in published maps and institutional affiliations.

This Springer imprint is published by the registered company Springer Nature Switzerland AG
The registered company address is: Gewerbestrasse 11, 6330 Cham, Switzerland

To my parents, Konstantinos and Margarita, and my brother Stefanos.

To Manto, for her love, encouragement, and being an inspiration to me.

Acknowledgements

This book is based on the research conducted in the framework of the project "The Identification and Critical Analysis of Potential Ways of Communicating Europe's Parliament to its Citizens More Effectively" at the University of Central Lancashire.

I would like to thank the journalists and the officers at the European Parliament Liaison Offices in Greece and the UK, who kindly agreed to be interviewed and provided valuable input for the book.

I am also grateful to the anonymous reviewer appointed by the publisher for the comments provided to the initial version of the text.

Last, but definitely not least, I wish to thank Niko Chtouris and Parthiban Gujilan Kannan at Springer for their patience, understanding, and support.

Any weaknesses and errors in the text are mine alone.

Contents

1	**Introduction**		1
	1.1	The Setting and the Intellectual Rationale of the Book	1
	References		5
2	**The European Parliament**		7
	2.1	The European Parliament in the EU Context	7
		2.1.1 Brief History of the European Parliament and Its Empowerment	7
		2.1.2 The Current Institutional Powers of the European Parliament	15
		2.1.3 Internal Organization and Operation of the European Parliament	17
	References		18
3	**European Parliament's Legitimacy: Conceptualization and Empirical Assessment**		21
	3.1	Legitimacy in Political Theory and in Social Sciences	21
		3.1.1 The Approach of Legitimacy in Normative Political Theory	22
		3.1.2 The Approach of Legitimacy in the Political and Social Sciences	24
	3.2	Legitimacy Beyond the Nation-State	26
	3.3	Legitimacy in the Context of the EU	27
	3.4	The Perceived Performance of the EP as Determinant of Popular Legitimacy	31
	3.5	Trust Towards a Political Institution as a Determinant of Legitimacy	33
	3.6	Electoral Turnout and the Feeling for the Impact of Vote as a Determinant of Legitimacy of the EP	34
	3.7	Empirical Data for Assessing the Social Legitimacy of the EP in the UK and Greece	35

		3.7.1	Declining Trust in the European Parliament	35
		3.7.2	European Parliament Perceived as an Inefficient Institution	40
		3.7.3	Electoral Turnout in the European Parliament Elections	45
		3.7.4	Dissatisfaction with the European Parliament and Belief that European Parliament Vote Has No Consequences	47
		3.7.5	Concluding Remarks	48
	References			49
4	**European Parliament and the News Media**			53
	4.1	The Role of the News Media in Shaping Public Perceptions Towards the EP		53
	4.2	Characteristics of the Media Coverage		56
	4.3	The EU and the EP Affairs in the UK News Media		57
	4.4	The EU and EP Affairs in the Greek News Media		58
	4.5	Communication Deficit of the EU and Its Institutions		59
	4.6	EP Information, Communication, and Media Relations Competences		61
	4.7	EU Media Relations		69
	4.8	Online News Media and Online News Journalists		71
		4.8.1	The Online News Media Context and the Unique Characteristics of the Online News Media Environment (Hyperlinks and Multimedia)	72
		4.8.2	The Use of Hyperlinks and Multimedia in Online Journalism	73
		4.8.3	Online Coverage of the European Parliament	74
		4.8.4	Online News Journalism	75
		4.8.5	Conclusion	76
	References			76
5	**Content Analysis and Semi-Structured Interviews as Assessment Tools**			85
	5.1	Use of Content Analysis for Examining the Coverage of the EP in News Websites in the UK and Greece		85
		5.1.1	Defining the Research Problem	86
		5.1.2	Review of Relevant Literature and Research	86
		5.1.3	Selection of the Media Sample	86
		5.1.4	Defining Analytical Categories	90
		5.1.5	Constructing a Coding Schedule and Protocol	92
		5.1.6	Piloting the Coding Schedule and Checking Reliability	92
		5.1.7	Data Preparation and Analysis	93

		5.2	Use of Semi-Structured Interviews	93
			5.2.1 Building the Set of Themes and Questions	94
			5.2.2 Sampling of the Online Journalists	95
			5.2.3 Sampling of the EPLO Officers	97
			5.2.4 Data Analysis	97
		References		98
6	**European Parliament's Media Coverage in the News Websites**			101
	6.1	European Parliament's Media Coverage in the Selected News Websites in Greece		101
		6.1.1	The Visibility of the European Parliament's Institutional Powers in Greece	101
		6.1.2	The Tone Towards the EP (or any Equivalent)	104
		6.1.3	The Visibility and the Patterns of Visibility of the European Parliament's Output	104
		6.1.4	The Tone of the Coverage of the European Parliament's Powers Output	105
		6.1.5	The Existence of Additional Internet-Facilitated Information Provided in the Coverage of the EP	107
		6.1.6	Conclusions from the Examination of the EP Media Coverage in the Selected Greek News Websites	111
	6.2	European Parliament's Media Coverage in the Selected News Websites in the UK		112
		6.2.1	The Visibility of the European Parliament's Institutional Powers in the UK	112
		6.2.2	The Tone Towards the EP (or any Equivalent)	114
		6.2.3	The Visibility and the Patterns of Visibility of the European Parliament's Output	116
		6.2.4	The Tone of the Coverage of the European Parliament's Powers Output	117
		6.2.5	The Existence of Additional Internet-Facilitated Information Provided in the Coverage of the EP	117
		6.2.6	Conclusions from the Examination of the EP Media Coverage in the Selected UK News Websites	124
	6.3	Conclusions for the Greek and the UK Case		125
	References			127
7	**Assessment of the Media Relations Performance of the EPLOs**			129
	7.1	Assessment of the Media Relations Performance of the EPLO in Greece		130
		7.1.1	The Extent to which the EPLO's Communication Material Either in Written or in Oral Form Fits Online Journalist's Needs and Expectations	130

	7.1.2	The Extent to which the EPLO's Media Relations Activities Facilitate Online Journalists' Work when Producing EP News Stories....................	132
	7.1.3	The Extent to which the EPLO Implements an Adequate "Source Strategy"...................	133
	7.1.4	The Extent to which the EPLO Media Relations Activities Take into Consideration the Changes in the Journalistic Practices of the Online Journalists.......	134
	7.1.5	Conclusions of the Assessment of the EPLO Media Relations Performance in Greece................	136
7.2	Assessment of the Media Relations Performance of the EPLO in the UK.......................................		137
	7.2.1	The Extent to which the EP Communication Material Either in Written or Oral Form Fits Online Journalist's Needs and Expectations......................	137
	7.2.2	The Extent to which the EPLO's Media Relations Activities Facilitate Online Journalists' Work when Producing EP News Stories....................	138
	7.2.3	The Extent to which the EPLO Implements an Adequate "Source Strategy"....................	138
	7.2.4	The Extent to which the EPLO Media Relations Activities Take into Consideration the Changes in the Journalistic Practices of the Online Journalists.......	139
	7.2.5	Conclusions of the Assessment of the EPLO Media Relations Performance in the UK...............	140
7.3	Conclusions Concerning the Assessment of the EPLO's Media Relations Performance in Greece and in the UK.......		141
References..			143

8 Identification and Critical Analysis of the Problems in the Online Media Coverage and Media Relations Performance of the EP in Greece and in the UK.................................. 145

8.1	Lack of Collective Representation or Voice for the EP in the Media and Co-Existence of Different News Management Policies Between the EP and the MEPs..................	145
8.2	Not Newsworthy Information Provided by the EP/EPLOs.....	148
8.3	Inefficient Source Strategy by the EPLOs..................	150
8.4	Communication Strategy Not Taking into Consideration Online Journalists' Needs...........................	151
8.5	Problems Related to the Operation: Function of the EPLOs....	151
8.6	Conclusion......................................	152
References..		153

9 Identification of Potential Ways of Communicating the EP more Effectively in Greece and in the UK ... 155
- 9.1 Greece ... 155
- 9.2 UK ... 160
- 9.3 Conclusions Concerning the Identification of Potential Ways of Communicating the EP more Effectively in Greece and in the UK ... 164
  - 9.3.1 In the Case of Greece ... 164
  - 9.3.2 In the Case of the UK ... 165
- References ... 166

10 Critical Analysis of the Potential Ways of Communicating the EP More Efficiently ... 169
- 10.1 The EP as a More Effective Communicator ... 169
  - 10.1.1 An Institution with a Communication Strategy Customized for News Websites ... 169
  - 10.1.2 An Institution that Applies (Via the EPLOs) a More Aggressive Source Strategy towards Online Journalists ... 170
  - 10.1.3 An Institution that Does More to Facilitate Contacts Between Online Journalists and MEPs or High-Profile EP Executives ... 170
  - 10.1.4 An Institution that Provides Information Customized for Domestic Audiences ... 170
  - 10.1.5 An Institution with the EPLO Website Structured in an Online Newsroom Format ... 171
  - 10.1.6 Conclusion ... 171
- 10.2 Barriers in the Way of the EP Becoming a More Effective Communicator ... 172
  - 10.2.1 Institutional Mind-Sets ... 172
  - 10.2.2 Barriers Deriving from Institutional Characteristics ... 173
  - 10.2.3 Resource Limitations ... 174
  - 10.2.4 The Competition from Non-Media-Related Tasks in the Daily Routine of EPLO Officials ... 174
  - 10.2.5 Insufficient Media and Public Relations Training of the EPLO Officers ... 174
  - 10.2.6 Barriers Deriving from the Political Nature of the European Parliament ... 175
- 10.3 Filtering the Various Possibilities for Reform ... 176
- References ... 178

11 Overall Conclusion ... 179

Appendix A 183
    Questions Asked in the Semi-Structured Interviews with Online
    Journalists in the UK and Greece 183

Appendix B 187
    Questions for Semi-Structured Interviews with Officers in EPLO's 187

About the Author

Dimitrios Souliotis is a public communication expert. He has worked at the Greek Public Administration and the European Commission. He has teaching experience in the University of Central Lancashire, the University of Patras, the Greek National School of Public Administration and Local Government, and the Training Institute for Public Administration. His professional and academic interests focus on mass media, public relations, and government communication. He has participated in several academic international conferences, and he has published relevant articles. He is currently Research Fellow at the Journalism Studies and Communication Applications Lab, in the Department of Communication and Media Studies, at the National and Kapodistrian University of Athens.

Chapter 1
Introduction

1.1 The Setting and the Intellectual Rationale of the Book

Almost 70 years since its establishment, the European Union (EU) is still confronted with the deep problem of the perceived gap between the EU institutions and the EU citizens. Relevant research shows that the majority of the Europeans do not trust the EU (European Commission, 2021; Pew Research Center, 2012; 2013; Inglehart et al., 2014) and they think of it as an inefficient institution that does not listen to them and does not understand their needs (Wike et al., 2019; Pew Research Center, 2014; Manchin, 2014). In addition, a large percentage of the EU citizens express their dissatisfaction with the way by which democracy works in the EU (European Parliament, 2018) while among the most popular reasons for abstention from the 2009, 2014, and 2019 European Parliament (EP) elections was the feeling of the EU citizens that their vote has no consequences and does not change anything (European Parliament, 2012, 2014, 2018). The steadily growing support for Eurosceptic and far right parties across member states (e.g. Italy, Germany, Austria, the Netherlands) (Oltermann, 2017; Mudde, 2017a, b; Henley & Malkin, 2017), the desire of citizens in different EU member states to have their voice heard through referendums on their own EU membership and their desire to have some of the EU key powers returned back to their national governments (Stokes, 2016; Pew Research Center, 2017) are also some of the facts that indicate the gap between the EU and its citizens.

This popular frustration towards the EU is also evident in the distrust levels and negative feelings regarding the EU's separate institutions, for example, the European Commission and the European Parliament. Trust in these institutions has been declining. In autumn 2012 and autumn 2013, these trust levels have reached record lows (European Commission, 2013a, b, c)—while nowadays Europeans remain significantly divided on trusting them (European Commission, 2020).

All the aforementioned negative feelings and attitudes have raised concerns and doubts about the legitimacy of the EU and its institutions; in other words, they have raised concerns regarding the justification of the right of the EU and its institutions to hold the power to make decisions that affect the everyday life of EU citizens.

The majority of scholars support that the EU legitimacy inadequacies are due mainly to (a) the "undemocratic" character of the EU governance and decision-making process and (b) the lack of support, trust, and recognition by the citizens towards the EU and its institutions. From this "recognition" point of view, this legitimacy deficit is considered, inter alia, a communication deficit; meaning that there is lack, both quantitative and qualitative, of adequate information—concerning the EU and its institutions—in the news media and in the national public spheres of the member states. Consequently, this lack of adequate EU information in the news media is considered a result of the inefficient EU communication and media relations performance which has been identified as one of the factors, among others, that affects the media coverage of the EU and its institutions, and thus enhances the relevant EU communication deficit.

However, in the relevant literature, little attention has been paid to the institution of the European Parliament per se, despite the fact that: (a) the European Parliament is the only directly elected institution of the EU, (b) the EP's increasing institutional powers, especially after the Lisbon Treaty, have made it nowadays a co-legislator along with the Commission and the Council, and (c) throughout EU history the EP has always been seen as the institution that gave public justification and moral authority to the EU.

Based on the aforementioned and considering that in order to improve the social legitimacy (the legitimacy from the "recognition" point of view) deficit of the European Parliament, one should face the relevant communication deficit by addressing the inadequacies of the communication and media relations performance, this book aims to identify and critically analyse the problems that the EP faces in communicating itself to the news media. Then, after having detected and explained these problems, potential solutions are proposed and discussed in order for the EP to overcome these problems and to improve its communication and, consequently, its social legitimacy deficit.

The empirical data which is used for the analysis and the assessment of the EP social legitimacy deficit covers the time period 2011–2013. This is the period when record low levels of EU citizens' trust and satisfaction, regarding the EP, have been observed, and that is why these data will serve as relevant indicators that will help us to propose and suggest potential solutions for the improvement of the social legitimacy deficit of the EP. In addition, since the aforementioned record low levels of the EU citizens' perceptions regarding the EP have been observed mainly in the United Kingdom and in Greece—for example, the highest levels of distrust and dissatisfaction towards the EP have been observed in these countries—the analysis will focus on these two EU member states (the United Kingdom was still an EU member state during the period under analysis) as case studies.

Following the above rationale, the study assesses empirically whether the EP faces a social legitimacy deficit in the UK and Greece. After the in-depth examination of the concept of legitimacy in the political theory and political and social sciences, selected empirical data serve as key indicators in order to investigate

1.1 The Setting and the Intellectual Rationale of the Book

whether the EP faces a social (popular) legitimacy deficit in the UK and Greece. The analysis proceeds by examining the news media coverage of the institutional powers of the EP in the specific countries, while taking into consideration the fact that the visibility of the impact of the EP's institutional powers is also a crucial element for the enhancement of its popular legitimacy. The way by which the output of EP is covered in the UK and Greece is also examined. Taking into consideration the fact that there is an increasing use of the Internet, in the EU as a source for obtaining information on European political matters and the European Parliament, the examination of the coverage of the European Parliament's institutional powers and their output—along with the identification and the analysis of the communication and media relations problems—will focus on selected news websites in these countries.

The crucial role of the European Parliament Liaison Offices (EPLOs) (the former European Parliament Information Offices—EPIOs) in delivering EP message to the news media of the member states is also taken into account; for the scope of the analysis, the examination focuses on the EPLOs in the UK and Greece and their media relations performance specifically towards news websites.

In short, the book sets out to examine: (1) issues of legitimacy of the EP in the UK and Greece, with a focus on social legitimacy (legitimacy which is mainly linked to the perceptions of citizens for the EP), (2) issues of media coverage of the EP's institutional powers and output in selected news websites in the UK and Greece, (3) issues of communication and media relation activities of the EP specifically towards news websites journalists in the UK and Greece, and (4) issues regarding the role of the EPLOS in the EP communication activities in the two countries.

Based on the examination of the aforementioned issues, the book identifies and critically discusses (a) the problems that the EP faces in communicating, via news websites, with the citizens in the UK and Greece and (b) potential ways to address these problems.

Against this background, the main questions to be addressed are the following:

RQ1: What is the coverage of the European Parliament's institutional powers and their output in selected news websites in the UK and Greece?

RQ2: What are the problems that the EP faces in communicating its institutional powers and their output to the selected news websites in the UK and Greece?

RQ3: What solutions could be proposed to the EP to enhance its communication performance in relation to the news websites of the UK and Greece and which of these solutions could be applied with some potential for success?

In short, this book aims to shed light on the EP social legitimacy deficit by addressing the communication and media relations inadequacies of the EP and by suggesting some potential solutions for them. Under this approach, it is argued that if the EP overcomes some of the problems that is facing in its communication and media relations performance, it will have greater chances to enhance its social legitimacy.

In addition, the book provides an initial comparison of the scale of the EP's task in two of the most "difficult" states as far as the communication of its messages is concerned (specifically for the case of the UK, the 2016 Brexit referendum and the relevant withdrawal agreement come to confirm, among others, the relevant communication difficulties of the EP) while it also tries to form a foundation upon which other studies can build similar comparisons of the EP's communication performance problems (and possible solutions) in other EU member states. These issues have not been adequately addressed in the relevant literature; thus, the present study aspires at making a significant contribution in the field of EU communication.

The structure of the book on a chapter-to-chapter basis is the following:

Chapter 2 provides a brief history of the European Parliament and its empowerment, its current institutional powers and its internal organization and operation.

Chapter 3 presents the concept of legitimacy, as it has been explored in political theory (normative approach) and the political and social sciences, respectively (empirical and descriptive approach). Given that legitimacy has been, till recently, mainly conceptualized in the framework of the nation-states, the chapter proceeds with the examination of the issue of legitimacy at the EU level. It explains how this concept has been approached, and it examines the debate on the EU democratic and legitimacy deficit. With a focus on social legitimacy, a selection of empirical data is made in order to assess the popular legitimacy of the EP in the UK and Greece.

Chapter 4 starts with the examination of the role of the news media in shaping public perceptions towards the EU and its institutions by analyzing the characteristics of the relevant media coverage. Then, it focuses on the communication deficit of the EU and its institutions, which is directly linked to the their social legitimacy deficit, and it examines the factors that contribute to this deficit, the communication and media relations performance of these institutions, and the way by which journalists produce EU news stories.

Specific emphasis is placed on the EP and the role of the EPLOs in delivering the EP information in the news media and the audience in the member states. Last but not least, issues relevant to online journalism (for example, specific features of online journalism and digital news production) are also discussed.

Chapter 5 outlines the key dimensions of the methodological approach that is used in the present study. The first section focuses on content analysis, while the second one explains how semi-structured interviews have been used as a tool to fill in some of the gaps in understanding the media coverage of the EP, gaps that an application of content analysis on its own would leave. The selected research methods contribute to the examination and analysis of (a) the way by which the EP is covered in the selected news websites in the UK and Greece, (b) the problems that the EP is facing in communicating itself in the selected news websites in the UK and Greece, and (c) the potential solutions for the EP in order to overcome these problems.

Chapter 6 presents the research findings from the analysis of the EP coverage in selected news websites in the UK and Greece, regarding the visibility of the European Parliament's institutional powers, the tone towards the EP (or any equivalent) and its institutional powers, the visibility and the patterns of visibility of the European Parliament's output, the tone of the coverage of the European Parliament's powers output, and the extent to which there is additional Internet facilitated information provided in the coverage of the EP (hyperlinks, audiovisual material) in both countries.

Chapter 7 presents the research findings from the semi-structured interviews that have been conducted with online news journalists in the UK and Greece, regarding the assessment of the communication and media relations performance of the European Parliament Liaison Offices (EPLOs) in Greece and in the UK. The assessment focuses on: the extent to which the EPLO's communication material either in written or in oral form fits online journalist's needs and expectations, the extent to which the EPLO's media relations activities facilitate online journalists' work when producing EP news stories, the extent to which the EPLO implements an adequate "source strategy" towards journalists, and the extent to which the EPLO media relations activities overall take into consideration the changes in the journalistic practices of the online journalists.

Chapter 8 provides a synthesis of the research findings of the examination of the EP online media coverage in the selected news websites in the UK and Greece and presents the results of the assessment of the EPLOs' media relations performance. This evidence helps to identify and critically analyse the reasons behind the observed problems in both the EP online media coverage and the EPLOs' media relations performance.

Chapter 9 presents a set of potential solutions for overcoming the problems of low visibility of the EP institutional powers and output. The identification of the suggested solutions has been based on: (a) elements of the research findings of the content analysis, (b) the working routines of the online journalists along with what the online journalists have said that they actually would want from the EPLOs, and the (c) the working routines of the EPLO officers in the UK and Greece.

Chapter 10 considers some practical problems that might arise in the implementation of the proposed solutions, together with an assessment of their prospects of success. The prerequisites for the EP to become a much more effective communicator with the selected news sites—and to achieve a much higher degree of visibility within them, are presented here along with an analysis of the barriers which may stand in the way of the EP being an effective communicator, an analysis of the various possibilities for reform, and an examination of which of them come out at the end as having a potential for working in the "real" as opposed to the "ideal" world.

Chapter 11 presents a brief summary of the findings, along with a critical discussion and the final conclusions of the book.

References

European Commission. (2013a). *Standard Eurobarometer 78*. DG Communication. https://europa.eu/eurobarometer/surveys/detail/1069

European Commission. (2013b). *Standard Eurobarometer 79*. DG Communication. https://europa.eu/eurobarometer/surveys/detail/1120

European Commission. (2013c). *Standard Eurobarometer 80*. DG Communication. https://europa.eu/eurobarometer/surveys/detail/1123

European Commission. (2020). *Standard Eurobarometer 93*. DG Communication. https://europa.eu/eurobarometer/surveys/detail/2262

European Commission. (2021). *Standard Eurobarometer 94*. DG Communication. https://europa.eu/eurobarometer/surveys/detail/2355

European Parliament. (2012). *2009 European elections desk research*. DG Communication. https://www.europarl.europa.eu/cyprus/resource/static/files/2012-11-13-desk-research-abstention-principaux-enseignements-en.pdf

European Parliament. (2014). *European elections 2014, post-election survey*. DG Communication. https://www.europarl.europa.eu/at-your-service/files/be-heard/eurobarometer/2014/post-election-survey-2014/analytical-synthesis/en-analytical-synthesis-post-election-survey-2014.pdf

European Parliament. (2018). *Democracy on the move: European Elections-one year to go. Eurobarometer Survey 89.2*. DG Communication. https://www.europarl.europa.eu/at-your-service/files/be-heard/eurobarometer/2018/eurobarometer-2018-democracy-on-the-move/report/en-one-year-before-2019-eurobarometer-report.pdf

Henley, J., & Malkin, B. (2017, May 19). Macron beats Le Pen in French presidential election – as it happened. *The Guardian*. https://www.theguardian.com/world/live/2017/may/07/french-presidential-election-emmanuel-macron-marine-le-pen

Inglehart, R., Haerpfer, C., Moreno, A., Welzel, C., Kizilova, K., Diez-Medrano, J., Lagos, M., Norris, P., Ponarin, E., & Puranen, B. et al. (eds.). (2014). *World values survey: Round six - country-pooled datafile version:* www.worldvaluessurvey.org/WVSDocumentationWV6.jsp. Madrid: JD Systems Institute.

Manchin, A. (2014, January 8). *EU leadership approval at record low in Spain, Greece*. News Gallup Inc. Retrieved November 13, 2018, from: https://news.gallup.com/poll/166757/leadership-approval-record-low-spain-greece.aspx?g_source=link_NEWSV9&g_medium=&g_campaign=item_&g_content=EU%2520Leadership%2520Approval%2520at%2520Record%2520Low%2520in%2520Spain%2c%2520Greece

Mudde, C. (2017a, March 19). Good' populism beat 'bad' in Dutch election. *The Guardian*. https://www.theguardian.com/world/2017/mar/19/dutch-election-rutte-wilders-good-populism-bad

Mudde, C. (2017b, September 24). What the stunning success of AfD means for Germany and Europe. *The Guardian*. https://www.theguardian.com/commentisfree/2017/sep/24/germany-elections-afd-europe-immigration-merkel-radical-right

Oltermann, P. (2017, December 18). Muted protests in Vienna as far-right ministers enter Austria's government. *The Guardian*. https://www.theguardian.com/world/2017/dec/18/thousands-protest-as-far-right-ministers-enter-government-in-austria.

Pew Research Center. (2012). *European unity on the rocks. Greeks and Germans at polar opposites. Global Attitudes Project*. Retrieved November 13, 2018, from http://www.pewresearch.org/wp-content/uploads/sites/2/2012/05/Pew-Global-Attitudes-Project-European-Crisis-Report-FINAL-FOR-PRINT-May-29-2012.pdf

Pew Research Center. (2013). *The new sick man of Europe: The European Union*. Retrieved November 13, 2018, from http://www.pewresearch.org/wp-content/uploads/sites/2/2013/05/Pew-Research-Center-Global-Attitudes-Project-European-Union-Report-FINAL-FOR-PRINT-May-13-2013.pdf

Pew Research Center. (2014). *A fragile rebound for EU image on eve of European Parliament Elections. Number, facts and trends shaping the world*. Retrieved November 13, 2018, from http://www.pewresearch.org/wp-content/uploads/sites/2/2014/05/2014-05-12_Pew-Global-Attitudes-European-Union.pdf

Pew Research Center. (2017). *Post-Brexit, Europeans more favorable toward EU*. Retrieved December 15, 2018, from http://www.pewglobal.org/wp-content/uploads/sites/2/2017/06/Pew-Research-Center-EU-Brexit-Report-UPDATED-June-15-2017.pdf

Stokes, B. (2016) *Euroscepticism beyond Brexit: Significant opposition in key European countries to an even closer EU*. Pew Research Center. Retrieved March 15, 2020, from https://www.pewresearch.org/global/2016/06/07/euroskepticism-beyond-brexit/

Wike, R., Fetterolf, J. & Fagan, M. (2019). *Europeans Credit EU with Promoting Peace and Prosperity, but Say Brussels is out of touch with its citizens*. Pew Research Center. Retrieved March 15, 2020, from https://www.pewresearch.org/global/2019/03/19/europeans-credit-eu-with-promoting-peace-and-prosperity-but-say-brussels-is-out-of-touch-with-its-citizens/

Chapter 2
The European Parliament

This chapter provides a brief history of the European Parliament and its empowerment, its current institutional powers, and its internal organization and operation.

2.1 The European Parliament in the EU Context

The European Parliament (EP) is considered to be nowadays the most democratic institution of the European Union (EU), since its 705 members (MEPs) are being directly elected every 5 years by the EU citizens through the European Elections.

During its history, and especially in the past few decades, the EP has empowered itself from being a forum and a consultative assembly composed of delegations from national parliaments to a co-legislator, along with the EU Council, for the majority of the European law.

2.1.1 Brief History of the European Parliament and Its Empowerment

The empowerment of the EP could be seen as a continuous process during the history of EU integration, depicted in the relevant EU Treaties and Treaty amendments: a history of continuous "struggle" from the side of the EP for the acquaintance of more and more institutional powers (Corbett et al., 2011; Jones, 2011; Kreppel et al., 2002; Dedman, 1996, 2010; Duncan, 2008). In order to better understand the evolution of the role of the European Parliament, this has to be examined in parallel with the history of the EU and the evolution of the EU integration.

The European Coal and Steel Community (ECSC) Treaty (1951)

This establishment provided for the unification of the coal and steel industries of France and Germany (industries that were of major importance for the production of weapons and war equipment) and the creation of an independent authority to govern the steel and coal production of these countries. The main institutional actor in the ECSC, which included beyond France and Germany, also Italy, Luxembourg, Belgium, and the Netherlands, was the "High Authority", which was a supranational institution with significant powers and control over the production and distribution of coal and steel. In order to balance the power of this supranational "High Authority" a nationally oriented Council of Ministers was introduced while a High Court was also established in order to manage any appeals or disputes by members of the coal and steel industry. As a "tool" for the public acceptance of the new ECSC, a Common Assembly (this is how the parliament was named in the ECSC) was introduced; it was felt that the presence of a Common Assembly (CA) in the ECSC would be very crucial for the public acceptance of the new Community. However, the Common Assembly, which was a body consisting of representatives selected by the national parliaments of the member states of the ECSC, was mentioned in only 10 over the 100 articles of the ECSC Treaty (Articles 20–25, 38, 78, 94, 95); this is an indicative fact of the limited role of the CA. In addition, in terms of its powers, the CA had no legislative powers at all and had very limited supervisory powers (in the form of oral-written questions to the High Authority, or of an open discussion of a general report that was submitted to it by the High Authority, or in the form of the power to ask for the resignation of the members of the High Authority) (Corbett et al., 2011; Dedman, 1996, 2010; Duncan, 2008).

The Treaty of Rome (1957): The Creation of the European Economic Community and the Euratom Treaty

After the creation of the European Coal and Steel Community, many attempts have been made in order to expand the cooperation of the countries—members of the ECSC in new policy areas. The most successful of them led to the "Resolution Adopted at Messina by the Foreign Ministers of the Member States of the ECSC" (June 1955) which called for the six-member states of the European Coal and Steel Community to draft a new treaty with the scope of a broad European cooperation in the economic, atomic energy, and social areas. In its turn, the aforementioned resolution led to the adoption of two separate treaties: (1) the EEC Treaty which dealt with further economic integration between the member states and the creation of an internal market and (2) the Euratom Treaty which focused on atomic energy and its use, in a peaceful manner, in Europe. These two aforementioned communities joined the European Coal and Steel Community in order to form the European Communities. The High Authority remained for the ECSC; however, two new supranational commissions were created for each of the two new communities,

2.1 The European Parliament in the EU Context

with the relative intergovernmental Councils (Corbett et al., 2011; Dedman, 1996, 2010).

As far as the Common Assembly is concerned, at this point it was decided to create a single assembly for all the three communities. Thus, the previous known Common Assembly changed to an enlarged "European Parliamentary Assembly", which had some differences in comparison to the previous Common Assembly. The new treaties (the EEC Treaty and the Euratom Treaty) required the MEPs to be directly elected and they called on the EP to draft a plan for universal direct elections [(EEC Treaty Article 138(3) and Euratom Treaty Article 108(3)].

In terms of institutional power, an increase in the power of the new EP, compared to the old Common Assembly, was the fact that the EP now could censure the Commission at any time, over any issue although the previous voting requirements still applied. The new treaties also included the EP in the legislative process, by including a consultation process for some policy areas. In this way the Council was required to consult the parliament and get its opinion, although there was no requirement for the Council to follow the EP's suggestions.

This new "European Parliamentary Assembly" was a step forward compared to the previous Common Assembly. However, despite the fact that the Members of the Common Assembly had been lobbying for further increase in the powers, role, and responsibilities of the new "European Parliamentary Assembly", having in mind a European Parliament modelled after the national parliaments of the member states, the reality fell far short of this idea (Corbett et al., 2011).

In addition, the call of the Treaties of Rome for direct elections of its members (MEPs) in the member states was ignored by the Council, and in fact, there was little effort by the Council to fulfil the requirements laid down on the specific treaties during that period.

As a reaction, the EP attempted to improve its relative institutional position through increased internal organization and informal extensions of the few powers granted to it in the aforementioned treaties. It was during that time, when the parliament incorporated the party groups formally into the rules and began to use the groups as a basis of internal organization. In addition, the EP incorporated into its Rules of Procedure several institutional powers not officially granted to it by the treaties. For example, the parliament called on the President of the Commission to present an annual programme formally to the parliament to garner its approval, the parliament requested that the Council should respond to parliamentary questions and report to the EP regularly on Community activities, and it also attempted to use the consultative powers granted to it by the treaties in the most extensive way possible [e.g. since the treaties allowed the Commission to incorporate the parliament's suggestions (Article 149(2)) into its proposals, the parliament began in the early 1960s to request that the Commission do so on a regular basis] (Corbett et al., 2011).

Last but not least, the EP attempted to increase its authority and influence within the Community by publicly redefining itself, and passing a resolution (1962) to formally rename the "Assembly" of the Treaties to "European Parliament".

The Budgetary Treaties (1970) and (1975)

As a result of the budgetary treaties of 1970 and 1975, the European Parliament gained the institutional power/right to reject the Council's proposed budget and to modify the level of expenditure and approve/disapprove accounts ("discharge") (Peterson and Shackleton, 2006). The new budgetary process provided a moderate role for the European Parliament while still maintaining the dominance of the Council. The parliament had little or no control or impact over this portion of the budget. Instead, the parliament was given partial control over the remaining "non-compulsory" portions of the budget as well as the ability to increase or decrease the overall budget within certain restricted margins. The Budget Act was adopted by the Council in September 1970 and quickly ratified by all member states. The Budget Act was not to be implemented until 1975 and by then an additional set of rules and amendments were adopted that also granted the parliament the power of discharge and added a "conciliation procedure" for future bills with significant financial impact. Thus, the revised Budget Act also added the requirement that the President of the Parliament sign the budget for it to be officially adopted (Corbett et al., 2011).

The First European Elections (1979)

A cornerstone in the EP's history was the 1979 first direct European elections which were designed to give a kind of moral authority to the EP deriving from its legitimacy through direct voting by the citizens, and the greater debate on European issues, despite the fact that the legislative powers of the EP were not expanded that time (Duncan, 2008).

However, despite a great deal of active campaigning and press attention, voter turnout was generally much lower than expected, ranging from a low of 33% in Great Britain to a high of 85% in Italy, with an overall average of 63%. In all cases, turnout was significantly lower than the average turnout for national elections.

With direct elections the total membership of the EP more than doubled, growing from 198 to 410. The numerical requirements and organizational structure of the previously appointed parliament could not be maintained given this increase in membership. A far more contentious process than originally expected, an entirely new and reorganized set of Rules of Procedure was finally adopted in 1981, over 2 years after the first attempt by the previous parliament.

After the first European Parliament elections, the parliament continued to push for greater legislative authority. It was argued that the EP was the only direct representative of the people of Europe and as such should have a greater influence on the legislative output of the Community. This sentiment increased still further with the accession of three new states: Greece (1981) and Portugal and Spain (1986) that had recently suffered under totalitarian rule and were somewhat wary of a community system in which the only democratically elected body was subjugated to the legislative will of the other institutions. The new members joined in the parliament's long-standing battle for increased legislative and political authority (Corbett et al., 2011; Dedman, 1996, 2010). This long-standing battle of the EP for increased legislative and political authority led to the signing of the Single European Act (1987).

The Single European Act (1987)

The Single European Act (SEA) was signed in February 1986 and went into effect in July 1987. The SEA was important for the European Parliament in several respects. It was the first official document to recognize the EP's chosen name, which had been a bone of contention between the Council and the parliament since the latter had changed its name 25 years earlier. The SEA also granted the parliament veto power over the accession or association of new states. By far, however, the most important increase in the EP's power was the addition of the cooperation procedure for certain legislative topics, which gave the EP the power to amend legislation directly. The new legislative procedure added a second reading to the previous consultation procedure and allowed the EP to directly impact legislative outcomes through its amendments. In order to understand the increased role and impact of the EP in the legislative process, there should be a reference to the cooperation procedure, which includes seven steps: In the first stage, the Commission initiates legislation and sends it to both the EP and the Council. The parliament then (after referral to the appropriate committee) holds a first reading, during which a simple majority can adopt amendments and the proposal as a whole. After the parliament's first reading the initiative goes back to the Commission, which can revise its original proposal by adopting any or all of the EP's amendments. The Council then decides on a Common Position based on the Commission's (possibly revised) proposal. The Council can adopt the Commission's proposal by qualified majority, but unanimity is required to modify it (including any EP amendments incorporated into the Commission's revised proposal). In the fifth step, the EP is once again given the opportunity to amend the proposal in light of the Council's Common Position. By its own rules, the EP can offer amendments only if they were adopted by the EP previously (during the first reading) or if the text of the proposal had been significantly revised so as to be substantively different from what existed during the first reading. If the EP feels that its views are wholly ignored or that the proposal for whatever reason should not pass, it can, by an absolute majority of its members, reject the proposal. A rejection by the EP can only be overturned by a unanimous vote in the Council. After the EP's second reading, the previous process is repeated. The Commission reviews the proposal and decides to adopt the EP's amendments or not (with explanations) and sends the proposal to the Council. In the final stage, the Council can once again adopt the Commission's proposal by qualified majority or change it by unanimity. The decision of the Council during the second reading of the proposal is final (Peterson and Shackleton, 2006; Corbett et al., 2011; Dedman, 1996, 2010).

The Treaty of Maastricht (1992)

The Maastricht Treaty was signed in 1991, but it was not officially ratified until 1992 (because of an initial negative vote by the Danes during a national ratification referendum) and not fully implemented until November 1993. The new treaty created a new "European Union" to replace the previous European Communities. The Maastricht Treaty marked the first time that integration was pursued in political as well as economic arenas. The previous European Councils and Summits, which had always existed outside the scope of the Community and the Treaties of Rome, were incorporated into the new European Union. The Maastricht Treaty officially brought European political and defence cooperation under the same roof with economic cooperation. It also officially recognized the concept of a European citizenry for the first time, as well as the need for European political parties. On the economic front, deadlines for a European Monetary Union and a single currency were created that forced a higher level of economic coordination between the member states than ever before.

For the European Parliament, the biggest change introduced by the Maastricht Treaty was the addition of the co-decision procedure, which gave it absolute veto power in some areas of legislation. The new legislative procedure was more complicated than the cooperation procedure introduced by the SEA because of the creation of a "conciliation committee" and the possibility for a third reading. As in the consultation and cooperation procedures, the Commission was still responsible for the initiation of all proposals. The initial stages of the new procedure were similar to the old cooperation procedure. A new proposal was forwarded to the EP and the Council at the same time; the parliament made its first reading amendments after the appropriate committee had reviewed the proposal. The amended version of the bill was then forwarded to the Commission. The Commission once again could incorporate those EP amendments that it approved of and then send the (modified) proposal to the Council. The Council adopted a Common Position (qualified majority to adopt the commission proposal and unanimity to amend it). After the Council submitted its Common Position, the EP could announce its intention to reject the proposal (absolute majority), adopt the Common Position (simple majority), or amend the Common Position (absolute majority). If the EP intended to reject the proposal, the Council could call for a "Conciliation Committee", which consisted of an equal number of MEPs and Council members. If a joint proposal was agreed to, then the proposal was sent back to the floor of the EP for approval (an absolute majority being required to reject the proposal). If no accord could be reached between the Council and the EP during conciliation, then the Council could revert to its previous Common Position (modified or not). The EP could then either definitively veto the proposal (by an absolute majority of its members) or adopt it. If upon receiving the Common Position the EP merely amended it (no intention to reject), the proposal went back to the Council. The Council could then either adopt it as amended (by qualified majority) or, if it could not or would not adopt the EP's version (including all amendments), a Conciliation Committee was called and the procedure continued as described above for an intended EP rejection (Peterson and Shackleton, 2006).

Although the most important, the new co-decision procedure was not the only addition to the powers of the EP included in the Maastricht Treaty. By including foreign and security policy within the broad structure of the new European Union, the treaty gave the EP some limited authority in these areas as well. The power of assent granted to the EP in the SEA was modified by the Maastricht Treaty to include all "important" international agreements. These were defined as those with important budgetary implications, requiring a formal institutional framework, or which require the amendment of Community legislation under the co-decision procedure (Corbett et al., 2011).

In the period after the signing of the Maastricht Treaty, the European Union expanded still further, with the accession of Austria, Finland, and Sweden (in 1995).

By the end of 1996, the percentage of EP amendments adopted by the other institutions was significantly higher than had been the case under either the consultation or cooperation procedures. The Commission, despite its reduced role in the procedure as a whole, adopted a higher percentage of EP amendments under the co-decision procedure than under the cooperation procedure. Relations between the Council and the EP have continued to improve as a result of the increased contact initiated by the co-decision procedure (Judge and Earnshaw, 2003; Kreppel et al., 2002).

The Treaty of Amsterdam (1997)

Although the focus of the Amsterdam Treaty (adopted in 1997 and ratified in 1999) was not specifically on re-evaluating the powers of the European Parliament, it did increase these through a restructuring of the legislative processes. The co-decision procedure was extended to 32 "legal bases" and was simplified. More specifically, the new co-decision procedure provides for the adoption of legislation at first reading if the EP and Council agree at this stage. Second, the phase whereby the EP could vote an "intention to reject" the Council's common position was dropped. If the EP now votes to reject the common position, the legislation fails. Third, the so-called third reading, whereby the Council could re-propose its common position after a breakdown of conciliation, was also dropped. Fourth, as a result of the change to the third reading, the reformed procedure provided for the proposal to fail if an agreement is not reached in conciliation. This deletion of the third-reading phase put the parliament on an equal footing with the Council in every stage of the procedure (Tsebelis and Garrett, 1997). The "equalization" of both legislative branches now implied a balanced set of veto powers. With the entry into force of Amsterdam, both the Council and the parliament share the responsibility for the adoption as well as for the failure of a proposed legislative act (Maurer, 2003). In addition to the aforementioned, in the Treaty of Amsterdam, the EP was given the right to approve the President of the Commission (Article 214 of the Treaty), while it also set the maximum number of members of the European Parliament, in line with parliament's request, at 700 (Article 189 of the Treaty).

The Treaty of Nice (2001)

The Treaty of Nice (signed in 2001, entry into force 2003) prepared the European Union for the important enlargements to the east and south on 2004 and 2007. In addition, there was an effort to produce a new legal basis for the Union in the form of the treaty establishing a Constitution for Europe. However, following "no" votes in referendums in France and the Netherlands, that treaty was not ratified. Among other provisions, and with an eye to enlargement, the number of MEPs for each member state was revised and the maximum number of MEPs was set at 732. According to the Treaty of Nice, parliament was also enabled (like the Council, the Commission, and the member states) to bring a legal challenge to acts of the Council, the Commission, or the European Central Bank on grounds of lack of competence, infringement of an essential procedural requirement, infringement of the treaty or of any rule of law relating to its application, or misuse of powers; in other words, it gave the EP the right to take other institutions to the European Court of Justice. In addition, parliament's legislative powers were increased through a slight broadening of the scope of the co-decision procedure and by requiring parliament's assent for the establishment of enhanced cooperation in areas covered by co-decision. Last but not least, parliament should also be asked for its opinion in case where the Council adopted a position on the risk of a serious breach of fundamental rights in a member state (Peterson and Shackleton, 2006; Dedman, 2010).

The Treaty of Lisbon (2007)

The latest cornerstone in the development of the European Parliament was the Treaty of Lisbon (signed in 2007, entry into force 2009) which enhanced to a greater extent the role of the EP, since it made the "co-decision procedure" the ordinary legislative procedure for the EU; with the Treaty of Lisbon the "co-decision procedure" now applies to more than 40 policy areas. In addition, it extended the scope of the consent procedure (previously known as assent procedure) to policy areas not subject to the ordinary legislative procedure, it provided for the President of the Commission to be elected by the EP (on a proposal from the European Council, which is obliged to select a candidate by qualified majority, taking into account the outcome of the European elections), it brought all expenditure under parliamentary control (e.g. the multiannual financial framework has to be agreed by the parliament), and it extended the supervision of the Commission by the EP and gave the EP a formal right to propose treaty revisions (Corbett et al., 2011; Jones, 2011).

It should be noted that since the early stages of the establishment of the European Coal and Steel Community (ECSC) (the predecessor of the EU), the European Parliament (or the Common Assembly as it was first known) was introduced as a "tool" for the public acceptance of this new supranational Community. It was felt that the presence of a Common Assembly in the ECSC would be very crucial for its public acceptance. In contrast to the European Commission, which is an appointed body with no direct connection to the EU citizens and to the Council members, who although they are accountable to their national parliaments, they are not directly accountable to the electorate either; the European Parliament has a unique character in the EU governing system, in the sense that it is more representative of the EU population in terms of ideological breadth.

The EP is considered by many scholars the institution that is most likely to generate direct legitimacy, through the direct European elections, and enhance the character of representative democracy at the EU level (Warleigh, 2003; Shackleton, 2017).

2.1.2 The Current Institutional Powers of the European Parliament

Based on the aforementioned, the European Parliament nowadays has more competences than ever in its history, since it exercises legislative powers, budgetary powers, powers of appointment and dismissal, and powers of scrutiny/control of the EU executive. In a more analytical view, there is the following categorization:

Legislative Powers With the co-decision procedure (which is the ordinary legislative procedure) the EP has the same weight with the Council in legislating for a number of policy areas such as economic governance, immigration, energy, transport, environment, and consumer protection. The EP has also a consultation role (for a limited number of areas such as internal market exemption, competition law, and in the adoption of international agreements under the Common Foreign and Security Policy) since it is asked for its opinion on proposed legislation before the Council adopts it. In other areas (e.g. ratification of association agreements or of agreements for accession to the EU, legislation combating discrimination) the EP is also asked to give its consent with the right of veto, approving or rejecting legislative proposals, and the Council cannot overrule its decision. In addition, the EP gives its opinion, adopts resolutions (its own initiative resolutions could also be part of the political forum function of the EP; see below), and votes on reports for issues such as implementing and delegating provisions, the codification of acts into one single act, agreements between management and labour, or voluntary agreements on the functioning of the monetary union. Last but not least, the EP has the right of legislative initiative by asking the Commission to "submit any appropriate proposal on matters on which it considers that a Union act is required" or by calling on the Commission to "take action of one sort or another" (Corbett et al., 2011; European Parliament, 2014a).

Budgetary Powers The EP decides with the Council of the European Union on the entire annual budget of the EU. The spending limits of the annual EU budget are set in the EU's long-term financial plan, the Multiannual Financial Framework. In addition, the EP exercises budgetary control to make sure that the Commission and the other EU institutions manage properly the European funds (Corbett et al., 2011; European Parliament, 2014b; Staab, 2008).

Appointment and Dismissal Powers The EP has the right to be consulted on the appointment of the members of the Court of Auditors, it approves the nominee for Commission President, it is asked for the approval of the entire College of the Commissioners, it has the right of being consulted on the President and the members of the Executive Board of the European Central Bank, it has the power to appoint the EU Ombudsman, and it is further involved in a number of appointments related to other EU bodies and agencies such as the Director of the European Anti-Fraud Office (OLAF) (Corbett et al., 2011).

Scrutiny and Control of the Executive Powers The EP exercises scrutiny and control over the EU executive through debates, questions, and reports. For example, the EP regularly asks the Commission to make a statement in the plenary session on important issues of current interest and this statement is followed by a debate. Debates with other institutions also take place in parliamentary committees, while in the same framework for each summit the President of the European Council presents a report to the EP on the outcome, ministers from the member state which holds the presidency might also appear in the EP, and the High Representative on Foreign Affairs and Security Policy reports, twice a year, on policies and financial implications. MEPs can also make use of written questions, questions at question time, and questions for oral answer with debate in order to exercise control and scrutiny over the EU executive (mainly the Commission), while a "question hour" with the President of the Commission is also used as a tool for scrutinizing the executive. In the same framework, annual and periodic activity reports are also provided by the Commission and the other EU institutions to the EP. Last but not least, any EU citizen, resident, company, or organization can submit a petition to the European Parliament on issues related to EU law, and the parliament can set up a committee of inquiry to look into violations of EU law by member states (Corbett et al., 2011; European Parliament 2014c).

Other Functions of the EP Along with the above-mentioned powers, the EP also functions as a political forum and a channel for communication. Through this role the EP tries to broaden its political agenda with set-piece debates, resolutions adopted at its own initiative, hearings, activities in the field of human rights, and the right of petitions. In addition, it maintains a network of contacts through contact channels to the other EU institutions, through contacts with individual governments, and through formal sittings such as addresses by Heads of State or similar. Finally, the European Parliament also has the potential to promote constitutional changes at the EU level (Corbett et al., 2011; Staab, 2008; European Parliament, 2014a).

2.1 The European Parliament in the EU Context

Thus, the European Parliament constitutes a policy-making, controlling, elective, and system developing actor in the EU governance system (Maurer, 2007; Wessels and Diedrichs, 1997; Bourguignon-Wittke et al., 1985).

The aforementioned powers determine the tasks and the daily activities of the EP, while they are also the core elements that constitute the institutional performance and the output of the European Parliament. The EP performance is directly linked to the way in which the above powers are exercised, the assigned tasks are fulfilled, and the output that is produced. For example, activities such as making parliamentary amendments through the co-decision procedure, approving or rejecting draft documents, approving or rejecting the EU budget or budget-related measures of EU legislation, setting stricter regulation, etc., along with the consequences that have either to the legislation process or directly to the EU citizens, constitute the institutional performance and output of the EP (Maurer, 2003, 2007). In addition, following Grabitz et al. (1986) and Grabitz and Läufer (1980), the aforementioned parliamentary powers and tasks, as key elements of the EP performance, are critical institutional functions necessary for the existence, preservation, and social acceptance of the institution itself or even of the broader political system in which the EP operates.

As it will be shown in Sect. 3.4, the perceived performance of an institution, in the specific case of the EP, is a source of support by the citizens, and thus a source of social legitimacy (Easton, 1965). This institutional performance is linked to the (perceived by the citizens) capacity of the institution to deliver economic benefits and other "goodies" effectively via the pursuit of appropriate purposes and the exercise of the institutional powers and tasks (Beetham and Lord, 1998; Schmitt and Thomassen, 1999; Marsh, 1999). In addition, as it will be shown in Sect. 3.4, trust towards the EP (which is also a crucial source for its social legitimacy) is further affected by the performance of it as an institution (Schmitt and Thomassen, 1999; Uslaner, 2002; Arnold et al., 2012). In the case of the EU institutions—and specifically of the EP—trust is increasingly determined by evaluations and perceptions of the performance outcomes of the EU or its institutions themselves (Torcal et al., 2012).

2.1.3 Internal Organization and Operation of the European Parliament

The internal organization and operation of the European Parliament is defined by the relevant Rules of Procedure which refer, inter alia, to the role of the MEPs in the operation of the EP, the different bodies in the EP (such as the President, the Vice-President, the Bureau, and the Conference of Presidents), the establishment and the rules that govern the operation of the political groups in the EP, the external relations of the EP, the relations with other institutions and bodies in the EU, the relations with the national parliaments in the member states, the various committees and delegations in the EP, and the organization and structure of the parliament's Secretariat.

The Secretariat is the administrative and organizational pillar of the EP whose task is to coordinate legislative work, organize plenary sittings and meetings, and provide technical and expert assistance to parliamentary bodies and MEPs in order to support them in the exercise of their mandates. The EP's secretariat is organized in 12 Directorates-General, each with its own tasks and responsibilities (Corbett et al., 2011; European Parliament, 2014d).

As regards the competent structures for the communication policy of the EP, in Sect. 4.6 there will be a more analytical presentation of the Directorate-General for Communication of the European Parliament, whose core business is to raise awareness of the European Parliament, its powers, its decisions, and activities among media, stakeholders, and the general public.

References

Arnold, C., Sapir, E.V., & Zapryanova, G. (2012). Trust in the institutions of the European Union: A cross-country examination. In L. Beaudonnet, & D. Di Mauro (Eds.), *Beyond Euroskepticism: Understanding attitudes towards the EU*. European Integration online Papers (EIoP). Special Mini-Issue 2, 16(8), Retrieved February 25, 2015, from http://eiop.or.at/eiop/texte/2012-008a.htm

Beetham, D., & Lord, C. (1998). *Legitimacy and the EU*. Longman.

Bourguignon-Wittke, R., Grabitz, E., Schmuck, O., Steppat, S., & Wessels, W. (1985). Five years of the directly elected European Parliament - Performance and prospects. *Journal of Common Market Studies, 24*(1), 39–59.

Corbett, R., Jacobs, F., & Shackleton, M. (2011). *The European Parliament* (8th ed.). John Harper Publishing.

Dedman, M. (1996). *The origins and development of the European Union 1945–1995: A history of European integration* (1st ed.). Routledge.

Dedman, M. (2010). *The origins and development of the European Union 1945–2008: A history of European integration* (2nd ed.). Routledge.

Duncan, W. (2008). *The European Union*. Edinburgh University Press.

Easton, D. (1965). *A systems analysis of political life*. Wiley.

European Parliament. (2014a). *About Parliament/Powers and procedures – Legislative powers*. Retrieved November 27, 2014, from: https://www.europarl.europa.eu/about-parliament/en/powers-and-procedures/legislative-powers

European Parliament. (2014b). *About Parliament/Powers and procedures – Budgetary powers*. Retrieved November 27, 2014, from: https://www.europarl.europa.eu/about-parliament/en/powers-and-procedures/budgetary-powers

European Parliament. (2014c). *About Parliament. Powers and procedures-supervisory powers*. Retrieved November 27, 2014, from: http://www.europarl.europa.eu/aboutparliament/en/00b9de8689/Oversight-and-control-functions.html

European Parliament. (2014d). *About Parliament/Organisation and work*. Retrieved November 27, 2014, from: http://www.europarl.europa.eu/aboutparliament/en/0025729351/Organisation-and-work.html

Grabitz, E., & Läufer, T. (1980). *Das Europäische Parlament*. Europa Union Verlag.

References

Grabitz, E., Schmuck, O., Steppat, S., & Wessels, W. (1986). Das Europäische Parlament – verurteilt zur Machtlosigkeit? Auf der Suche nach einem neuen Leitbild. *Aus Politik und Zeitgeschichte, No. B, 28*(26), 22–37.

Jones, A. C. (2011). The legal and institutional framework of the 2009 European Parliament elections in the shadow of the Lisbon Treaty. In M. Maier, J. Stromback, & L. Lee Kaid (Eds.), *Political communication in European parliamentary elections*. Ashgate.

Judge, D., & Earnshaw, D. (2003). *The European Parliament: The European Union Series*. Palgrave Macmillan.

Kreppel, A., Lange, P., Bates, R., Comisso, E., Hall, P., Migdal, J., & Milner, H. (2002). *The European Parliament and Supranational party system: A study in institutional development. Cambridge studies in comparative politics*. Cambridge University Press.

Marsh, M. (1999). Policy Performance. In H. Schmitt & J. Thomassen (Eds.), *Political representation and legitimacy in the European Union*. Oxford University Press.

Maurer, A. (2003). The legislative powers and impact of the European Parliament. *Journal of Common Market Studies, 41*(2), 227–247.

Maurer, A. (2007). The European Parliament between policy-making and control. In B. Kohler-Koch & B. Rittberger (Eds.), *Debating the democratic legitimacy of the European Union*. Rowman & Littlefield Publishers.

Peterson, J., & Shackleton, M. (Eds.). (2006). *The institutions of the European Union* (2nd ed.). Oxford University Press.

Schmitt, H., & Thomassen, J. (Eds.). (1999). *Political representation and legitimacy in the European Union*. Oxford University Press.

Shackleton, M. (2017). Transforming representative democracy in the EU? The role of the European Parliament. *Journal of European Integration, 39*(2), 191–205.

Staab, A. (2008). *European Union explained: Institutions, actors, global impact*. Indiana University Press.

Torcal, M., Muñoz, J., & Bonet, E. (2012). Trust in the European Parliament: From affective heuristics to rational cueing. In D. Sanders, P. Magalhaes, & G. Toka (Eds.), *Citizens and the European polity: Mass attitudes towards the European and national polities*. Oxford University Press.

Tsebelis, G., & Garrett, G. (1997). Agenda setting, vetoes and the European Union's co-decision procedure. *The Journal of Legislative Studies, 3*(3), 74–92.

Uslaner, E. M. (2002). *The moral foundations of trust*. Cambridge University Press.

Warleigh, A. (2003). *Democracy and the European Union. Theory, practice and reform*. Sage.

Wessels, W., & Diedrichs, U. (1997). A new kind of legitimacy for a new kind of parliament-The evolution of the European Parliament. *European Integration Online Papers (EIoP), 1*(6) http://www.eiop.or.at/eiop/texte/1997-006.htm

Chapter 3
European Parliament's Legitimacy: Conceptualization and Empirical Assessment

This chapter presents the concept of legitimacy, as it has been explored in political theory (normative approach) and the political and social sciences, respectively (empirical and descriptive approach). Given that legitimacy has been, till recently, mainly conceptualized in the framework of the nation-states, the chapter proceeds with the examination of the issue of legitimacy at the EU level. It explains how this concept has been approached, and it examines the debate on the EU democratic and legitimacy deficit. With a focus on social legitimacy, a selection of empirical data is made in order to assess the popular legitimacy of the EP in the UK and Greece.

3.1 Legitimacy in Political Theory and in Social Sciences

Before moving to the assessment of the EP social legitimacy in the UK and Greece it is necessary to examine the concept of legitimacy, in its various approaches, both in political theory and in political and social science. Then, having discussed the concept of legitimacy at the EU level, the relevant—for the assessment of social legitimacy—indicators will be selected.

Despite the fact that it is difficult to find an absolute and clear definition of the specific concept, legitimacy is, more broadly, defined as the justification of the right of a government/authority to hold and exercise power and make decisions that affect the lives of the citizens who are governed.

In a historic perspective, the concept of legitimacy has been approached both by political theory (normative approach) and by social and political science (empirical approach). On the one hand, the approach of the normative political theory seeks to define the ideal criteria and standards that need to be met for a government to be legitimate (or in other words tries to answer the question of when an authority/government/polity is legitimate). On the other hand, literature from the social and political science provides more descriptive/empirical explanations of what actually is legitimacy in the real world and in real social situations and power relations.

3.1.1 The Approach of Legitimacy in Normative Political Theory

The ancient Greeks were the first ones to speak of democracy and legitimacy. They considered that governance is legitimate when it is exercised by the "many", by "the people". In practical terms this approach was related to the direct involvement of the Athenian citizens in the decision-making process of the city through their in-person participation in the local assembly. Their participation gave the specific decision and the relevant governing authority the necessary legitimacy. Following that, citizens were obliged to obey to the decision made by the majority in the assembly (even if this was not their choice) (Held, 1987).

After the period of Roman Empire where the political thought was keeping up with a theological framework and the period of the Middle Ages (fifth to fifteenth century AC) where the political thinking regarding the nature of political communities was not developed, liberal democratic ideas have started to emerge.

In the writings of the first thinkers of the liberal democratic ideas of the sixteenth century, such as Hobbes and Locke, the establishment and the function of a legitimate democratic liberal government ought to be based on the "consent" of the citizens, who give their individualistic rights of self-government to a powerful single authority/government—authorized to act on their behalf—under the condition that the government will protect and secure their life, their liberty, their estate, their rights, their ends, their interests (Ashcraft, 1991). This "consent" of the citizens creates the unique relation of the sovereign to subject and the unique political power, the sovereign power or else sovereignty, which is the authorized use of state powers by a person or assembly established as sovereign. Under this approach the rule by the people (by the demos)—which is the core precondition for a democratic political system—is realized through the sovereign, which is at the same time the citizen's representative (Held, 2006). Under this approach, the "consent" of the citizens is the step that creates the specific relation of sovereign and subject; however, it is the precondition that the government ought to protect and secure their life, liberty, estate, rights, ends, and interests, which makes its power legitimate. If the government (sovereign) fails to represent and secure citizens' interests, its legitimacy should be accordingly called into question by the citizens who are the final judges and can dispense both with their deputies and, if need be, with the existing form of government itself. In addition, Hobbes and Locke also referred in their works to the necessity of a legislative body, in a legitimate democratic political system, which enacts rules as the people's agent in contradiction to the executive which enforces the legal system (De Baecque, 1995; Held, 1987; Ashcraft, 1991).

Following the above rationale, Baron de Montesquieu (1689–1755) argued that the liberty and welfare of the citizens could only be secured and realized, in a political system, by the existence of an institutionalized separation (divisions of power) and balance of powers within the state. He argued that legitimate political authority could only be exercised within the framework of the rule of law and constitutionalism that would give the citizens the right to hold the executive accountable for unlawful acts and power abuse (Vile, 1998; Held, 2006). Thus, under this approach and in addition to the liberal thinking of Hobbes and Locke, Montesquieu linked the legitimacy of a political authority to constitutionalism.

For normative political theorists such as Jeremy Bentham (1748–1832) and James Mill (1773–1836) the creation of policies and institutions, in a democratic political system, is legitimate to the extent that they all upheld the principle of utility; that is to say the achievement of the greatest happiness for the greatest number of people (Held, 2006).

They also argued that political mechanisms such as the secret ballot, regular voting, and competition between potential representatives are crucial in a democratic political system since they enhance and sustain its legitimacy, by giving citizens satisfactory means for choosing, authorizing, and controlling political decisions, and at the same time ensure the accountability of the governors (Held, 2006).

Following the aforementioned rationale, John Stuart Mill (1806–1873) focused on representativeness as a crucial element of legitimacy in a democratic political system. According to him, the institution of parliament which is the core institution that incarnates the representative character of the political system, has some distinct advantages: it provides the mechanism whereby central powers can be watched and controlled; it establishes a forum to act as a watchdog of liberty; it is a centre of reason and debate; and it harnesses, through electoral competition, leadership qualities with intellect for the maximum benefit for all the members of society. Mill argued that the representative character of the democratic political system, along with its legitimacy potential, is also important as an aspect of the free development of individuality (this argument is also known as developmental democracy). According to Mill's view, representativeness drives participation in political life—for example, through voting or through involvement in local administration—and is vital for the creation of (a) a direct interest in government, (b) for an informed and developing citizenry, and (c) a dynamic developmental polity (Mill & Gray, 1991; Held, 2006).

In a similar vein, social-political theorists such as Weber and Schumpeter having as a starting point the fact that the size, the complexity, and the diversity of modern (industrial) societies make direct democracy inappropriate as a general model of political regulation and control, argued that a necessary mechanism for ensuring the legitimacy of an authority and its right to exercise power, under these specific circumstances of the (industrial) society, is the mechanism of parliament. For Weber strong parliaments would serve as a balance to public and private bureaucracy, would maintain a degree of openness in government, would be an important testing ground for future leaders, and would provide the space for negotiation about entrenched positions (Weber, 1978; Held, 2006; Mommsen, 1974). For Schumpeter, parliaments are a crucial element of a system that establishes and maintains legitimate leadership and authority; this system also involves political mechanisms such as general elections, parties, cabinets, and Prime ministers (Schumpeter, 1976).

David Beetham (1991) identifies a set of three criteria which he considers have to be satisfied for any governmental system to be considered as legitimate. According to Beetham, political authority is legitimate to the extent that it is (1) acquired and exercised according to established rules, (2) justifiable according to socially accepted norms and beliefs about the rightful source of authority and the proper ends and standards of government, and (3) confined through actions expressive of the people's consent to it, such as elections. Beetham sees these legitimizing criteria as important for the degree of cooperation and the quality of performance that the powerful can secure from the people.

Based on the aforementioned approaches, parliaments are considered as the political institutions that ensure the representative nature of liberal democratic political systems (since they express the public will). Parliaments are seen, since the ancient times, as the space for direct involvement in the decision-making process of the city (as this was the case, for example, in the ancient Athenian democracy), as the legislative body which enacts rules and as the people's agent (for example, as seen in the theory of Locke), as the mechanism whereby central powers can be watched and controlled, as a forum for the expression of different opinions and the debate of discussions, as a watchdog of liberty and as a centre of reason and debate (as seen in Stuart Mill's view), and as a solution to the over bureaucratization in modern industrial societies, a mechanism for keeping the balance between public and private bureaucracy and maintaining a degree of openness in government and a space for negotiation over entrenched positions (as seen in Weber's view).

Parliaments are—in the theorization of liberal democracies—the political mechanisms that, apart from the aforementioned responsibilities, ensure the representativeness and the expression of public will as an important and stable element of a legitimate democratic political system. Especially from the nineteenth century onwards, the steadily expanding franchise in the western European polities has made political theorists to consider the legitimacy of a political system as dependent on the expression of the franchise's popular will, through the mechanism of elections of legislative national parliaments.

Given that the scope here is not to examine in depth the normative criteria that have to be met in order for a political authority (in our case the European Parliament) to be legitimate, rather than to investigate how legitimacy is conceptualized in the real world and in real social context, it is necessary to also review legitimacy under a more empirical approach.

3.1.2 The Approach of Legitimacy in the Political and Social Sciences

A very influential conceptualization of political legitimacy, under the empirical approach, is provided by Weber (1964). According to him, the condition that a political entity is legitimate means that the people governed believe that it is legitimate. As he argues: "the basis of every system of authority, and correspondingly of every kind of willingness to obey, is a belief, a belief by virtue of which persons exercising authority are lent prestige" (Weber 1964: 382). And he develops his view by identifying three main sources (ideal types) of legitimacy of a political authority: (a) tradition (people have faith to the political order since this order has been there for a long time), (b) charisma (people have faith to the rulers/leaders), and (c) legality (people have faith and respect in the rationality of the rule of law) (Weber, 1964).

However, the legitimacy sources as set out by Weber are not of great use for the assessment of the EP legitimacy in our case. There is no influential tradition regarding the EP institution that could trigger popular legitimacy for the EP, and there are not any charismatic MEPs or EP institutional actors in the sense of Weber's ideal type that could make the EU citizens to have faith in the EP. Evidently, the EP is part of the EU polity whose development is, in a large extent, based on legality. People have faith in legality (in the rule of law) since this has been an important element and prerequisite of the democratic liberal political systems.

In David Beetham's (1991) second criteria of the legitimacy, a political authority is legitimate to the degree that it is justifiable according to socially accepted norms and beliefs about the rightful source of authority and the proper ends and standards of government. These criteria, in contrast to the other two which are of a more normative nature (legality and representativeness), seem to be more relevant for the scope of this book since it refers to social acceptance and social beliefs about the political authority and its performance. These elements of legitimacy (socially accepted norms and specifically the beliefs about the rightful source of authority and the proper ends and standards of government) can be assessed by empirical data regarding people's feelings and people's perceptions for a political institution; in our case the European Parliament.

In another approach regarding the description and the assessment of the legitimacy of a political authority in an empirical manner, David Easton (1965) distinguishes, as sources of popular (social) legitimacy, three objects of support: the political community, the political regime, and the performance of the authorities. Following his approach, the relevant indicators of social legitimacy that are going to be used, as it will be shown in Sect. 3.7, are: (1) support for the performance or the policy output of the authority (of the EP) in the UK and Greece, and (2) support for the political institution itself (the EP itself), by the citizens of the UK and Greece.

In other relevant conceptualizations of social legitimacy, Nedergaard (2006), when defining the key concepts of formal and societal legitimacy, argues that societal (or popular) legitimacy implies that decisions of an authority/government are in accordance with the expectations and support of the majority of the population. In that case, legitimacy is what the majority of citizens regard as right or wrong, acceptable or unacceptable, democratic or undemocratic, and so on. The basis for determining the degree of societal legitimacy is the general attitude towards the authority's decisions.

Based on the aforementioned, it is clear that the conceptualizations of social (or else popular) legitimacy consider the public consent towards an authority as a basic source of legitimacy; not the only one though. The positive evaluative stance towards the political authorities, the positive perceptions and the belief from the side of governed for the right of the exercise of power by a political authority is a basic source of its legitimacy.

Thus, since legitimacy under the empirical approach is usually defined in terms of what is believed in a society (citizen's perceptions), this understanding has greater relevance and applicability for the assessment of the degree of EP's social legitimacy.

3.2 Legitimacy Beyond the Nation-State

The political thinking and the development of the theories regarding legitimacy (both normative and societal) had at their core the dominant political association of the nation-state. And this is natural if we consider that the nineteenth and early twentieth century in Europe was marked by the awakening of the national consciousness of the nations of central Europe and the rise of the nation-states (De Baecque, 1995; Nedergaard, 2006). It was expected that the idea of the nation-state would unite those people living in the same communities to form nations along territorial lines. Elements such as common language, values, myths, shared history and culture, etc., would allow the people to come to identify with the national state and accept its authority and its relevant exercise of power as legitimate. In addition, and in a parallel process, the development of a sense of national identity (over time) would also allow the state to further base its claim to exercise authority. Since the nineteenth and early twentieth century, the modern nation-state has become the principal type of political entity across the globe and thus the concept of legitimacy was directly related to this entity.

However, today the dynamics of global economy, the rapid growth of transnational links along with the existence of regional and global interconnectedness, and the problems of the modern world that necessitate more global approaches have made many scholars to rethink about the traditional approach of nation-state and its legitimacy, and to explore alternative paths that these conceptualizations might follow.

The territorial boundaries of the nation-states specify the basis on which individuals are included and excluded from participation in decisions affecting their lives, but the outcomes of these decisions and of the decisions of those in other political communities and agencies often go beyond national boundaries. The implications of these interdependences are troubling not only for the concepts of consent and legitimacy but also for other concepts of democratic theory such as representation, proper participation, accountability, etc. According to Held (2006), in this new reality among these concepts that have to be re-examined and reconceptualized is the concept of legitimacy.

Held (2006) has underscored the importance of reconceptualizing politics and democratic theory and argues that political alternatives to the aforementioned state of affairs could be developed by deepening and extending democracy across nations, regions, and global networks. Such a process can be referred to as the entrenchment of democratic autonomy on a cosmopolitan basis—or else a "cosmopolitan democracy". This would involve the development of administrative capacity and independent political resources at regional and global levels as a necessary complement to those in local and national polities (Held, 2006). A model of cosmopolitan democracy, according to Held, would seek to entrench and develop democratic institutions at regional and global levels as a necessary complement to those at the level of nation-state.

Before Held, Habermas (1984) in a similar vein has also sought to move democratic theory away from its focus on the "people" conceived as part of a nation. According to Habermas, legitimate rule emerges instead where rational discourse, not bonds of ethnicity or culture, informs collective action.

In the same direction, Charles Taylor (1992), by addressing the implications of national, ethnic, and cultural diversity for democracy, argues that the mutual recognition of difference, both within and across societies, is vital for political legitimacy (Taylor, 1992).

Despite the fact that the aforementioned political theorists, among others, have not developed new approaches to recognition and legitimacy explicitly in the context of the European Union, their alternative thinking provided a starting point for thinking about legitimacy and the EU.

3.3 Legitimacy in the Context of the EU

As far as the case of the EU and the EU institutions is concerned, the debate on legitimacy derives from the fact that more and more competences that previously were under national sovereignty have now been transferred to the EU level. The creation of binding legislation for the EU citizens and the decisions made on issues such as economy, foreign policy, social policy, the environment, etc., necessitate a kind of justification of the power on behalf of the EU decision-making machinery.

The literature on EU legitimacy focuses mainly on: (a) the analysis of the democratic structure and elements (e.g. representativeness, accountability) of the EU polity and decision-making process (this is where the term EU democratic deficit is usually used), and (b) the analysis of the popular identification (or in other words recognition) of the EU citizens with the EU and its institutions. Under these approaches the EU legitimacy crisis is reflected in the lack of popular identification with the EU and/or in the undemocratic structure of its institutions (Weiler, 1991; Banchoff and Smith, 1999; Decker, 2002).

During the first four decades of the existence of the EU, the issue of democracy and legitimacy was not intensely debated. Few had questioned the democratic and legitimate character of the EU since it was assumed by academics and politicians that the EU was democratic and legitimate, mainly through the presence of the national ministers in the Council. Thus, there was a "permissive consensus" of the legitimacy of the EU; a passive acceptance of the EU integration by the public opinion (Lindberg and Scheingold, 1970; Schweiger, 2016).

The debate over the democratic character and the legitimacy of the EU started during the period of the ratification of the Maastricht Treaty in 1992. The Maastricht Treaty was rejected at the relevant referendum in Denmark (51% to 49% in 1992), it was barely passed in the French referendum (51% to 49%), while in the case of the UK the House of Commons passed the treaty only with great difficulty in 1993. These events revealed that the EU was distant from its citizens and triggered the debate on the EU legitimacy. It has to be mentioned here that the term democratic deficit was first used by the British MEP, Bill Newton-Dunn who employed this phrase in a pamphlet back in the 1980s; there, he was referring to the widely held belief that there was a lack of democratic control and accountability within the EU and that these deficiencies were said to prevent its institutions from acquiring political legitimacy and widespread recognition and acceptance (Watts, 2008).

On the one hand of the relevant debate, there are scholars who support that the EU is adequately democratic and thus does not suffer from a legitimacy deficit, as far as its democratic character is concerned. For example, Majone (1998) first argues that one should not apply to European institutions standards of legitimacy that derive from the theory and practice of parliamentary democracies because: (a) the institutional architecture of the Community has been designed by Treaties duly ratified by all national parliaments and (b) one of the characteristic features of the European Community is the impossibility of mapping functions onto specific institutions (the European Community has no legislature but a legislative process in which different political institutions have different parts to play; there is no identifiable executive, since executive powers are exercised for some purposes by the Council acting on a Commission proposal, for other purposes by the Commission, and overwhelmingly by the Member States in implementing European policies on the ground). Then he argues that the process of European integration is inherently non-majoritarian, and thus the depoliticization (in other words, the lack of need for democratic contestation and popular identification) of European policy-making is the price that has to be paid in order to preserve national sovereignty largely intact. In this respect, for Majone, the EU does not face a democratic deficit.

In the same vein, Moravcsik (2002) argues that if we judge the EU against existing advanced industrial democracies, the EU seems to be democratic since constitutional checks and balances, indirect democratic control via national governments, and the increasing powers of the European Parliament are sufficient to ensure that EU policy-making is, in nearly all cases, clean, transparent, effective, and politically responsive to the demands of European citizens. And he develops his argument by supporting that: (1) there is a set of substantive, fiscal, administrative, legal, and procedural constraints on EU policy-making process and EU governance which are embedded in treaty and legislative provisions and have the force of constitutional law that guarantee that the EU will not become a despotic "superstate", (2) there are democratic procedures that prevent the EU from becoming an arbitrary and unaccountable technocracy (direct and indirect democratic accountability via two robust mechanisms: the stronger EP and the elected national officials in the case of the European Council and the Council of Ministers), (3) there are legitimate reasons for shielding certain EU decision-makers from direct democratic contestation in precisely those areas—such as central banking, constitutional adjudication, criminal and civil prosecution, technical administration, and economic diplomacy—in which many advanced industrial democracies insulate themselves from direct political contestation, (4) the EU governance is not substantively biased in a neo-liberal direction. Moravcsik (2002) supports that the neo-liberal bias of the EU, if it exists, is justified by the social welfarist bias of current national policies; at the same time nor is there much evidence that the EU is driving social protection downward, as he argues that by contrast, the EU has often permitted high standards and supportive institutional reform, and thus has tended to reregulate at a high level.

Last but not least, from a social acceptance approach, Moravcsik argues that there are underlying social reasons explaining why political participation in the EU could not be radically expanded. He says that: (a) insulated institutions—such as constitutional courts and administrative bureaucracies—are often more popular with the public than legislatures, (b) EU legislative and regulatory activity is inversely correlated with the salience of issues in the minds of European voters, (c) even if a common European "identity" and the full panoply of democratic procedures existed, it would be very difficult to induce meaningful citizen participation. Moravcsik (2002) makes the conclusion that the fact that the EU seems to be unpopular is because of the subset of functions it performs such as: central banking, constitutional adjudication, civil prosecution, economic diplomacy, and technical administration—matters of low electoral salience commonly delegated in national systems. Thus, according to him, the EU is not undemocratic; it is simply specialized in those functions of modern democratic governance that tend to involve less direct political participation.

In the same vein, Banchoff & Smith (1999) challenge the legitimacy crisis within the EU. However, they do not deny that the EU is engaged in a difficult legitimation process, and as far as the recognition element is concerned, they agree that some Europeans still refuse to acknowledge the EU as an appropriate venue for politics and policy-making. By defining a legitimate polity as a broadly recognized framework for politics with representative institutions, they argue, first, that while Europeans do not strongly identify with the EU, they increasingly recognize the EU as a framework for politics alongside existing national and sub-national arenas; and, second, that while the EU lacks strong central democratic institutions, the integration process has created significant informal and pluralist forms of representation.

More specifically they argue that an increasing range of actors has come to acknowledge the EU as an appropriate framework for politics, alongside and not in place of national and sub-national levels of government. The activities in which these actors engage—and their capacity to combine existing identities with participation in Europe—have contributed to EU legitimacy conceived as recognition. At the same time they also argue that interactive, decentralized institutions have given rise to complex links between state and society in Europe. Interest groups and parties, while still anchored in national politics, have become more active at the

European level. These new forms of representation constitute an important, often overlooked source of political legitimacy (mainly viewed from the approach of democratic character) within the European Union.

On the other side of the relevant debate, scholars who indicate an EU legitimacy deficit point to either the undemocratic structure of the EU government system (thus they talk for a democratic deficit) or to the lack of recognition of the EU citizens to the EU.

For example, for Follesdal and Hix (2006), the EU "democratic deficit" is evident in the following five main claims: (1) the European integration has meant an increase in executive power and a decrease in national parliamentary control. The design of the EU means that policy-making at the European level is dominated by executive actors such as national ministers in the Council, or government appointees in the Commission, and the actions of these executive agents at the European level are beyond the control of national parliaments, (2) the European Parliament is still too weak—compared to the governments in the Council—despite the successive reforms of the EU treaties, since the mid-1980s, that have dramatically increased the powers of the European Parliament, (3) there are no "European" elections, since neither national elections nor European Parliament elections are really "European" elections: they are not about the personalities and parties at the European level or the direction of the EU policy agenda. Protest votes against parties in government and steadily declining participation in European elections indicate that they are actually "second-order national contests" for domestic issues in the member states, (4) the EU is simply "too distant" from voters, both in institutional and psychological terms. Institutionally, electoral control over the Council and the Commission is too weak. Psychologically, the EU differs too much from the domestic democratic institutions that citizens are used to. Thus, citizens cannot understand the EU, and so will never be able to assess and regard it as a democratic system nor to identify with it, (5) the European integration produces policies that are not supported by a majority of citizens in many or even most member states. Governments are able to undertake policies at the European level that they cannot pursue at the domestic level, where they are constrained by parliaments, courts, and corporatist interest group structures (and these policy outcomes include a neo-liberal regulatory framework for the single market, a monetarist framework for Economic Monetary Union, and massive subsidies to farmers through the common agricultural policy). These feature skew EU policy outcomes more towards the interests of the owners of capital than is the case for policy compromises at the domestic level in Europe.

In addition, Follesdal and Hix (2006) argue that the EU is undemocratic since there is no electoral contest for political leadership at the European level or the basic direction of the EU policy agenda. (National elections are about domestic political issues, where the policies of different parties on issues on the EU agenda are rarely debated while European Parliament elections are not in fact about Europe, but are "second-order national contests"). Follesdal and Hix (2006) continue by saying that there is a need for full transparency of the amendment procedures, the agenda-control rules and even the recording of roll-call votes when votes fail, inside the EU

Council in order for the academics or the media and the general public to follow what goes on inside the EU Council.

Last but not least, another problem of the EU democracy, according to Follesdal and Hix (2006), from the social acceptance point of view, is the lack of a connection between the growing democratic politics inside the European Parliament and EU Council and the views of the public. They argue that without an electoral contest connected to political behaviour in these EU institutions it is impossible for voters to punish MEPs or governments for voting the "wrong way".

According to the aforementioned views, scholars who either argue that there is a democratic deficit in the EU or support that the EU does not suffer from a democratic deficit acknowledge that legitimacy is a multidimensional concept that consists of elements which have to do both with the procedural-legal dimension of the political authority and with the recognition (social acceptance) of it as well. More specifically, as far as the social acceptance (social legitimacy) element is concerned, a general consensus exists that there is a lack of recognition with the EU and its institutions.

For example, both Majone and Moravcsik defend the EU's democratic character since they support that the EU decision-making system embeds basic elements and characteristics of transparency, accountability, representativeness, and efficiency. However, in terms of recognition and social "acceptance" they argue that there is a lack of recognition with the EU. In the same vein, Banchoff & Smith, despite the fact that they challenge the legitimacy crisis, they acknowledge that, as far as the recognition element is concerned, some Europeans still refuse to acknowledge the EU as an appropriate venue for politics and policy-making; and thus, there is, in some extend, a social acceptance (social legitimacy) deficit of the EU and its institutions.

The European Parliament is part of a polity whose legitimacy cannot be easily assessed, based on the normative criteria of democratic theory (which has as a reference the nation-state). Thus, as it has been mentioned before, the assessment of the EP's social legitimacy seems to be of greater relevance and use. However, in order to assess its popular legitimacy (social acceptance), by using relevant empirical data as indicators, one should first determine which aspects of the political system people's feelings and perceptions are relevant for it.

The selection of the specific elements of support (public perceptions) that have been employed in order to assess the EP popular legitimacy is explained in Sect. 3.4.

3.4 The Perceived Performance of the EP as Determinant of Popular Legitimacy

Scholars suggest that public evaluations of the EU's (and the EU institutions') performance are crucial empirical indicators of the EU's (and its institutions) popular legitimacy (Thomassen, 2009; Beetham and Lord, 1998; Schmitt and Thomassen, 1999).

In Beetham and Lord's (1998) view, and in terms of social acceptance, legitimacy depends, inter alia, on the perceived performance of the EU and its institutions in terms of the extent to which the EU as a political system is perceived, by the EU citizens, to provide benefits and other goods via the pursuit of appropriate purposes. As far as the EU (and its institutions) popular legitimacy is concerned, they indicate that this can be weak or absent even though power and accountability might be present.

Other researchers, such as Schmitt and Thomassen (1999), having defined EU legitimacy as the belief that the existing political order is right, based their assessment of people's attitudes towards the EU on several factors, such as (a) whether European citizens have developed a European "sense of community" and a collective European identity, (b) whether and in what policy areas voters accept policy-making at the European level, (c) whether people are satisfied with the way in which the EU and its various policy processes function, and (d) whether they trust its institutions to represent their interests and concerns at the EU level. On the basis of the empirical evidence, Schmitt and Thomassen conclude that if people feel that they have benefited directly from EU membership and the EU institutions, then they are more likely to support the EU and its institutions.

In the case of judgments and support towards the EU and its institutions, there is a strong utilitarian basis, since this perception is related to the material benefits gained by the EU membership and the performance of the EU institutions. This influence of policy and institution performance output on the level of both general and specific support for a political system and a political institution, and thus its popular legitimacy, has also been highlighted by other scholars (Easton, 1965; Marsh, 1999). For example, as argued in Marsh (1999) well-performing institutions are invested with more authority; thus, states and polities like the EU and its institutions are judged on their relative effectiveness in performing a service.

In the same vein, Easton (1965) distinguishes, as sources of popular legitimacy, three objects of support towards: the political community, the political regime, and the performance of the authorities. Easton's framework was also used by Thomassen (2009) for the assessment of the EU legitimacy after the 2004 EU enlargement. In his approach Thomassen interpreted the Eastonian concept "political regime" in terms of the EU political institutions, while he also argued that the three objects of support towards the political community, towards the political regime, and towards the performance of the authorities are matched, respectively, to the normative dimensions of democratic legitimacy (identity, representation and accountability, performance). However, it has to be mentioned here that Thomassen used this framework in order to assess the legitimacy of the whole EU polity after the 2004 EU enlargement and not the legitimacy of specific EU institutions.

In line with the above perceptions and given that the focus here is on the assessment of the popular legitimacy of the European Parliament—and not of the whole EU as a polity—the following indicators will be used: (1) the people's support for the performance or the policy output of the European Parliament in the UK and Greece, and (2) the support/satisfaction for the EP as an institution by the citizens of the UK and Greece. Easton (1965) also considers, as a source of popular legitimacy, the support towards the political community; in our case this would mean the EU as a political community. However, the perceptions of the EU citizens regarding the EU as a political community are not of great relevance for the purposes of this book, since the focus is on the assessment of the social (popular) legitimacy of the EP.

3.5 Trust Towards a Political Institution as a Determinant of Legitimacy

The perceived performance of the EU (and its institutions), as a determinant of popular legitimacy, is also closely related to the variable of trust towards the EU (and its institutions). And as far as the EU (and its institutions) legitimacy is concerned, scholars such as Schmitt and Thomassen (1999) also consider trust of the EU citizens towards the EU and its institutions as a crucial indicator of their popular legitimacy.

The level of trust that citizens have for political institutions is a measure of the perceived gap between their political preferences and the outputs of the specific political institutions. Perceptions of political institutions' performance reflect the voters' evaluations and trust towards the specific institutions and policies, meaning that when the institutions do not produce the outcomes envisaged, trust for them is expected to be lower (Uslaner, 2002; Arnold et al., 2012; Mishler and Rose, 2001).

In the case of the EU institutions (thus in the case of the EP as well) relevant research shows that along with determinants such as (a) the level of trust and evaluations of the national institutions (de Vries & van Kersbergen, 2007; Rohrschneider, 2002; Ilonszki, 2009; Hobolt, 2012), (b) the perceived status of the economy (Hooghe & Marks, 2005; Ehrmann et al., 2013), (c) the utilities people perceive that they gain from membership in the EU (Arnold et al., 2012), and (d) perceived levels of transparency (Van der Cruijsen & Eijffinger, 2008), trust is increasingly determined by subjective instrumental perceptions—thus, evaluations and perceptions of the performance outcomes of the EU or its institutions themselves (Torcal et al., 2012; Bellucci and Memoli, 2012).

Trust in political institutions is an essential element of the democratic legitimacy of decision making and the regime as such. Trust can be regarded as a resource or an asset of a political system allowing for relative autonomy of governance. Trust is, with regard to political actors or institutions, an advance "payment" resulting from the expectation that they (political actors and institutions) will do a proper job or function properly in the future (Luhmann, 1968; Preisendörfer 1995). It is based on retrospective evaluations that are translated into expectations for the future. Repeated positive experience translates into generalized attitudes; that is, trust (Wessels, 2009).

Based on the aforementioned and taking into consideration the close relationship between the perceived performance of the EU (and its institutions) and trust towards the EU and its institutions, the variable of trust towards the EP in the UK and Greece will also be used as an indicator for the assessment of the popular legitimacy of the EP in both countries.

3.6 Electoral Turnout and the Feeling for the Impact of Vote as a Determinant of Legitimacy of the EP

The extent of the EU's (and the EP's) legitimacy has also been assessed in relation to the electoral turnout at the European elections. For example, Blondel, Sinnott, and Svensson (1998) after having defined legitimacy as a variable quantity, which depends on the support of people for the institution in question, they use survey data from the 1994 European elections in order to assess popular perceptions of the EU and its Parliament. Their main argument is that, for example, the EP's legitimacy depends both on the extent and kind of voter participation, whereby low turnout is presumed to reflect and accentuate low levels of legitimacy, and that to understand why people abstain in EP elections requires the writers rejecting the received "second-order election" model.

There has also been an opposite view to the use of EP elections turnout level as an indication for the EU or the EP's popular legitimacy. For example, prior to the first EP direct elections in 1979, Herman and Lodge (1978) identified a number of problems which they thought might hinder the extent to which electoral turnout could be taken as a measure of the public's acceptance of, and support for, the EP's authority. These problems were related to the EP's limited role within EU decision making and to the lack of visibility and intelligibility of its powers and functions to the ordinary public. According to them, in this context, a low turnout could not be taken as an indication of a low level of public acceptance, and, therefore, of the EP's legitimacy. In the same vein, Cees van der Eijk and Hermann Schmitt (2009) argue that not voting (abstention from the EP elections) is not a manifestation of the EU (or the EP) lacking legitimacy in the eyes of the voters.

However, taking into consideration the fact that: (a) popular legitimacy in the relevant political and social science literature (as seen in Sect. 3.1) is conferred by some public act of acceptance or participation and (b) the EP elections turnout has been used in the past as an indicator for assessing the EP legitimacy, in our case the EP elections turnout will also be used, in parallel with the other relevant indicators.

In addition to the above and as far as the EP elections are concerned, another interesting issue to be noticed is that a key problem according to Schmitt and Thomassen (1999) to the EU and EP social legitimacy, is the fact that European elections do not provide voters with the opportunity to determine which party/parties should form a government and the kind of policies that government should pursue (as this is the case in national elections). According to them, despite the existence of a directly elected EP, if people do not think their votes make a difference, "this might be detrimental to the legitimacy not only of the EP, but of the whole European project as well".

Thus, in order to supplement the use of the electoral turnout indicator the empirical indicator of how the EU citizens think of their vote in the EP elections (whether it makes a difference, or not) will be also used for the assessment of the popular legitimacy of the EP.

In short, based on the aforementioned analysis, the following indicators will be used in Sect. 3.7 in order to empirically assess the popular legitimacy of the EP:

1. Trust level for the EP,
2. Perception of the EP's institutional efficiency,
3. Level of satisfaction with the EP as an institution,
4. EP elections voter turnout,
5. Feeling of EU citizens regarding the impact of their vote.

3.7 Empirical Data for Assessing the Social Legitimacy of the EP in the UK and Greece

3.7.1 Declining Trust in the European Parliament

According to the relevant data, as seen in Fig. 3.1 and since 1993 (a year after the rejection of the Maastricht Treaty in Denmark and the starting point of the debate in the literature regarding the EU legitimacy and democratic deficit) there is a trend of declining trust towards the institution of the European Parliament. For example, in 1993, approximately 54% of the EU citizens trusted the European Parliament, while in the first semester of 2018, approximately 49% of the EU citizens trusted the EP—and more recently in winter 2021, approximately 50% of European citizens trust the EP (European Commission, 2021). There is a general decrease of trust of the EU citizens towards the EP despite the fact that there have been slight fluctuations, with relevant increases mainly in the periods close to the European elections (June 1999, June 2004, June 2009, May 2014, May 2019) (these increase could be explained by the European elections campaigns in the specific periods) and in the periods of the EU enlargements in 2004 and 2007 (with the citizens of the new EU member states increasing the general trust levels towards the EU). However, the record low trust levels have been observed during the period 2011–2013. More specifically, in autumn 2011, distrust rates for the European Parliament had increased by seven percentage points (+7%), compared to autumn 2010, with 41% of Europeans trusting the European Parliament, and 45% distrusting it (European Commission, 2012a) while in spring 2012, 40% of the respondents (−1%) trusted the European Parliament, and 46% (+1) distrusted it (European Commission, 2012b). Despite a slight increase in the EP trust levels, only 44% of Europeans trusted the European Parliament, in autumn 2012 (European Commission, 2013a). The declining trust trend continued in autumn 2013 (39% of the EU citizens trusted the EP) and in spring 2014 with only 37% of Europeans trusting the European Parliament (these

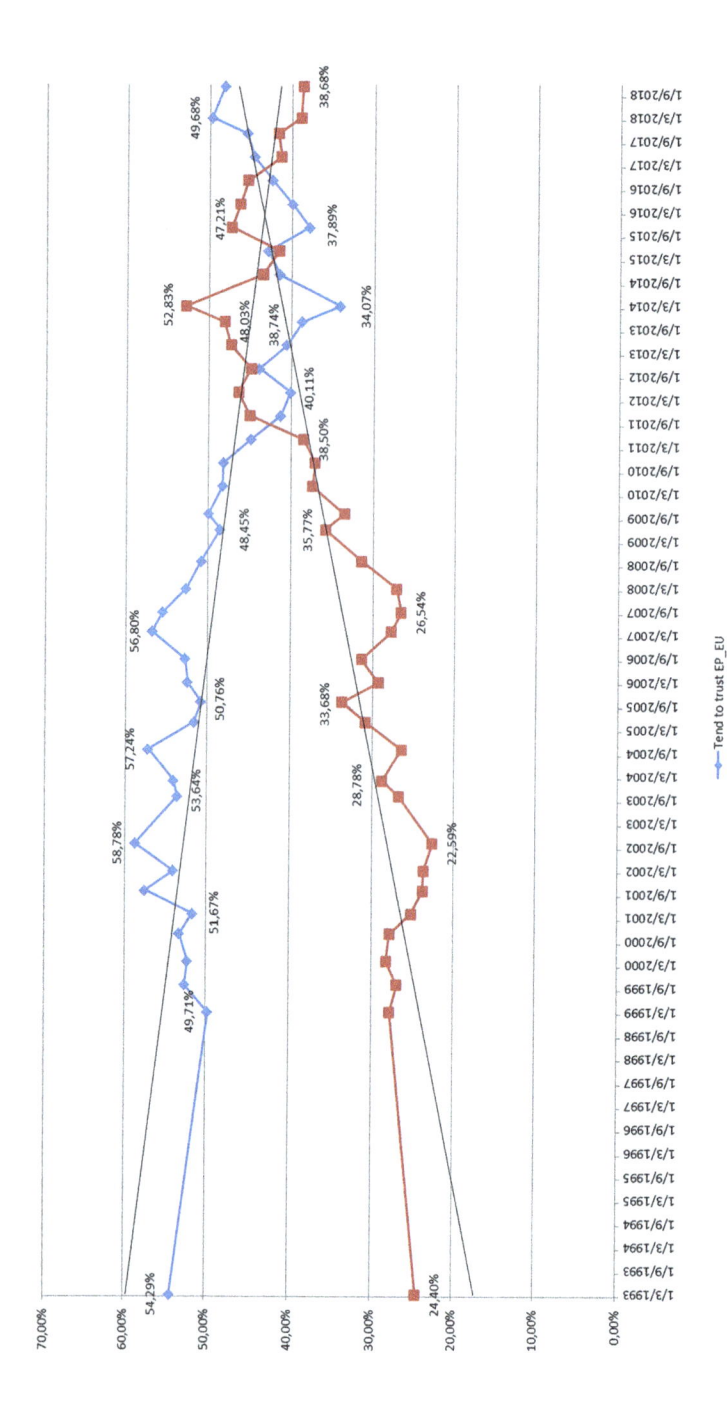

Fig. 3.1 Trust for the European Parliament at EU level (1993–2018) (Elaboration of Eurobarometer Interactive data by author)

data were drawn a few months after the 2014 EP elections) (European Commission, 2014).

As far as the case of the UK is concerned, since 1993, there is also a trend of declining trust towards the EP, by the UK citizens. According to the relevant data, as seen in Fig. 3.2, since 1993, there is a consistent trend of declining trust by the UK citizens, towards the institution of the European Parliament. In 1993, approximately 48% of the UK citizens trusted the European Parliament, while in the first semester of 2018, approximately 35% of the UK citizens trusted the EP—and more recently in November 2019, 33% of the UK citizens trusted the EP (European Commission, 2019). There is a general decrease of trust of the UK citizens despite again the fact that there are slight fluctuations of trust levels, with relevant increases mainly in the periods close to the European elections.

Relevant record low trust levels have also been observed during the period 2011–2013. More specifically during autumn 2011 in the United Kingdom the distrust level towards the European Parliament was the highest in the EU (68%) (European Commission, 2012a), while in spring 2012, the UK had the second highest—following Greece—distrust scores for the European Parliament (65%) (European Commission, 2012b). In autumn 2012, the UK also had one of the highest distrust scores for the EP (65%) following Greece and Spain (European Commission, 2013a). In spring 2013, the distrust score for the EP in the United Kingdom remained one of the highest in the EU (62%) (European Commission, 2013b), while during autumn 2013, the UK had again one of the highest distrust scores for the EP (60%) (European Commission, 2013c). In spring 2014, 57% of UK citizens distrusted the EP (European Commission, 2014). Adding to the above and regarding the same time period (spring 2014) a relevant Pew Research Center survey also reveals low support score (32%) for the European Parliament in the UK (Pew Research Center, 2014).

Similar is the case in Greece, where a trend of decreasing trust towards the EP is observed over the past decades. According to the relevant data, as seen in Fig. 3.3, since 1993, there is a consistent trend of declining trust by the Greek citizens, towards the institution of the European Parliament. In 1993, approximately 65% of the Greek citizens trusted the European Parliament, while in the first semester of 2018, approximately 30% of the Greek citizens trusted the EP—and more recently in winter 2021, approximately 43% of Greek citizens tend to trust the EP (European Commission, 2021). Thus, there is a general decrease of trust of the Greek citizens despite again the fact that there are slight fluctuations of trust levels, with slight relevant increases in the trust mainly in the periods close to the European elections. Relevant record low trust levels have also been observed during the period 2011–2013. More specifically, during autumn 2011, the distrust score towards the European Parliament (64%) was the second highest in the EU following that of the UK (European Commission, 2012a). In spring 2012, Greece was the country with the highest distrust score for the European Parliament (70%) (European Commission/DG Communication, 2012b). It was a similar case during autumn 2012, since Greece continued to be the member state with the highest distrust scores towards the EP (70%) (European Commission, 2013a). In spring 2013, the distrust score for the

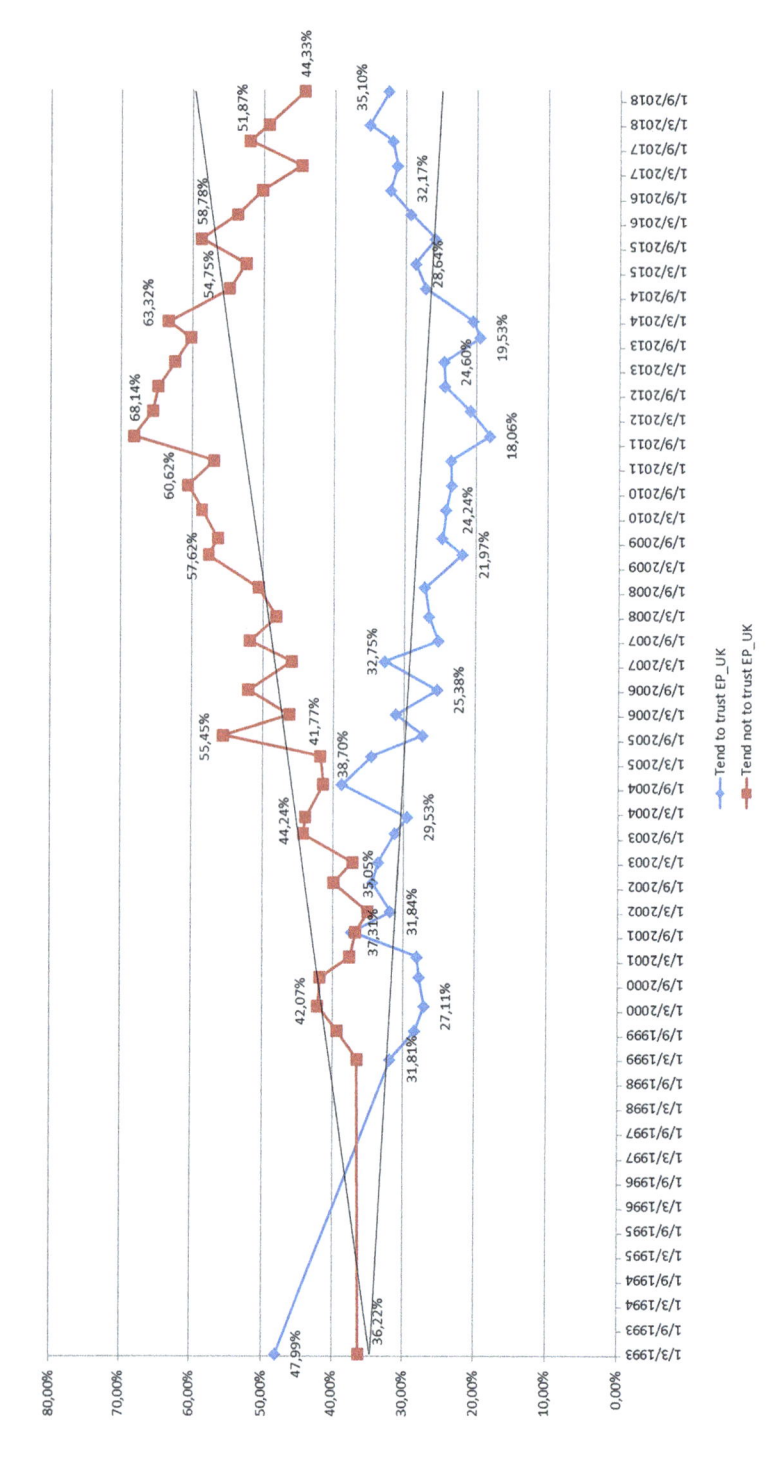

Fig. 3.2 Trust for the European Parliament in UK (1993–2018) (Elaboration of Eurobarometer Interactive data by author)

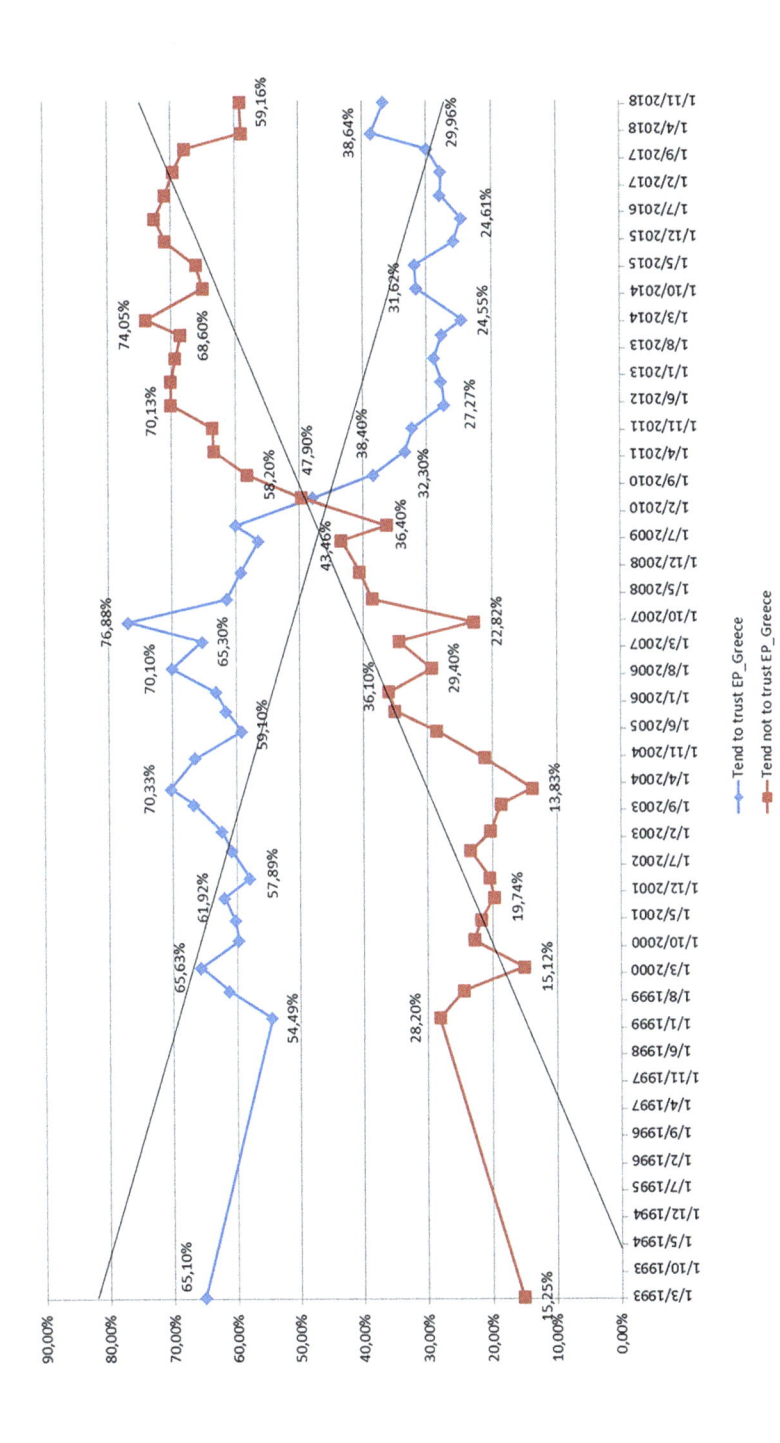

3.7 Empirical Data for Assessing the Social Legitimacy of the EP in the UK and... 39

Fig. 3.3 Trust for the European Parliament in Greece (1993–2018) (Elaboration of Eurobarometer Interactive data by author)

EP in Greece remained one of the highest in the EU (69%) (European Commission, 2013b), while in autumn 2013, Greece had again the highest score in the EU concerning the distrust in the European Parliament with 68% of Greek respondents distrusting the EP (European Commission, 2013c). In spring 2014, 64% of the Greeks distrusted the EP (the second highest score in the EU (European Commission, 2014). In addition, regarding the same time period (spring 2014), a relevant Pew Research Center survey reveals the lowest—in the EU—support score (26%) for the European Parliament in Greece (Pew Research Center, 2014).

3.7.2 European Parliament Perceived as an Inefficient Institution

Apart from the trust level towards the institution of the EP, relevant data also reveal that the EU citizens and more specifically the UK and Greek citizens perceive the EP as an inefficient institution.

The perceived effectiveness of the European Parliament was first examined in the Eurobarometer 42 (EB42) (Fieldwork December 1994) and continued till autumn 2000 (EB54). Although not defined directly, the specific EB42 report examined the perceived efficiency of the EP, by combining the variables of trust towards the EP (EB Question: Do you feel you can rely on the EP?) and the perception of the EU citizens that the EP protects their interests (EB Question: Does the European Parliament protect your interests?). As it was mentioned in the following Eurobarometer report (EB43) these two variables (trust and perception that the EP protects the EU citizens' interests) were combined for examining the perceived EP effectiveness.

Since trust towards the EP has already been examined in Sect. 3.7.1 as an independent variable, in this section (regarding specifically the time period 1994–2000) the perception of the EU citizens that the EP protects their interests will be analysed as a determinant more related to the effectiveness of the EP.

The perceived efficiency of the EP was again examined in autumn 2007 (EB68.1) and continued till Nov.–Dec. 2012 (EB78.2) where the EU (and the UK and Greek) citizens were asked whether they believed that the word "inefficient" describes well the EP. (The empirical data regarding the aforementioned variable—perceived efficiency of the EP—are only available for the period 2007 till 2012. From the 2014 European Parliament Eurobarometer—EB/EP82.4—onwards the detailed attributes of the EP's image are not examined/questioned in the public opinion poll).

Based on the aforementioned, regarding the period 1994–2000, and as shown in Fig. 3.4, since autumn 1997, the proportion of the EU citizens who believe that the European Parliament can protect their interests is steadily higher than the proportion of the EU citizens who believe that the European Parliament cannot protect their interests.

3.7 Empirical Data for Assessing the Social Legitimacy of the EP in the UK and... 41

Fig. 3.4 EU citizens' perception that the EP can protect their interests (1994–2000)

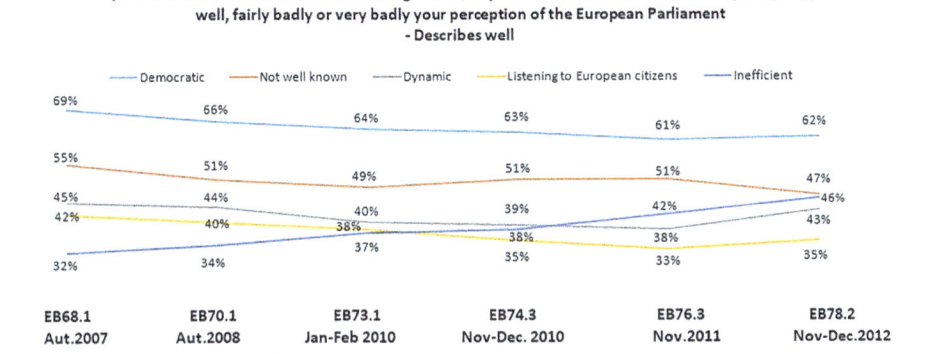

Fig. 3.5 European Parliament perceived as inefficient institution by the EU citizens (2007–2012)

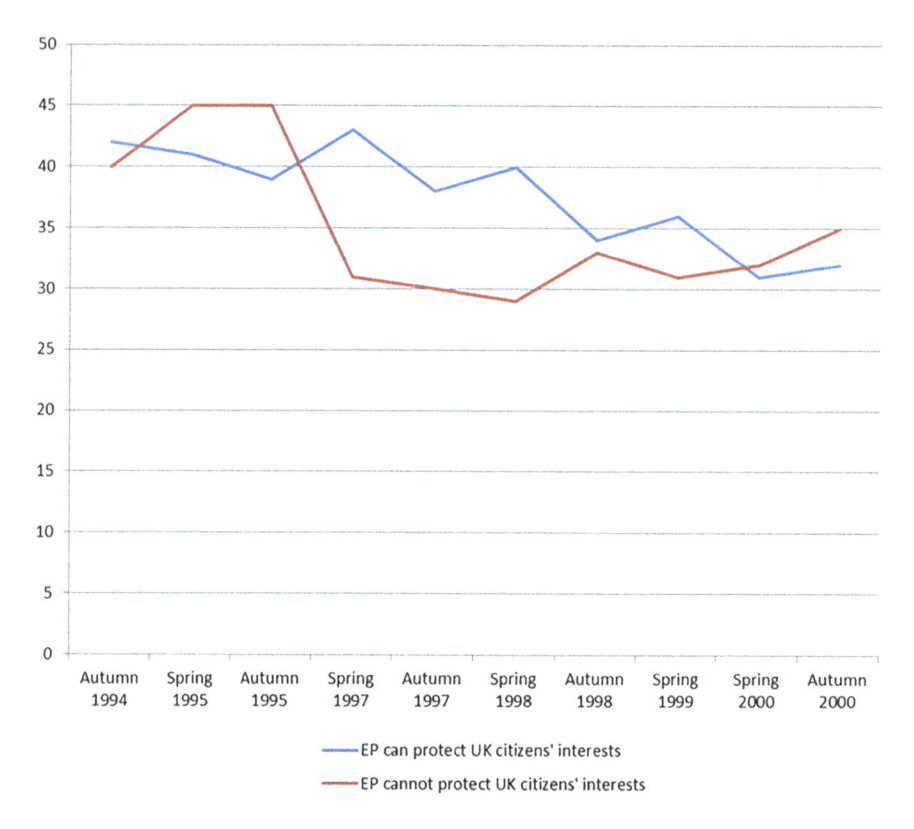

Fig. 3.6 UK citizens' perception that the EP can protect their interests (1994–2000)

However, and as can be seen in Fig. 3.5, for the period 2007–2012, there is an increasing trend regarding the proportion of the EU citizens who believe that the word "inefficient" describes well the European Parliament. Since autumn 2007, when 32% of the EU citizens considered the EP as an inefficient institution, this figure climbed at 46% in autumn 2012 (European Parliament, 2013), indicating an increase of 14% during this 5-year period.

As far as the UK is concerned, and as seen in Fig. 3.6, despite the fact that for the time period 1996–2000, the proportion of UK citizens who believed that the EP can protect their interests is higher than the proportion of the UK citizens who believe that the EP cannot protect their interests, since spring 1998, there is an increasing trend of the proportion of the UK citizens who consider that the EP cannot protect their interests. Since spring 2000, this specific proportion is higher than the opposite one. In spring 2000, 31% of the UK citizens felt that the EP can protect their interests very/fairly well while 32% of the UK citizens felt that the EP cannot/not at all protect

3.7 Empirical Data for Assessing the Social Legitimacy of the EP in the UK and... 43

Term "inefficient" describes well the EP

[Chart showing an increasing line from approximately 46% in Autumn 2007 to 56% in Autumn 2012, with data points at Autumn 2007, Autumn 2008, Autumn 2010, Autumn 2011, and Autumn 2012. Y-axis ranges from 0 to 60.]

——Term "inefficient" describes well the EP

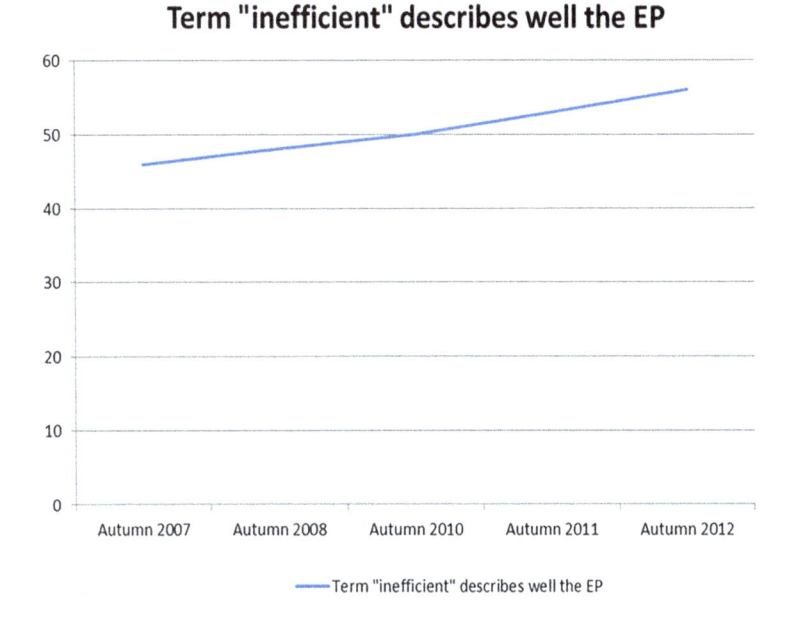

Fig. 3.7 European Parliament perceived as inefficient institution by the UK citizens (2007–2012)

their interests (EB53) (European Commission, 2000a). In autumn 2000, 32% of the UK citizens felt that the EP can protect their interests very/fairly well while 35% of the UK citizens felt that the EP cannot/not at all protect their interests (EB54) (European Commission, 2001).

In addition, as seen in Fig. 3.7, for the period 2007–2012, there is an increasing trend regarding the proportion of the UK citizens who believe that the word "inefficient" describes well the European Parliament. Since autumn 2007, when 46% of the UK citizens considered the EP as an inefficient institution (European Parliament, 2008), this figure reached at 56% in autumn 2012 (European Parliament, 2013) indicating an increase of 10% during this 5-year period.

As far as Greece is concerned, and as seen in Fig. 3.8, for the time period 1994–2010, the proportion of the Greek citizens who believe that the EP cannot protect their interests (despite some slight fluctuations) is steadily higher from the proportion of people who consider that the EP can actually protect their interests. This statistical difference is even higher since spring 2000. In spring 2000, 39% of the Greek citizens felt that the EP can protect their interests very/fairly well, while 41% of the Greek citizens felt that the EP cannot/not at all protect their interests (EB53) (European Commission, 2000a). In autumn 2000, 33% of the Greek citizens felt that the EP can protect their interests very/fairly well while 53% of the Greek

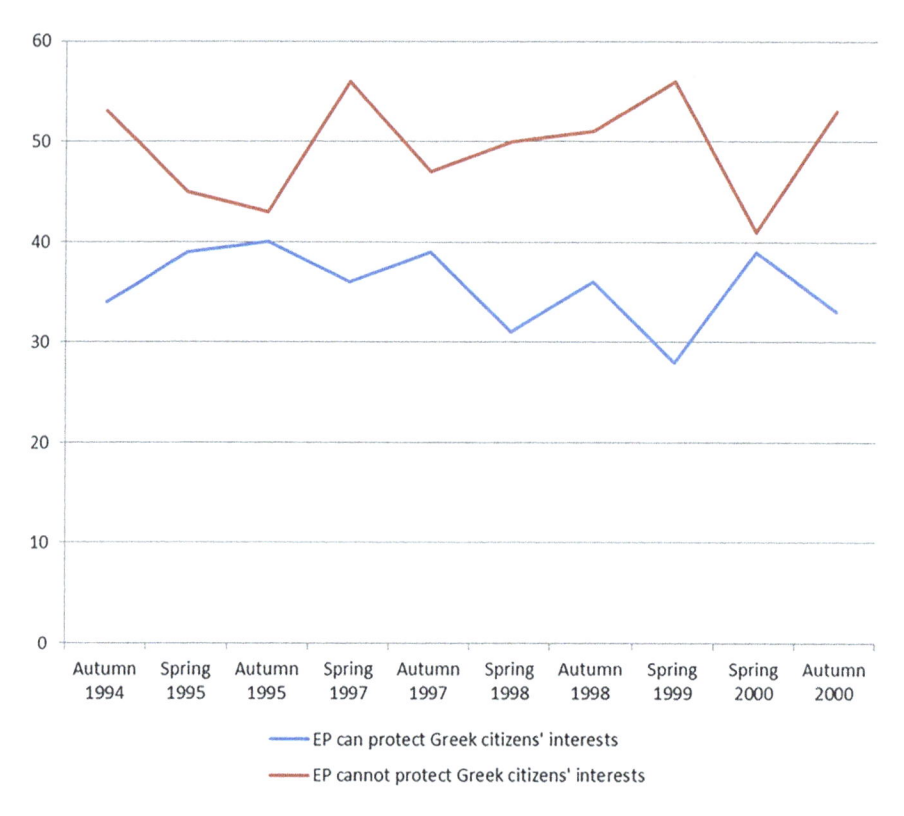

Fig. 3.8 Greek citizens' perception that the EP can protect their interests (1994–2000)

citizens felt that the EP cannot/not at all protect their interests (EB54) (European Commission, 2001).

In addition, as seen in Fig. 3.9, for the period 2007–2012, there is an increasing trend regarding the proportion of the Greek citizens who believe that the word "inefficient" describes well the European Parliament. More specifically, since autumn 2007, when 29% of the Greek citizens considered the EP as an inefficient institution (European Parliament, 2008), this figure reached at 64% in autumn 2012 (European Parliament, 2013) indicating an increase of 35% during this 5-year period.

Term "inefficient" describes well the EP

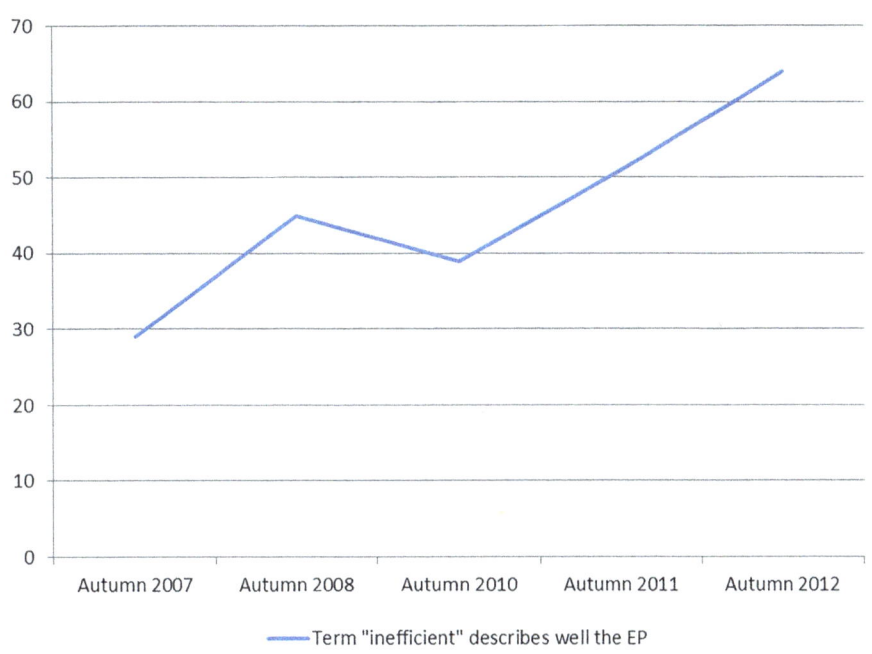

Fig. 3.9 European Parliament perceived as inefficient institution by the Greek citizens (2007–2012)

3.7.3 Electoral Turnout in the European Parliament Elections

As far as the electoral turnout in the EP elections is concerned—this is an indicator that will be used in parallel and supplementary to the other relevant indicators—and as seen in Fig. 3.10, since the first EP elections in 1979, there is a consistent trend of decreasing turnout in the European Elections (This decreasing trend is halted in the last 2019 EP elections where the turnout rate has increased 8% in comparison to the 2014 EP elections).

As far as the case of the UK is concerned, as seen in Table 3.1 and in Fig. 3.11, despite some slight fluctuations there is a stable turnout level in the EP elections, which is approximately 35–36%.

As far as the case of the Greece is concerned, as seen in Table 3.1 and in Fig. 3.12, since the first EP elections in Greece in 1981, there is a decreasing trend for the turnout till 2009. However, this decreasing trend halted in the two last EP elections in 2014 and 2019, where there was an increase in the turnout level.

Fig. 3.10 Turnout (EU level) in the European Parliament Elections (1979–2019) (European Parliament, 2019)

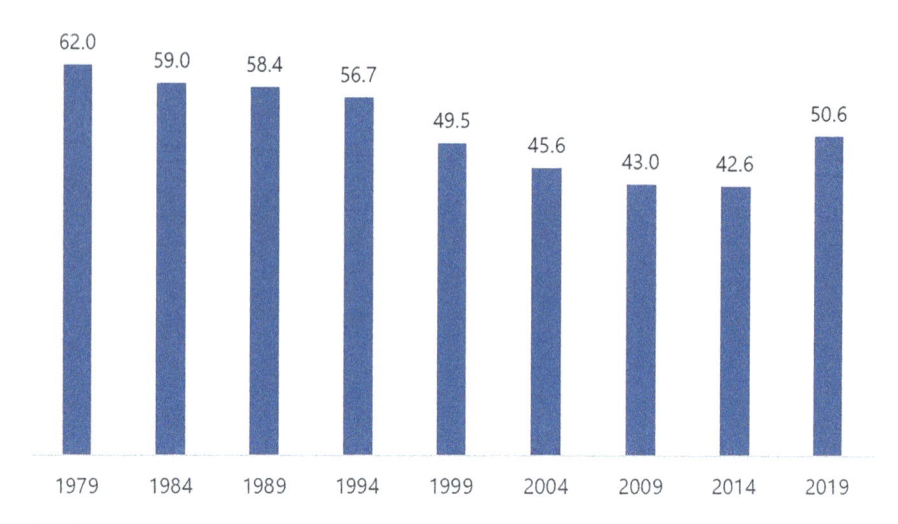

Table 3.1 Turnout in the EP elections in UK and Greece

Country	1979	1981	1984	1989	1994	1999	2004	2009	2014	2019
UK	32.35		32.57	36.37	36.43	24.00	38.52	34.70	35.60	36.90
Greece		81.48	80.59	80.03	73.18	70.25	63.22	52.54	59.97	58.69

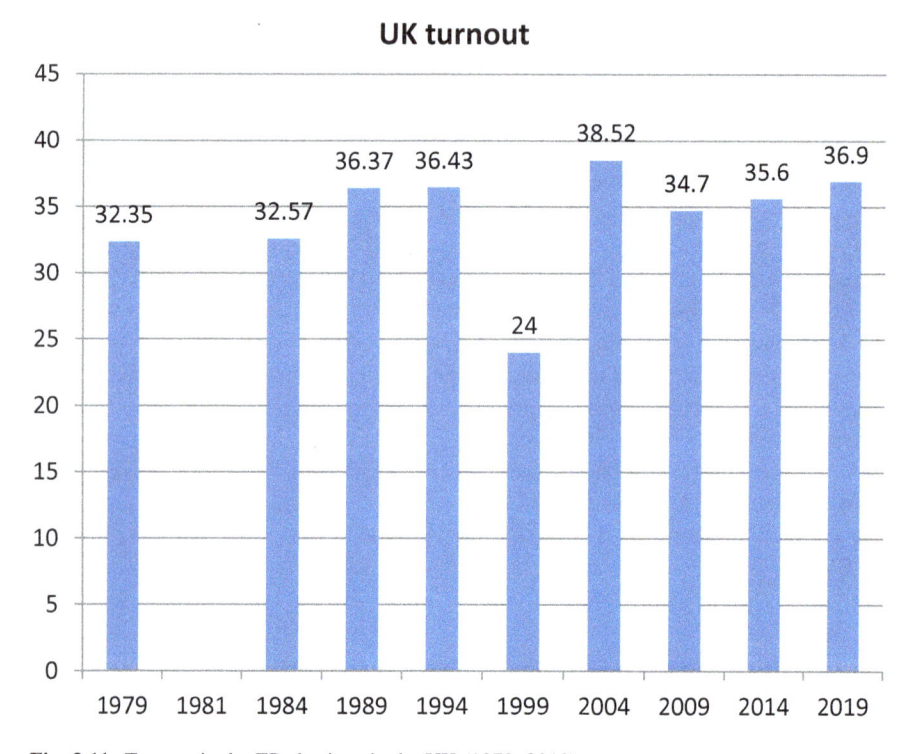

Fig. 3.11 Turnout in the EP elections in the UK (1979–2019)

Greek turnout

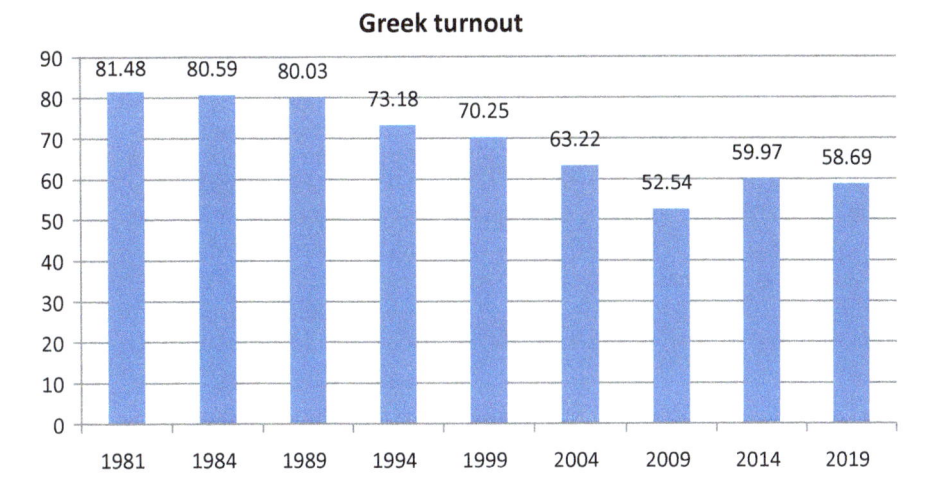

Year	Turnout (%)
1981	81.48
1984	80.59
1989	80.03
1994	73.18
1999	70.25
2004	63.22
2009	52.54
2014	59.97
2019	58.69

Fig. 3.12 Turnout in the EP elections in Greece (1979–2019)

3.7.4 Dissatisfaction with the European Parliament and Belief that European Parliament Vote Has No Consequences

Relevant empirical data also reveal that there is a feeling of dissatisfaction of the European citizens with the EP as an institution. According to the Eurobarometer data, one of the reasons for the abstention of the EU citizens from the EP elections in 1999, 2004, 2009, and 2014 was the dissatisfaction towards the EP as an institution. Since 1999 EP elections, when 5% of the non-voters felt that way (European Commission, 2000), this proportion increased to 8% in the 2014 EP elections (European Parliament, 2014).

As far as the UK is concerned, among the main reasons for not voting in the 1999 EP elections was the dissatisfaction with the EP as an institution, with 5% of the respondents-abstainers in the UK supporting that view (European Commission, 2000), a percentage that remained stable in the 2014 EP elections (European Parliament, 2014).

In Greece, among the main reasons for not voting in the 1999 EP elections was the dissatisfaction with the EP as an institution (3%) (European Commission, 2000), while this percentage reached at 11% as a reason for not voting in the 2014 EP elections (European Parliament, 2014).

It has to be mentioned here that in EB32 (Commission of the European Communities, 1989) (fieldwork autumn 1989) in the reasons of the people who did not vote in the 1989 EP elections there was no reference to the dissatisfaction towards the EP as a reason for not voting in the European elections. Similar is the case in the EB22 regarding the 1984 EP elections, and in the EB12 regarding the 1979 first EP elections (Commission of the European Communities, 1979, 1984).

In supplementing the aforementioned data, it should be also noted that among the most popular reasons for abstention from the 2009 and 2014 EP elections was the feeling of the EU citizens (and the citizens in the UK and Greece) that their vote has no consequences and does not change anything.

In the UK, 9% of the respondents-abstainers supported that view regarding the 2009 EP elections, while 6% of the respondents-abstainers in the UK supported that view regarding the 2014 EP elections) (European Parliament, 2014).

In addition, in Greece, 24% of the respondents-abstainers supported this view regarding the 2009 EP elections, while 20% of the respondents-abstainers in Greece supported this view regarding the 2014 EP elections (European Parliament, 2012, 2014).

3.7.5 Concluding Remarks

The scope of this section was to assess the social legitimacy of the EP in the UK and Greece through the use of relevant empirical data. These data reveal that during the selected time period (2011–2013) negative public perceptions—in most cases the highest negative scores in the EU—towards the EP in the UK and Greece are observed, as seen in the declining trust levels for the EP, in the increasing public perception of the EP as an inefficient institution, in the increasing dissatisfaction with the EP as an institution, and in the feeling of the EU citizens that their vote in the EP elections does not change anything and has no consequences. These negative public perceptions indicate that the EP—during the period under examination—faces a serious social legitimacy deficit, in the UK and Greece.

Before proceeding to Chap. 4, it has to be mentioned here that scholars such as Banchoff and Smith (1999) argue that there are grounds for doubt in using public opinion polls for explaining an EU legitimacy crisis, from the recognition point of view. According to them: (a) such a conclusion obscures important changes in the meaning of European integration over time, (b) negative responses to general questions about the EU may represent dissatisfaction with particular EU policies, and not the integration process as a whole, and (c) the examination of political attitudes and views cannot capture recognition expressed through patterns of activity.

However, in our case these empirical data—specifically related to the EP—are not used for the assessment of the social legitimacy of the EU as a whole polity or the integration process, but are used for the assessment of the social acceptance levels of a specific EU institution. In addition, the use of the turnout level in the EP elections, as a relevant supplementary indicator, also takes into consideration and captures recognition expressed through patterns of activity (in the specific case patterns of participation—or non-participation—in the EP elections).

References

Arnold, C., Sapir, E. V., & Zapryanova, G. (2012). Trust in the institutions of the European Union: A cross-country examination. In L. Beaudonnet, & D. Di Mauro (Eds.), *Beyond Euroskepticism: Understanding attitudes towards the EU. European Integration online Papers (EIoP)*. Special Mini-Issue 2, 16(8). Retrieved February 25, 2015, from http://eiop.or.at/eiop/texte/2012-008a.htm.

Ashcraft, R. (Ed.). (1991). *John Locke: Critical assessments*. Routledge.

Banchoff, T. F., & Smith, M. P. (1999). *Legitimacy and the European Union the contested polity*. Routledge.

Beetham, D. (1991). *The legitimation of power*. Macmillan.

Beetham, D., & Lord, C. (1998). *Legitimacy and the EU*. Longman.

Bellucci, P., & Memoli, V. (2012). The determinants of democracy satisfaction in Europe. In D. Sanders, P. Magalhaes, & G. Toka (Eds.), *Citizens and the European Polity: Mass attitudes towards the European and national polities* (pp. 9–39). Oxford University Press.

Blondel, J., Sinnott, R., & Svensson, P. (1998). *People and parliament in the European Union: Participation, democracy, and legitimacy*. Oxford University Press.

Commission of the European Communities. (1979). *Euro-Barometer 12. European Parliamentary Elections October-November 1979*. ZA1037/ICPSR 7778. Brussels.

Commission of the European Communities. (1984). *Euro-Barometer 22. October-November 1984. Energy Problems and the Atlantic Alliance*. ZA 1321.Brussels.

Commission of the European Communities. (1989). *Standard Eurobarometer No.32 – December 1989. Public Opinion in the European Community*. Directorate-General Information, Communication, Culture. Brussels. Available at: https://europa.eu/eurobarometer/surveys/detail/1428

De Baecque, A. (1995). *A history of democracy in Europe*. Columbia United Press.

De Vries, C. E., & van Kersbergen, K. (2007). Interests, identity and political allegiance in the European Union. *Acta Politica, 42*, 307–328.

Decker, F. (2002). Governance beyond the nation-state. Reflections on the democratic deficit of the European Union. *Journal of European Public Policy, 9*(2), 256–272.

Easton, D. (1965). *A systems analysis of political life*. Wiley.

Ehrmann, M., Soudan, M., & Stracca, L. (2013). Explaining European Union Citizens' Trust in the European Central Bank in normal and crisis times. *Scandinavian Journal of Economics, 115*(3), 781–807.

European Commission. (2000). *Eurobarometer 52, Public Opinion in the European Community (Spring, 2000)*. ZA No. 3204. Directorate-General for Communication. Brussels.

European Commission. (2000a). *Eurobarometer 53, Public Opinion on the European Community*. ZA No. 3296. Directorate-General for Communication. Brussels.

European Commission. (2001). *Eurobarometer Report 54, Europeans and Languages. Executive Summary*. ZA No. 3389. Directorate-General for Communication. Brussels.

European Commission. (2012a). *Standard Eurobarometer 76. Public Opinion in the European Union*. ZA No. 5567. Directorate-General for Communication. Brussels.

European Commission. (2012b). *Standard Eurobarometer 77. Public Opinion in the European Union*. ZA No. 5612. Directorate-General for Communication. Brussels.

European Commission. (2013a). *Standard Eurobarometer 78. Public Opinion in the European Union, (Autumn 2012)*. ZA No. 5685. Directorate-General for Communication. Brussels.

European Commission. (2013b). *Standard Eurobarometer 79. Public Opinion in the European Union, (Spring, 2013)*. ZA No. 5689. Directorate-General for Communication. Brussels.

European Commission. (2013c). *Standard Eurobarometer 80. Public Opinion in the European Union, (Autumn, 2013)*. ZA No. 5876. Directorate-General for Communication. Brussels.

European Commission. (2014). *Standard Eurobarometer 81. Public Opinion in the European Union, (Spring, 2014)*. ZA No. 5928. Directorate-General for Communication. Brussels.

European Commission. (2019) *Standard Eurobarometer 92. Public Opinion in the European Union. (Autumn, 2019)*. Directorate-General for Communication. Brussels. https://europa.eu/eurobarometer/surveys/detail/2255
European Commission. (2021) *Standard Eurobarometer 94*. DG Communication. https://europa.eu/eurobarometer/surveys/detail/2355
European Parliament. (2008). *Eurobaromètre Spécial 288/Vague 68.1 - Le Parlement Européen/ Rapport*. L'opinion publique dans l'union Europeenne. Direction Générale Communication. Brussels.
European Parliament. (2012). *2009 European Elections Desk Research: Abstention and voting behaviour in the 2009 European elections*. Directorate-General for Communication. Brussels. Available at: https://www.europarl.europa.eu/cyprus/resource/static/files/2012-11-13-desk-research-abstention-principaux-enseignements-en.pdf
European Parliament. (2013). *European Parliament Eurobarometer (EB/EP 78.2, November 2012)*. Directorate -General for Communication. Brussels.
European Parliament. (2014). *European Elections 2014, Post-election survey*. Directorate-General for Communication. Brussels. Available at: https://www.europarl.europa.eu/at-your-service/files/be-heard/eurobarometer/2014/post-election-survey-2014/analytical-synthesis/en-analytical-synthesis-post-election-survey-2014.pdf
European Parliament. (2019). *The 2019 Elections. A pro-European -and young-electorate with clear expectations. First results of the European Parliament post-electoral survey*. DG Communication. Brussels. Available at: https://www.europarl.europa.eu/at-your-service/files/be-heard/eurobarometer/2019/election2019/EB915_SP_EUROBAROMETER_POSTEE19_FIRSTRESULTS_EN.pdf
Follesdal, A., & Hix, S. (2006). Why there is a democratic deficit in the EU: A response to Majone and Moravcsik. *Journal of Common Market Studies, 44*(3), 533–562.
Habermas, J. (1984). *The theory of communicative action, 2 vols*. Beacon.
Held, D. (1987). *Models of democracy*. Polity Press.
Held, D. (2006). *Models of democracy* (3rd ed.). Polity Press.
Herman, V., & Lodge, J. (1978). *The European parliament and the European community*. Palgrave Macmillan.
Hobolt, S. B. (2012). Citizen satisfaction with democracy in the European Union. *Journal of Common Market Studies, 50*(s1), 88–105.
Hooghe, L., & Marks, G. (2005). Calculation, community and cues: Public opinion on European integration. *European Union Politics, 6*(4), 419–443.
Ilonszki, G. (2009). National discontent and EU support in Central and Eastern Europe. *Europe Asia Studies, 61*(6), 1041–1057.
Lindberg, L., & Scheingold, S. (1970). *Europe's would-be polity*. Prentice-Hall.
Luhmann, N. (1968) *Vertrauen. Ein Mechanismus der Reduktion sozialer Komplexität. Soziologische Gegenwartsfragen, N.F., Nr. 28*. Stuttgart: F. Enke.
Majone, G. (1998). Europe's democratic deficit: The question of standards. *European Law Journal, 4*(1), 5–28.
Marsh, M. (1999). Policy performance. In H. Schmitt & J. Thomassen (Eds.), *Political representation and legitimacy in the European Union*. Oxford University Press.
Mill, J., & Gray, J. (1991). *On liberty and other essays*. Oxford University Press.
Mishler, W., & Rose, R. (2001). What are the origins of political trust? Testing institutional and cultural theories in post-communist societies. *Comparative Political Studies, 34*(1), 30–62.
Mommsen, W. J. (1974). *The age of bureaucracy*. Blackwell.
Moravcsik, A. (2002). In defence of the "democratic deficit": Reassessing legitimacy in the European Union. *Journal of Common Market Studies, 40*(4), 603–624.
Nedergaard, P. (2006). *European Union administration: Legitimacy and efficiency. Nijhoff Law Specials, 69*. Brill Academic Publishers.
Pew Research Center. (2014). *A fragile rebound for EU image on eve of European Parliament Elections. Number, facts and trends shaping the world*. Retrieved November 13, 2018, from:

http://www.pewresearch.org/wp-content/uploads/sites/2/2014/05/2014-05-12_Pew-Global-Attitudes-European-Union.pdf

Preisendörfer, P. (1995). Vertrauen als soziologische Kategorie. Möglichkeiten und Grenzen einer entscheidungstheoretischen Fundierung des Vertrauenskonzepts. *Zeitschrift für Soziologie, 24*(4), 263–272.

Rohrschneider, R. (2002). The democratic deficit and mass support for an EU-wide government. *American Journal of Political Science, 46*(2), 463–475.

Schmitt, H., & Thomassen, J. (Eds.). (1999). *Political representation and legitimacy in the European Union*. Oxford University Press.

Schumpeter, J. (1976). *Capitalism, socialism and democracy*. Allen and Unwin.

Schweiger, C. (2016). *Exploring the EU's legitimacy crisis: The dark heart of Europe*. Edward Elgar Publishing.

Taylor, C. (1992). *Multiculturalism and the "politics of recognition"*. Princeton University Press.

Thomassen, J. J. A. (Ed.). (2009). *The legitimacy of the European Union after enlargement*. Oxford University Press.

Torcal, M., Muñoz, J., & Bonet, E. (2012). Trust in the European Parliament: From affective heuristics to rational cueing. In D. Sanders, P. Magalhaes, & G. Toka (Eds.), *Citizens and the European polity: Mass attitudes towards the European and national polities*. Oxford University Press.

Uslaner, E. M. (2002). *The moral foundations of trust*. Cambridge University Press.

Van der Cruijsen, C. A. B., & Eijffinger, S. C. W. (2008). From actual to perceived transparency: The case of the European Central Bank. *Journal of Economic Psychology, 31*(3), 388–399. https://doi.org/10.1016/j.joep.2010.01.007

van der Eijk, C., & Schmitt, H. (2009). *Legitimacy and electoral abstention in European Parliament elections*. Oxford University Press.

Vile, M. (1998). *Constitutionalism and the separation of powers* (2nd ed.). Liberty Fund.

Watts, D. (2008). *The European Union*. Edinburgh University Press.

Weber, M. (1964). In T. Parsons (Ed.), *The theory of social and economic organization*. Free Press.

Weber, M. (1978). *Economy and society, 2Vols*. University of California Press.

Weiler, J. (1991). Problems of legitimacy in post 1992 Europe. *Aussenwirtschaft, 46*(3–4), 411–437.

Wessels, W. (2009). *Das politische System der Europäischen Union*. Springer.

Chapter 4
European Parliament and the News Media

This chapter starts with the examination of the role of the news media, in shaping public perceptions towards the EU and its institutions, by analyzing the characteristics of the relevant media coverage. Then, it focuses on the communication deficit of the EU and its institutions, which is directly linked to their social legitimacy deficit, and it examines the factors that contribute to this deficit, the communication and media relations performance of these institutions, and the way by which journalists produce EU news stories. Specific emphasis is placed on the EP and the role of the EPLOs in delivering the EP information in the news media and the audience in the member states. Last but not least, issues relevant to online journalism (e.g. specific features of online journalism and digital news production) are also discussed.

4.1 The Role of the News Media in Shaping Public Perceptions Towards the EP

As it has been discussed in Sects. 3.4, 3.5, and 3.6, the relevant literature identifies determinants that explain public opinion towards the EU and the EU institutions. For example, public support for European integration has been explained in terms of cognitive mobilization, which is based on a positive correlation between higher levels of political involvement and knowledge and support for European integration (Inglehart, 1970, 1977). In addition, utilitarian and economic considerations also explain EU support; according to this theory, EU citizens from different socio-economic situations (more specific determinants are income, education, and occupational skills) experience different costs and benefits from integrative policy and the EU and consequently have different perceptions towards the EU (Gabel and Palmer, 1995; Gabel, 1998). Another strand of research suggests that citizens resort to proxies when shaping their view on EU integration and EU in general and that these proxies are likely to be based on national political considerations and preferred parties (Anderson, 1998; Franklin et al., 1994).

However, in addition to the aforementioned public opinion determinants, relevant research indicates that news media have the potential to shape public perceptions and attitudes towards the EU, the EU institutions, and issues such as the EU enlargement or specific EU policies (Norris, 2000; De Vreese and Semetko, 2004; Vliegenthart et al., 2008; De Vreese and Boomgaarden 2006a; Schuck and de Vreese, 2006; Maier and Rittberger, 2008; De Vreese and Kandyla, 2009; Lubbers and Scheepers, 2010; Elenbaas et al., 2012).

For example, Maier and Rittberger (2008) showed that public attitudes towards EU enlargement are strongly affected by exposure to the mass media, since it affects the standards by which individuals evaluate the accession of potential candidate countries. They demonstrated that information on the economic, political, or social situation in a candidate country significantly changes the level of public support for EU accession by this country; positive information about a candidate country generally causes an increase in support for accession, whereas negative information leads to a decline in support for further EU enlargement.

In a similar vein, regarding the news media effects on EU citizens public attitudes towards EU enlargement, De Vreese and Boomgaarden (2006a) demonstrated that public attitudes about EU enlargement are conditioned by media coverage (visibility) and by the tone of the coverage (whether evaluations of EU enlargement are portrayed positively, negatively, or mixed). Their results suggested that media coverage of EU affairs mattered to change in public opinion about EU enlargement. For example, in the case where the news media coverage was considerable in amount and positive in tone they found respondents to be gain-seeking and endorse the enlargement of the EU, while in the situation where news media messages were less visible and mixed in character they did not find the news media to exert an influence on the dynamics of public opinion formation. In another study, Schuck and de Vreese (2006) employed evaluations of the 2004 EU enlargement in terms of risks and opportunities as "valence frames" in order to assess the influence of these frames on public support for EU enlargement. They found that the "risk frame" led to lower levels of support for EU enlargement among respondents than the "opportunity frame". In other words, if EU enlargement was presented as a risk, people's support was generally lower than if it was presented as an opportunity.

Brettschneider et al. (2003) in order to examine whether the media coverage played any role in the forming of the public opinion in Germany regarding the introduction of the Euro as a common EU currency, they had a systematic content analyses of television newscasts compared with representative opinion polls on the aggregate level. Their assumption was that mass media played in Germany an important role in the formation of public opinion on the Euro.

In another study, De Vreese and Boomgaarden (2006b) tested a model of how media message flows and interpersonal communication affect public opinion. They found that exposure and attention to news media affected public policy support. These were effects of a consistent negative bias, presenting an issue in terms of risks and losses, which led to lower levels of support for the policy, and effects of positive

4.1 The Role of the News Media in Shaping Public Perceptions Towards the EP

news coverage of the issue, focusing on the potential gains and advantages, which led to increased public policy support. According to them, the media mattered to change in public opinion but only in the context in which the news media reported considerable in amount and in a consistent tone about a political event.

In a similar vein, De Vreese and Semetko (2004) investigated how the information environment in the Danish 2000 euro referendum campaign served to crystallize opinion on the issue (within the context of a number of other hypothesized influences on the vote). They found that exposure to news significantly influenced vote choice when controlling for other predictors. Mediated sources of information in the final weeks of the campaign exerted a significant influence on crystallizing individual opinion on the vote (even after controlling for all other possible influences). They suggested that attention should be paid to the actual content and tone of the coverage.

Vliegenthart et al. (2008) examined, in seven EU member states for the period 1990–2006, whether the visibility and the framing of EU news coverage influences EU support at an aggregate level. By utilizing aggregated data on the content, analytical indicators, and aggregate public support measures in a time-series design, they related variation in news content to subsequent public opinion variation and dynamics. They found that the framing of EU news in terms of benefit and conflict mattered for EU public support; benefit framing increased EU public support, while conflict framing decreased EU public support.

In another study, De Vreese and Kandyla (2009), focusing on the impact of the news content itself rather than the amount of news (visibility), examined the effects of framing in terms of "risk" and "opportunity" on public support of a specific EU policy; they examined whether the effect of framing common foreign and security policy (CFSP) as a "risk for the nation-state" has more impact than "risk for the EU" framing. Drawing on a survey-embedded experiment they found that participants in the "risk" frame condition showed significantly lower levels of support compared to participants in the "opportunity" condition. In addition, those in the "risk for the nation-state" condition were significantly less supportive of CFSP than those in the "risk for the EU" condition.

Last but not least, Elenbaas et al. (2012) examined whether acquiring information following a real-world EU decision-making event alters citizens' judgements about the utilitarian and democratic performance of the EU. It was found that citizens who acquired performance-relevant information became more approving of the EU's utilitarian performance but did not change their judgements about its democratic performance.

The aforementioned studies indicate that the news media coverage has the potential to shape public attitudes towards the EU and EU institutions, or, in other words, they indicate that there is a link between the social legitimacy (public perceptions towards the EU and its institutions) and the relevant news media coverage. Exposure to media is an important factor in shaping opinion, while public attitudes about the EU are conditioned, in the vast majority of the relevant studies, by the amount of the media coverage (visibility) and the tone of the coverage.

4.2 Characteristics of the Media Coverage

Since the visibility and the tone of the EU and EU institutions' coverage are important factors for shaping public attitudes, the specific elements and characteristics of the relevant media coverage need to be further examined.

Research shows that in general the EU news accounts for a small proportion of news in national media with high visibility during key events (e.g. EU summits) and low visibility in routine periods (Norris, 2000; Peter et al., 2003; Gleissner and De Vreese, 2005; Kandyla and De Vreese, 2011; Peter and de Vreese, 2004; Machill et al., 2006; Kontochristou & Mascha, 2014).

There is a strong national orientation in the news media in member states (Gleissner and De Vreese, 2005; Machill et al., 2006; Souliotis, 2013) with the EU actors being usually absent from the EU coverage (Peter and de Vreese, 2004; Souliotis, 2013), while the tone of news is usually negative (Gleissner and De Vreese, 2005; Peter et al., 2003; Archontaki, 2012; Souliotis, 2013).

With reference to news framing (meaning which aspect is more salient in the news), studies show that major EU events, such as Council meetings, are covered more intensively because of the conflict, the tension, and the drama they involve, while EU events are also framed in terms of attribution of responsibility and the economic consequences, or via the "risk" and "opportunity" frames (De Vreese, 2001a; Norris, 2000; Semetko and Valkenburg, 2000; De Vreese et al., 2001; Archontaki, 2012; Kandyla and De Vreese, 2011).

As far as the thematic areas of coverage are concerned, economic policy and monetary policy are the most salient topics while foreign policy, the enlargement of the EU, and the various EU policies are also prominent issues (Trenz, 2004; Norris, 2000; Peter et al., 2003). During the Eurozone crisis, the media coverage of the EU was also focused on issues related to solidarity (Kontochristou and Mascha, 2014) or the handling of the crisis by the EU (Souliotis, 2013).

When it comes to the media coverage of the EU and the EU institutions' performance output, relevant research shows that coverage focuses predominantly on the national consequences of the EU output and policies. For example, the introduction of the euro was portrayed in the news via the economic consequences framed both in terms of the potentially severe economic repercussions or positive developments for the domestic macro-economies and individual businesses in the member states (Semetko et al., 2000; de Vreese et al., 2001), while the same kind of nationally focused framing has also been used when showing either the benefits or disadvantages of a country's EU membership (Vliegenthart et al., 2008). The media coverage of the effects of the European Union Constitution was similarly framed since the domestic relevance of the Constitution for the individual member states was most frequently discussed together with, in some cases, the evaluation of the Constitution's effect on EU candidate countries or the EU in general (Gleissner and de Vreese, 2005). Research also confirms that the central institutions of the EU are covered in the media predominantly with regard to how far their activities and their impact are for or against the interests of the individual member states (Lloyd and Marconi, 2014).

When it comes to the institution of the European Parliament, most of the studies focus on the EP elections and show that in general there is a lack of EP election news in the media (De Vreese, 2001b, 2003; MacLeod, 2003), with the exception of the 2004 EP elections which were more visible, than previous EP elections, in the "new" member states because of the novelty of the event (De Vreese et al., 2005, 2006). There is also a domestic point of view in the relevant EP election news (domestic political actors dominate the coverage) with an interest more in the social angle than the political one in the stories, while in some cases voter apathy is a dominant theme (Leroy and Siune, 1994; De Vreese, 2003; Kevin, 2001; Demertzis, 2006). As far as the tone of the news is concerned, the EP election campaign news is rather neutral (De Vreese et al., 2006; Michailidou, 2012). In routine periods, the daily European Parliament debates and workings remain largely invisible to the public (Anderson and Weymouth, 1999; Norris, 2000) even if in some countries there is a regularity of news provision following the parliamentary calendar (Gattermann, 2013).

4.3 The EU and the EP Affairs in the UK News Media

Existing studies on the EU and EP media coverage in the UK show that European affairs stories are far from salient, with few stories referring to the rights that the EU provides to the citizens and, in general, EU news stories being covered with a negative tone, with the exception of the relatively small UK Europhile press and to varying extents the BBC (Morgan, 1995; Gavin, 2000; Esser, 1999; Norris, 2000; De Vreese, 2001a; Gleissner and De Vreese, 2005). There is most predominantly an anti-European stance—with its discourse ranging from understandable concerns about EU integration to extreme historicism, emotionalism, and xenophobic patterns (Anderson and Weymouth, 1999).

In the UK, the media coverage of the output of the EU performance or policies focuses, as seen before, mainly on the domestic level and is predominantly covered with a negative tone. For example, in the past the relevant discourse in the predominant Eurosceptic titles of the British press has usually referred negatively to the economic consequences if Britain were to join the EMU, or were to sign the Social Chapter, together with the negative political implications of EU integration for British sovereignty and governance in the UK, or the allegedly negative EU impact at the international level (Anderson and Weymouth, 1999). In the case of the euro launch, the news reports in the UK presented it in terms of the potentially severe economic repercussions for the domestic macro-economy and the economic implications for the British pound sterling and for individual businesses (Semetko et al., 2000; de Vreese et al., 2001). The situation is similar with regard to the Constitution where the relevance of it for Britain was most frequently discussed and it was regarded mostly unfavourable (Gleissner and de Vreese, 2005), as was the case with the Common Foreign and Security Policy (CFSP) (Kandyla and de Vreese, 2011).

When it comes to the European Parliament, its profile in the British press is very low with a greater emphasis on the other two institutions, the European Commission and the Council of Ministers (Anderson and Weymouth, 1999).

4.4 The EU and EP Affairs in the Greek News Media

Research on the coverage of Europe or the European Parliament in the Greek media seems to be scarce. However, a study conducted in 2004 showed that European news became the main story just once in a month during a routine period of coverage by the Greek press and television stations and that the national interest and matters of domestic concern were the important selection criteria for European news (Theodosiadou et al., 2004). Other research shows that EU news is covered in a negative tone, through a domestic logic and within a responsibility or conflict framing (Archontaki, 2012; Souliotis, 2013).

In Greece, regarding the media coverage of the effectiveness and the impact of the EU performance or policies, the EU has been portrayed as a weak and dysfunctional mechanism with ineffective output which could not handle the Greek crisis and which was also criticized for its slow response (Souliotis, 2013).

When it comes to the coverage of the European Parliament in Greece, relevant research shows, for example, that during the period of the 2 weeks leading up to the 2004 European Elections 21% of the main evening news time was devoted to these specific elections, making it the biggest percentage of television news coverage in the EU (De Vreese et al., 2005). In addition, Demertzis (2006) has examined the coverage of the 2004 EP election campaign in the Greek media, by analysing the period covering the last 2 weeks of the campaign, and found that most of the EP elections news referred to the Greek political parties and domestic public issues rather than to European ones, that the tone of the news stories was highly ethnocentric, and that a non-conflictual framing dominated the coverage.

As discussed in Sect. 4.1, the visibility and tone in the news media coverage of the EU and its institutions has been identified as an important indicator to be taken into consideration, since it is argued that higher levels of visibility of news about European politics provide citizens with information about the issues at stake that they might otherwise miss and cue them about the importance of EU policies and EU institutions (Boomgaarden et al., 2013; De Vreese et al., 2006). In the same vein, the visibility and tone in the EU or the EP news is really crucial as an indicator as it shows how much and what kind of communication EU citizens actually receive about EU affairs (Trenz, 2004).

4.5 Communication Deficit of the EU and Its Institutions

The low visibility of EU (and EU institutions) news, the negative tone of the coverage, the strong national orientation in the news media in member states, and the conflict/tension and drama framing the coverage are characteristics that enhance the so-called communication deficit of the EU, which is directly linked to the legitimacy deficit of the EU and its institutions.

The EU communication deficit could be described as an absence of a corresponding (to the transfer of political power from European nation states to the EU) increase in public discourses in the member states about the EU and its institutions (Meyer, 1999; Sifft et al., 2007; Bijsmans and Altides, 2007; Laursen and Valentini, 2013). And this discrepancy, according to many scholars, also constitutes a major problem for the popular support to the EU, the EU institutions, and their relevant legitimacy.

For example, Meyer (1999) argues that the invisibility of the EU in public discourse and the consequent low public support deriving from this invisibility could be framed as a "legitimacy deficit". Laursen and Valentini (2013) argue that the EU communication deficit constitutes a barrier to public participation and public support for the EU and its institutions. Participation and public support are fundamental for democracy and specifically for the case of the EU are fundamental for its integration process. Karp et al. (2003) consider that the EU communication deficit is directly related to citizens' lack of knowledge about the EU, which is also one of the major reasons for low support towards the EU and its institutions. From an institutional legitimacy point of view, Anderson and McLeod (2004), after having examined the information and communication inadequacies of the EP, conclude that the European Parliament communication deficit could lead to the European Parliament's electoral support withering away to the extent that the institution loses all credible claims to legitimacy.

Regarding the causes of the alleged EU (and its institutions) communication deficit, the majority of scholars have linked it to the seeming inability of the EU (and EU's institutions) to communicate with the media (Meyer, 1999; Habermas, 2012; Anderson and McLeod, 2004; Blondel et al., 1998; Bijsmans and Altides, 2007).

For example, Meyer (1999), after having examined the EU public communications performance as a factor of influencing the political legitimacy of the EU, argued that EU communication deficit is linked to key aspects of the EU's decision-making structures and institutional set-up. In another relevant study, Statham (2010) argues that among other reasons that contribute, partially, to the EU communication deficit and the unlikelihood of a mass-mediated European public sphere (such as the restricted national market that results from low general readership demand for European news, the limited and national-focused sources of information that journalists receive from the political system, the low communicative qualities of EU politics) the feeble efforts of EU institutions to communicate to their citizens as general audiences through the national press are also to be blamed. In a similar vein,

Bijsmans and Altides (2007), from the perspective of the EU institutional communication performance, analyse how far both Commission communication and media news coverage contain information on (a) policy issues, (b) the policy process, and (c) the actors involved and the positions they take. Based on data on Commission communication output and the news coverage in two Dutch and two German newspapers with regard to two specific EU policies, they argue that the Commission and the national media emphasize different aspects of the EU political process. According to them, this differentiation could further enhance the public communication deficit of the EU and its institutions and pose problems in terms of the legitimacy of EU policies and the Commission's role.

Regarding specifically the institution of the European Parliament, Anderson and McLeod (2004) focused on the extent to which the parliament's press and information directorate, and to a lesser extent, MEPs, are successful in handling their relationships with the mass media, given that the latter is a crucial means of communicating images of the parliament to the electorate and enhancing its institutional legitimacy. They argued that a mass communication deficit of the EP and of its press directorate exists, which could be, partially, blamed for the limited and adverse media coverage of the EP activities. The specific problems experienced by the European Parliament as a communicator exist on every level of its political and bureaucratic structure, and they could lead to the European Parliament's electoral support withering away to the extent that the institution loses all credible claims to legitimacy. In a similar context, Blondel et al. (1998) consider the communication deficit of the European Parliament as responsible for the low turnout levels in the European Parliament elections. They argue that in order to facilitate and mobilize the electoral participation in the European Parliament elections, it will require improved information and communication activities on behalf of the European Parliament. According to them, the EP needs to be able to inform European citizens and to persuade them of the value of the process of European governance and of the significance of the European-level issues involved. In addition, strengthening the image of the parliament in the minds of the citizens, through higher profile activity by MEPs during inter-election periods, and an improvement in people's perceptions of the capacity of the parliament to look after the interests of the citizens, is necessary in order to overcome the communication deficit of the EP.

As shown above, many scholars argue that the EU and EU institutions are to be, partially, blamed for their relevant communication deficits. That is also the case for the European Parliament which, according to the relevant literature, has information and communication deficiencies.

Thus, there is a need to further examine the problems that the EU institutions are facing in communicating their messages, specifically to the news media and the journalists. In other words, it is necessary to explore, based on the relevant literature, what are the problems that are related specifically to the media relations performance of the EU and the EU institutions; these problems enhance their communication deficit and affect their social legitimacy. However, before moving to this discussion, one should first examine (a) the relevant EU policy documents that provide the rationale and the scope of the information, communication, and media relation competences of the EU and its institutions and (b) the EP's organizational and operational infrastructure regarding its information, communication, and media relation competences.

4.6 EP Information, Communication, and Media Relations Competences

The EU policy documents could provide useful input in understanding the rationale of establishing information, communication, and media relations competences at the EU level. As it will be shown, the need for the visibility of the European institutions and of the impact of their powers and activities in the media is revealed in a number of key policy documents, which describe relevant communication initiatives and developments.

Despite the fact that scholars such as Harrison and Pukallus (2015) recognize that the Community had a persistent concern from the 1950s onwards for a public communication policy addressed at an inclusive general European public—and that this was exemplified in both a populist approach and an opinion leader approach to public communication policy— the majority of scholars argue that the need for an effective EU public communication policy started to become recognized by the Community in its response to the Maastricht crisis in 1992/1993 (the Maastricht Treaty was rejected at the relevant referendum in Denmark in 1992; it was barely passed in the French referendum, while in the case of the UK the House of Commons passed the treaty only with great difficulty in 1993) or to the Santer Commission resignation crisis in 1999 (the Santer Commission, led by Jacques Santer, took office in 1995 and after an investigation into allegations of corruption concerning individual EU commissioners, the entire Commission resigned in March 1999) (Brüggemann, 2005; Bee, 2008; Meyer, 1999).

In 1993, the European Commission launched a review of its internal and external communication activities. Following a request by the European Council of Helsinki in 1999, the European Commission was asked to adopt a new framework of cooperation for future activities concerning information and communication policy, which became the first systematic initiative in the creation of a common EU communication agenda.

The first relevant document on EU information and communication policy, which was published in 2001, was the European Commission's Communication to the Council, the European Parliament, the Economic and Social Committee, and the Committee of the Regions on *"A new Framework for Co-operation on Activities concerning the Information and Communication Policy of the European Union"* (European Commission, 2001). This policy document recognized that there is a need to bring Europe closer to its citizens and aimed at setting up a new framework for inter-institutional relationship and cooperation on information and communication strategies and activities of the European Union. It is also mentioned that work with the press is a high priority in today's world and is the key to the immediate presentation of new information, policies, and opinions. The information and communication strategy should, whenever possible, facilitate this work with the media by assuring that factual and updated information on current topics is readily available. Under this framework each institution remains responsible for its press activities (and for the relevant press contacts) and for the presentation, promotion, and defence of its own policies and actions, since the autonomy and integrity of all of the institutions is fully respected in the new framework.

The specific policy document described the framework for cooperation between the European Commission and the European Parliament regarding the information and communication activities and identified three levels of actors in this effort: (1) the political level in the form of the Inter-institutional Group on Information (IGI), (2) the operational level where the responsible services (DG PRESS and Communication for the Commission and DG Information and Public Relations—DG III—for the Parliament) will decide and oversee activities, and (3) the decentralized level at which execution takes place in the member states (Commission Representations and European Parliament External Offices).

As far as the operational level is concerned, the relevant services of the two institutions (DG Press and Communication—DG PRESS—of the Commission and DG Information and Public Relations—DG III—of the European Parliament) are charged with preparing, implementing, monitoring, and evaluating information activities. As far as the decentralized level is concerned, under the new framework for cooperation a high degree of local coordination between the Commission Representations and the European Parliament External Offices in the Member States is a necessary condition for enhancing the efficiency of the actions taken on a local level. The Commission Representations and EP Offices are to be considered the centres for all decentralized cooperation in the member states within this new framework. This cooperation is to be based on systematic local contacts and regular exchange of forward plans and initiatives, and whenever possible the Offices and the Representations should seek common solutions to common problems. The Commission Representations and the EP external Offices have a key role to play in inter-Institutional cooperation on a decentralized basis; close working relationships between Representations and EP External Offices will be of growing importance in planning and carrying out their respective activities. Under this approach, partnerships with civil society and NGOs are critical, while there is a great need for the information to be modern and user-friendly, as well as to be addressed to people's real concerns.

As far as the EP specifically is concerned, besides the framework for cooperation with the Commission Representations, the specific policy document states that the European Parliament, when acting in its role as legislator, as budgetary authority, or as the democratic control authority, must have full independence to voice its opinion and its members to speak freely on any subject of their choice. It acknowledges that the parliament's External Offices are only marginally associated with communication networks and that there is much scope for closer involvement of the EP in two ways: (a) the Offices could be invited to use the networks for institutional

4.6 EP Information, Communication, and Media Relations Competences

information from the EP and should in time be invited to reflect on the location, the size, and the structure of the relevant networks and (b) MEPs should be invited to participate in local events organized by or through the networks.

In July 2002, another EU policy document described the strategy of information and communication in the EU through an information network which would expand to all member states. The European Commission's Communication to the Council, the European Parliament, the Economic and Social Committee, and the Committee of the Regions on *"An Information and Communication Strategy for the European Union"*, (European Commission, 2002), stated that one of the main objectives of the Information and Communication Strategy for the European Union is "to improve perception of the European Union and its Institutions and their legitimacy by enhancing familiarity with and comprehension of its tasks, structure and achievements and by establishing a dialogue with its citizens".

The specific policy document acknowledges that the ignorance or lack of public understanding about the European Union is due largely to the complexity of the European process but also to the absence of an EU information and communication policy on the part of both the European institutions and the member states. Under this approach, the Union must organize its information policy in such a way as to encompass a more comprehensive range of subjects.

Referring to the need of effective decentralization, the specific policy document states that the Commission representations and the European Parliament Information Offices will work together to adapt the Union's message to local and national situations within a joint framework drawn up jointly with the member state. As a part of the aforementioned attitude, the Commission's representations, together with the European Parliament information offices, will shoulder the main responsibility for conducting the various information campaigns. (As far as the more procedural issues are concerned, they will have to draw up the communication plan for each subject chosen by the IGI, where necessary with assistance from outside experts. The plan will incorporate the action programme drawn up jointly with the member state and the Union's independent action programme, in case where the member state does not go along with the priorities or messages selected.) In addition, drawing on support from the relevant DGs, the representations along with European Parliament Information Offices will also rework the message to meet national, regional, or local requirements adapting the content of the information campaigns to various target groups, selected media, and people's everyday concerns. The policy document recognizes that messages and presentations will need to be adapted and take into account the communications vector used. For example, radio and television clearly require a special format different from that required by the press.

The next EU policy document in April 2004 described the implementation of the previously mentioned information and communication strategy. It was the Communication from the Commission on *"Implementing the Information and Communication Strategy for the European Union"* (European Commission, 2004). In this policy document, it was reaffirmed that the principal aim of the EU information and communication strategy was to improve perception of the European Union and its institutions and their legitimacy by deepening knowledge and understanding of its tasks, structure, and achievements and by also establishing a dialogue with its citizens. According to this policy document, it is absolutely essential for the EU to update and reprogramme the strategies underlying the different priority information as these were mentioned on the relevant Communication of July 2002 (these are enlargement, the future of the Union, the area of freedom, security and justice, and the euro). In addition, it also proposes the use of Memorandums of Understanding (MoUs) in the EU-25 as the foundation tool for partnership between the member states and the Community institutions, while it also focuses on the preparation and development of different types of partnership for the implementation of the information and communication strategy.

One necessary comment that has to be done here is that several of the documents of this period (2004–2007) were produced specifically in response to the failed Constitutional ratification process (e.g. the French and Dutch rejection of the Constitutional Treaty in 2005), in an effort to identify and address the causes of the citizens' distrust towards attempts for EU institutional reform.

During the same period, structural changes within the Commission (establishment of a separate Directorate-General Communication in 2004 whose mission was to inform the media and the general public about the Commission's activities, to communicate the objectives and the aims of its policies and activities, and to inform the Commission about the developments and discussions on the EU in the member states) and a new College of Commissioners that took on its duties in November 2004 have also contributed to the shift of the Commission's public communication strategy. Margot Wallstrom was appointed Commission Vice-President with responsibility for Inter-institutional Relations and Communication and has driven these changes in the policy direction from the start (Michailidou, 2006).

In July 2005, the European Commission decided to reform its communication policy from the inside by publishing the *"Action Plan to improve communicating Europe by the Commission"* (European Commission, 2005a). The Commission's objective was to act more professionally. The new approach included three strategic principles: listening, communicating, and connecting with citizens by "going local". It also proposed the modernization and the improvement of the communication tools of the EU and the importance of cooperation among the institutions (European Commission, European Parliament, and the Council). For example, at the decentralized level, the Commission Representations would continue to cooperate closely with the member state and the Offices of the European Parliament in its member state on communication activities.

The next policy document initiative was developed in October 2005. It was entitled *"Plan D for Democracy, Dialogue and Debate"* (European Commission, 2005b). The objective of this policy document was to achieve a new political approach towards the challenges of the twenty-first century. This, according to Plan D, presupposed that Europeans were informed about the political choices at the EU level but first and foremost presupposed a public platform for debate and discussion of the political problems, for communication with all EU institutions. In "Plan D for Democracy, Dialogue and Debate" it was stated, inter alia, that these debates should involve civil society, social partners, national parliaments, and political parties and that these debates could only be a success if the mass media were engaged in the process (in particular television while equally the Internet was of prime importance for stimulating the debate). In addition, at the decentralized level, the Representations of the European Commission in the member states and the European Parliament Offices would have a key role in providing assistance during the period of reflection. The European Parliament could also play a key role in the national debate, both in terms of working with national institutions and through the involvement of individual members of the European Parliament.

In February 2006, the *White Paper on a European Communication policy* (European Commission, 2006) was presented, which focused on matching the EU's communication policy to the EU public's concerns and expectations of prosperity, solidarity, and security in the face of globalization. It stressed the need for involvement of more actors (EU institutions and bodies, national, regional, and local authorities, European political parties, and the civil society) and for establishing a strong partnership among them. It identified five areas of partnership: (1)"Defining common principles" starting from the right to information and the freedom of expression, (2) "Empowering citizens" through their education on European issues, (3) "Working with the media and new technologies" by giving Europe a "human face", (4) "Understanding European public opinion" through the extensive analysis of the results of the standard Eurobarometer and other national survey programmes, and (5) "Doing the job together", i.e. connecting the EU institutions with the local communities ("going local"). In order to achieve that, the institutions, according to the White Paper, should adopt a citizen-oriented approach for European dialogue.

The specific policy document identified that the media are key players in any European communication policy and that a European communication policy should encourage public bodies at European, national, and regional level to (a) supply the media with high-quality news and current affairs material, (b) work more closely with broadcasters and media operators, (c) establish new links with regional and local communication systems, and (d) proactively use new technologies.

In addition, according to this policy document, the European Parliament, the member states, and the representation of European citizens have a special role to play, as peoples' support for the European project is a matter of common interest.

The next year's (2007) European Commission's Communication to the Council, the European Parliament, the European Economic and Social Committee, and the Committee of the Regions on *"Communicating Europe in Partnership"* (European Commission, 2007) pointed to the need for further increasing the visibility of EU action at all levels and for demonstrating its utility to citizens. At the decentralized level, the Representations would step up their activities in organizing Commissioners' visits to the regions and in supporting efforts to offer information to regional and local journalists via modern media technology as well as traditional means. Under this approach, the significance of the Internet and media was stressed as a means to engage citizens in the European process. According to the policy document, the Internet has moved from a static information tool to an interactive platform, with social media, blogs, and websites offering access to millions of online material and resources.

During the period 2008–2012, the communication strategies proposed the enforcement of the EU by covering the audiovisual media market. The aim was still to create a European "public sphere" by covering a broad area of EU information through TV, radio, and national broadcast programmes. The innovations would include the creation of a network of TV channels, the audiovisual library, the EU events calendar, and the broadcasting of EU content through the European radio network (EURANET) with more language coverage. In the period 2012–2013, emphasis was placed on making the EU's presence on the Internet more coherent, cost-effective, and interactive and enforcing the role of citizens in the political process.

When it comes to the contribution of the European Parliament to the aforementioned policy documents, the following relevant documents should be taken into consideration:

The European Parliament's *Resolution on the Information and Communication Policy in the European Union* (European Parliament, 1998) which states that there is a need for measures aimed at information and communication with citizens ... in order to increase awareness of the achievements and advantages of the Union and foster public support for the forthcoming stages of the integration process. In addition, and as far as the media relations performance of the EU institutions is concerned it states, inter alia: "... whereas the following factors contributed to the lack of success of the European communication policy ... absence of a clear policy on relations with the media, which is partly the result of inadequate and occasionally counter-productive reactions on the part of the European Parliament's appropriate bodies", "the need in general to match the information made available more closely to the main target groups such as the press, educational establishments, industry and private citizens", and "considers that Parliament has nothing to hide and that therefore a professional but flexible relationship must be developed with the media and with journalists on the basis of maximum openness, taking into account, however, the right to privacy of Members and political groups".

The European Parliament's *Resolution on the Commission's communication on a new framework for cooperation on activities concerning the information and communication policy of the European Union* (European Parliament, 2002), which "stresses the need to make information more readily available to journalists, sub-editors and editors-in-chief" (focusing here on media relations).

The European Parliament's *Resolution on the Implementation of the European Union's information and communication strategy* (European Parliament, 2005), which considers that "the information and communication strategy must also actively demonstrate to citizens how belonging to the European Union brings positive benefits to them in their daily lives" and that one of the primary objectives of the EU's information and communication strategy should be "to keep the Union's citizens continually and properly informed about the functioning of the Union's Institutions in order to develop their knowledge, concern and participation in the Union's affairs and bring them closer to the Union". In addition, and as far as the media relations performance of the EU institutions is concerned it states, inter alia: "(the EP) invites the EU institutions to improve conditions for and working relations with accredited journalists and, more generally, to create the widest possible access to sources for all citizens seeking information on the European Union's policies and activities", "(the EP) stresses the need for the institutions to improve their press releases and the quality of all information intended for the press, in order to facilitate the work of all professional journalists closely following events in Brussels; calls also for the institutions' press releases to be prepared as far as possible by professional communications experts".

The European Parliament's *Resolution on the "White Paper on a European Communication policy"* (European Parliament, 2006), where the EP itself is of the opinion that "in order to reach the citizen, it is important to communicate better and show the relevance and impact of EU decisions for daily life", while referring to the media relations performance it states: "(the EP) recommends that the Commission use clear and concise language when communicating with the media and citizens".

The European Parliament's *Resolution on "Journalism and new media—creating a public sphere in Europe"* (European Parliament, 2010), in which the EP believes that "in order to be effective, communication must make it clear that political decisions taken at EU level are of direct relevance to the daily lives of EU citizens, who see the EU as still being too distant and having too little influence in terms of solving their real problems".

In total, the EU policy documents having acknowledged the need for better information, communication, and media relations performance from the EU institutions, in order to further increase the visibility of EU action at all levels and for demonstrating its utility to citizens, have provided the strategy, the mentality, and the guidelines towards an EU closer to the EU citizens. It should be mentioned here that despite the fact that they have not always referred specifically to the EP institution, one could argue that they do serve as a guide for the EP towards the establishment of its own information and communication competences.

At the operational level, the relevant policy documents suggest that each institution remains responsible for its press activities and for the presentation, promotion, and defence of its own policies and actions (e.g. the European Parliament, when acting in its role as legislator, as budgetary authority, or as the democratic control authority, must have full independence to voice its opinion and its members to speak freely on any subject of their choice), while the relevant institution services (General Directorates in the Commission and the European Parliament) are charged with preparing, implementing, monitoring, and evaluating information activities.

At the decentralized level, the role of the local offices (Commission Representations or the EPLOs) is very important for approaching EU citizens and the different stakeholders (the news media and the journalists as well). There is a need for Commission Representations or the EPLOs to work on the different message to meet national, regional, or local requirements adapting the content of the information campaigns to the various target groups, the media selected, and people's everyday concerns. In addition, a high degree of local coordination and cooperation between the Commission Representations and the European Parliament Offices seems to be necessary.

In any case, the aforementioned EU policy documents acknowledged that the press is a high priority in today's world and is the key to the immediate presentation of new information, policies, and opinions. The information and communication strategy of the EU and of the EU institutions should, whenever possible, facilitate the work with the media by assuring that factual and updated information on current topics is readily available. According to the EU policy documents a European communication policy should encourage public bodies at European, national, and regional level to (a) supply the media with high-quality news and current affairs material, (b) work more closely with broadcasters and media operators, (c) establish new links with regional and local communication systems, and (d) proactively use new technologies.

As seen above, the European Parliament itself acknowledges that the absence of a clear policy on relations with the media is partly the result of inadequate and occasionally counterproductive reactions on the part of the European Parliament's appropriate bodies, while it also considers that a professional but flexible relationship must be developed with the media and with journalists.

Nowadays, the EP's Directorate-General for Communication (DG COMM) communicates the political nature of the institution and the work carried out. Its core mission is to raise awareness of the European Parliament, its powers, its decisions, and activities among media, stakeholders, and the general public, bringing the work of the European Parliament closer to citizens on both centralized and decentralized levels. The main tasks of the Directorate-General are (a) to collaborate with the media, to inform, explain, and enhance the visibility of the European Parliament's work, (b) to increase the awareness on the European Parliament among citizens, stakeholders, and opinion leaders through bespoke communication and information campaigns and online channels, (c) to foster sustainable links with citizens through enhanced visitors' facilities in Brussels, Strasbourg, and the member states, (d) to provide expertise and services to members and political groups such as media and public opinion monitoring, training, conferences for visitors' groups, and offices in the member states, and (e) to go local and reach out to people through the European Parliament Liaison Offices (EPLOs) in the EU Member States and in Washington (Corbett et al., 2011).

At the decentralized level, the EPLOs are responsible for the local implementation of the EP communication activities, with the ultimate goal of ensuring that people understand the importance of the European Parliament well enough to engage in the European democratic process. The Offices engage with citizens and stakeholders, manage contacts with national, regional, and local media, and provide support to members of the European Parliament (MEPs) in the exercise of their official mandates in the member states. More specifically, as far as their task of engaging with media in the member states is concerned, the mission of the EPLOs is to proactively bring EU news, debates, and decisions to national, regional, local, and specialized media, by (1) assisting journalists in their work and making them aware of the impact of European issues, (2) organizing seminars for journalists, and inviting them to cover plenary activities, (3) creating media opportunities for MEPs in national, regional, local, and specialized media, and (4) monitoring inaccuracies and misleading news about the European Parliament, and rebutting them (European Parliament, 2018).

However, as indicated in Sect. 4.7, the EU's (and the EU institutions') media relations performance to a certain extent fails to accomplish their operational tasks and missions as these have been set in the EU policy documents.

4.7 EU Media Relations

Most of the existing literature on media relations focuses on the EU as a whole with only a relatively small amount focused specifically on the EP. However, it is still useful to look at literature regarding the general media relations situation within the EU, given that the EP is part of that overall picture.

Different elements of the EU institutions' media relations activities have been assessed so far by scholars who use as a research tool interviews with relevant journalists and the EU/EP press officers. These are mainly (a) the information/communication material (either in written or in oral form) provided to journalists by the EU institutions, (b) the EU institution's support to journalists in doing their job, (c) the EU institutions' "source strategies", and (d) the extent to which media relations between journalists and EU officers have been created and established.

The written communication material of the European Council (including background documents with information about each item in the agenda of the Council - history, motivations, aims, procedural matters) and the press releases provided to journalists have been assessed (Laursen and Valentini, 2013; Gleissner and De Vreese, 2005; Valentini, 2007) with the Council press officers evaluating them as bureaucratic, formal, and highly structured in a way that does not give them the freedom to decide which information to pass on (Laursen and Valentini, 2013). EC press officers evaluate themselves as "reactive providers of impartial information" with credibility, while they also characterize the information they provide as apolitical and non-partisan, which might not meet journalist's expectations (Laursen and Valentini, 2013). Commission staff members make a similar assessment of the Commission's spokespersons' written material (press releases) since it is also characterized by complex and bureaucratic language (Balcytiene et al., 2007).

Journalists, on their side, have also been criticizing the EU press releases for being dull and overly complicated (Gleissner and De Vreese, 2005), while EU communication in general has also been characterized by journalists in a variety of ways ranging from views that it is informative, to a lesser extent promotional and educational, or inefficient to bureaucratic, complex, and confused (Valentini, 2007). In another piece of research (Martins et al., 2012), EU correspondents are shown to have a negative attitude overall towards the voluminous information flow from the EU institutions, and, in some cases, for the absence of non-English versions of some press releases.

In the same vein, other relevant research shows that journalists, regarding the information-provision aspect of EU communications, highlight limitations due to the technocratic language, the complexity due to the number of countries and issues involved, and the remoteness of the EU institutions and their press offices (Statham, 2010). Journalists have also criticized negatively the suitability for news journalism of the information received from the EU institutions, while they have also characterized the political-communicative aspects of the EU's communication as problematic (Statham, 2010).

In another piece of research, journalists (correspondents in Brussels from the new member states) consider EU press material to be overly technical, vague, and too voluminous (Lecheler, 2008). Concerning specifically the European Parliament, journalists have in the past assessed the website of the institution in terms of site design, ease of use, and the extent to which information is presented in a form that would be likely to appeal to journalists working under pressure. Most of the journalists were happy with the site's ease of use; however, the information in the website was presented, according to journalists, in a form that could not grab the media's attention (Anderson and McLeod, 2004). In any case, the European Parliament has been rated by the Brussels correspondents as more media friendly—in comparison to the European Commission—with its party politics dimension leading to media-tailored press releases (Martins et al., 2012).

As far as the oral communication of the European Council is concerned, this is perceived by the relevant press officers to allow them more flexibility in terms of what and how information can be communicated, and it is in the oral communication when press officers might reveal information of a more sensitive political nature. Thus, oral communication is regarded as being less official and allowing for a more flexible way of communication between the Council press officers and the journalists (Laursen, 2012; Laursen and Valentini, 2013). In the same vein, the Commission's spokespersons prefer verbal interaction with journalists, since it leaves them considerable space for manoeuvre (Balcytiene et al., 2007; Spanier, 2010). However, even in the case of oral communication, the approach of the Council Press Officers is more reactive than proactive, since they usually do not make any statements on their own initiative (Laursen and Valentini, 2013). In contrast, the approach of the Commission's spokespersons, as far as oral communication is concerned, has been characterized as more proactive, specifically through the daily midday briefings in Brussels (Balcytiene et al., 2007).

The EU institution's support of journalists' work has also been assessed, by scholars, as another media relations dimension (Gleissner and De Vreese, 2005). Journalists have been negative, since they characterize the institution's efforts as not being very supportive of the correspondent's work. For example, TV journalists have made reference to the difficulties they face, due to their dependence on pictures, in trying to arrange filming possibilities (Gleissner and De Vreese, 2005). In addition, in the past scholars such as Morgan (1995) and Gavin (2001), who analysed the working conditions of EU correspondents, characterized their working relations with the EU institutions as problematic. For example, British EU correspondents in Brussels saw signs of growth in legal and administrative constraints on the release of news, while they also claimed that EU information officers frequently had a lack of technical knowledge or were unwilling to help them, or had a lack of influence with policy-makers (Morgan, 1995). However, at that time the European Parliament seemed to be the most accessible EU institution for the British EU correspondents in Brussels (Morgan, 1995).

The EU's "source strategies" and more specifically the frequency with which national and sub-national journalists are contacted by EU actors who want to get their message across and supply them with press statements (or other similar material) have also been assessed by scholars. Relevant research shows that European institutions try less compared to national actors to make themselves heard by national and sub-national journalists. Thus, Europe as a political actor makes relatively less effort to penetrate the information resource pool of journalists (Statham, 2010).

Last but not least, the extent to which satisfactory media relations between journalists and the EU representation offices in the member states have been created has also been assessed. Journalists in the past have been dissatisfied with the EU's media relations activities, citing difficulties in making contact with EU officers for interviews or for obtaining material for news reports. For example, journalists in the national and local press in Italy and Finland have stated that the quality of EU information is very poor and that the media relations between them and the EU representation offices are difficult and not well established (Valentini, 2007). In more general terms, EU officials self-criticize themselves for their EU-media relations performance; however, all the EP press officers considered their services to be of better quality than those of the Commission, and in fact several officials from the EC share this assumption as well (Martins et al., 2012).

The aforementioned literature proves to be really useful since it will provide the guidelines and will contribute, as it will be shown in Chap. 5, to the formation of the research background for the identification and critical analysis of the problems that the EP faces, specifically in the area of its media relations with journalists working online.

4.8 Online News Media and Online News Journalists

Given that the book is researching the European Parliament's problems in communicating with the citizens of the UK and Greece via online news sites, in this section the relevant literature, regarding the online news context both in terms of its specific characteristics and of the routines of the online journalists, will be discussed.

4.8.1 The Online News Media Context and the Unique Characteristics of the Online News Media Environment (Hyperlinks and Multimedia)

Online news content, due to the technological potentialities of the Internet, differs in a number of formal characteristics from the news content in the "so-called" traditional news media. The online news characteristics that have been most identified and examined, in the relevant literature, are hypertextuality, mutlimediality, and interactivity (Steensen, 2011; Deuze, 2003, 2004, 2005; Cover, 2006; Larsson, 2012), while other characteristics such as liquidity have also been noticed (Karlsson and Strömbäck, 2010; Karlsson, 2012).

However, the specific characteristics of hypertextuality and multimediality are the ones which are more related to the theoretically most desirable format of the news content, since they augment significantly the news text and they provide additional material (information) to the readers of the news stories. Thus, in the framework of the examination of the media coverage of the EP in the online news, in terms of content, the specific features of hypertextuality and multimediality are selected to be examined and analysed.

Hyperlinks and Multimedia

Hyperlinks are one of the core aspects of the World Wide Web which are used by online news media in order to augment journalistic text and allow the readers to access other related information material as well (Larsson, 2013). Hypertextuality refers to the ability to connect nodes of information within sites or other webpages through clicking on a word, phrase, or graphic image (Hall, 2001; Carpenter, 2010). Hyperlinks give the opportunity to the readers to have access to more related material, and an active role in deciding whether they access this material or not. Thus, hyperlinks have the potential to enrich users' online choices by adding background information and providing more contexts to a developing news story (Dimitrova and Neznanski, 2006). Hyperlinks could be internal, referring to additional information related to the same news item within the same website, or to another part of the same article (so-called bookmarks), or external, leading to a virtually unlimited amount of information on the same subject outside the specific website (Deuze, 2003; Beyers, 2006; Engebretsen, 2006; Karlsson, 2012).

Mutlimediality, on the other hand, refers to the extent of usage by news websites of content that includes a combination of text, graphics, sound, and image integrated in a single format. According to one definition, multimediality is "the quality, which consists of combining different communicative codes—text, image, sound—in one informative discourse" (Palacios and Diaz Noci, 2007), while a more media logic-based approach refers to multimediality as a common electronic language, based on the "bits" of the computer, with text, sound, voice, and still and moving images being translated in a common digital form (Dahlgren, 1996). Two of the most common ways of using multimedia in journalism according to Deuze (2004) are (a) the presentation of a news story package on a website using two or more media formats, such as spoken and written word, music, moving and still images, and graphic animations, including interactive and hypertextual elements, and (b) an integrated (although not necessarily simultaneous) presentation of a news story package through different media, such as a website, a Usenet newsgroup, e-mail, SMS, MMS, radio, television, teletext, print newspapers, and magazines.

4.8.2 The Use of Hyperlinks and Multimedia in Online Journalism

Early empirical studies show that the news websites did not employ in full the hyperlinking potential, and in the cases that this happened there were much more internal links offered rather than external ones (Neuberger et al., 1998; Massey and Levy, 1999; Dibean and Garrison, 2001). Findings from other research also show that despite the fact that news websites are developing their hyperlinking practices, they still do not take full advantage of the hyperlinking potential offered, as far as the external links are concerned (Dimitrova et al., 2003; Dimitrova and Neznanski, 2006; Van der Wurff, 2005; Larsson, 2013).

A similar situation arises with regard to the use of multimedia by news websites. For example, Van der Wurff et al. (2008), after having assessed online newspapers in Europe from a media evolutionary perspective, found that the usage of multimedia features remained very limited, since just 12% of the sample examined added an audio file to one or more important news items, and not more than 6% of the sample added a movie file. In the same vein, Schroeder (2004), after having examined 62 newspapers' sites from 15 European countries, found that interactive infographics played only a marginal role in European news sites, since despite the fact that many sites offered photo galleries, video and audio files, or cartoons and slide shows as multimedia assets, they (these multimedia assets) hardly represented an added value compared to the affiliated medium.

When it comes to the factors that affect the use (or not) and the extent of use of hyperlinks and multimedia in news websites, research indicates slight differences regarding linking practices between tabloids and broadsheets, and between news of different origin (Larsson, 2013), while financial considerations, commercial concerns, source hierarchy, and domesticity are also factors affecting the journalistic preference of using (and what kind of) hyperlinks or not (Chang et al., 2012; Ryfe et al., 2012). For the case of multimedia, Schroeder (2004) identifies specific factors that have an impact on the use of multimedia by news websites, such as availability of sources and assets; for example if there are affiliations with conventional media such as television, radio, or a newspaper, these will strongly determine the usage of the output of these media in the news website, the offered added value that multimedia assets are supposed to provide to the news content, usability of the multimedia assets by the readers, and profitability.

The examination of the visibility of hyperlinks and multimedia in the sampled news items regarding the online media coverage of the EP in the UK and Greece will reveal whether the readers of the specific news stories are provided with the option of additional information regarding the EP—and what kind of information is that.

In addition, by acknowledging that there are plenty of factors that shape the hyperlinking and multimedia practices in news websites, and following Weber (2012), it is argued that the extent of the hyperlinks and multimedia presence also serves as an indicator of the relationships between the news websites, or the journalists themselves, with content providers; under this approach the extent of the hyperlinks and multimedia presence in the EP news stories will be considered as a tool for assessing the relationship of the news websites with the European Parliament as a source of information or as a content provider.

4.8.3 Online Coverage of the European Parliament

Despite the fact that there is a significant amount of research which examines mainly from a political campaign perspective the use and the visibility, inter alia, of hyperlinks and multimedia assets by single candidates, or political parties in their campaigns for the European Parliament elections (Schweitzer, 2009, 2012; Pătruţ, 2015; Lilleker et al., 2016), there are only a few pieces of research concerning the coverage of the EU or the EP in news websites and the relevant visibility of hyperlinks or multimedia in them. For example, Kevin (2001) found that in the coverage of the 1999 EP elections the Internet versions of the media outlets (that were examined in the study) offered a deeper analysis of the news with hyperlinks to previous stories in the same websites, and political parties and NGOs involved in the debate and in the policy process. There was also an amount of shared and syndicated online news stories between European outlets, while the online coverage of the elections also allowed greater access to information about the campaign in other European countries.

In another piece of research, Michailidou (2012) analysed the online news coverage of the 2009 EP elections, in Greece, Sweden, and the UK. Concerning the material produced by online journalists in relation to the EP elections, she found that journalism websites offered plural thematic coverage through regular reporting and commentary, while in addition the news websites provided dedicated EP election "files", that is to say website sections with detailed information regarding not only the process of EP elections and practical issues but also extensive information on the history, set-up, and competencies of the EP and the wider institutional structure of the EU.

Concerning the relationship between multimediality (or the use of multimedia) and the European Parliament or the EU, studies examining from a political campaign perspective the use and visibility, inter alia, of multimedia features by single candidates, or political parties in their campaign websites for the European Parliament elections, have found that parties in the European and national elections provided a range of add-on materials in the articles (including PDFs, embedded audio and video streams, e-cards) (Schweitzer, 2012).

The aforementioned literature contributes to the formation of the background for the examination of the visibility of the additional hyperlinked/multimedia EP-related content (information), offered by the news websites, along with the text of the news item. In other words, it contributes to the examination of (a) whether EU citizens receive additional information in the coverage of EP affairs news stories and (b) what is the kind of this additional information (e.g. as other texts linked to the original one or multimedia content).

As it has been stated in Sect. 4.1, the higher visibility of news about European politics provides citizens with information about the issues at stake which can affect them and cues them about the importance of EU policies (Boomgaarden et al., 2013; De Vreese et al., 2006). Thus, it is argued that the visibility of EP news (and of additional information) is a crucial indicator which shows how much and what kind of communication EU citizens potentially observe about EP affairs specifically through the sampled news websites.

4.8.4 Online News Journalism

Since there is a focus on the examination of the media relations performance of the EP regarding specifically online journalists, it is also necessary to review the changing practices of online news production. These practices will contribute to the formation of the research background, in order to examine whether these are taken into consideration in the media relations activities of the EP regarding journalists working online.

Relevant research shows that the development of the Internet and the online news sites has brought changes in the journalistic practices of the journalists who work in them. The aspects of the changes that have been identified, inter alia, are modifications in the editorial workflow, alterations in news gathering practices, acceleration of temporal patterns of content production, and the convergence of the print, broadcast, and online operations (Mitchelstein and Boczkwoski, 2009).

Modifications in the Editorial Workflow The development of online journalism has increased journalists' workload and pressure to work and create content for different media platforms (Ursell, 2001). In this new news production environment, online journalists consider that multimedia elements are an important component of online news (Paulussen, 2004), and demand multimedia features such as graphics or visuals for the online news that they produce (Klinenberg, 2005) despite the fact that multimedia production in online newsrooms is not as developed as it needs to be (O'Sullivan, 2005; Quandt, 2008; Colson and Heinderyckx, 2008).

Alterations in News Gathering Practices Relevant research also shows that online journalists greatly and rapidly have increased the use of the Internet as a news gathering, source seeking, verification, and initiating news stories tool (Gulyas, 2013; O'Sullivan and Heinonen, 2008). In this aspect, social media is also a critical component in the daily practice of online journalists who use it for gathering information, initiating a story, finding sources, or even quoting from them (Agarwal and Barthel, 2015; Broersma and Graham, 2012).

Acceleration of Temporal Patterns of Content Production These changes are more related to the increased pressure that online journalists face to immediately upload their stories (Lewis and Cushion, 2009; Quandt et al., 2006; Lewis et al., 2005), while they also refer to the "publish-first-and-update-later" routines of online journalists (Karlsson and Strömbäck, 2010; Saltzis, 2012; Widholm, 2016). In the same vein, other research confirms the increased pace and frequency of work in online newsrooms (Boczkowski and De Santos, 2007; Cassidy, 2005; Klinenberg, 2005; Agarwal and Barthel, 2015).

4.8.5 *Conclusion*

In this chapter, the theoretical background of the book was formed, with the aim to identify and critically analyse the problems that the EP is facing in communicating, via news websites, with the citizens of the UK and Greece, and the potential solutions for the EP in order to overcome these problems. This theoretical background will guide the research parts in trying to answer the relevant research questions (RQ1: What is the coverage of the European Parliament's institutional powers and their output in selected news websites in the UK and Greece? RQ2: What are the problems that the EP is facing in communicating its institutional powers and their output to the selected news websites in the UK and Greece? RQ3: What solutions could be proposed to the EP to enhance its communication performance in relation to the news websites of the UK and Greece and which of these solutions could be applied with some potential for success?). In the following chapter (Chap. 5), the methodological aspects of the study are discussed.

References

Agarwal, S. D., & Barthel, M. L. (2015). The friendly barbarians: Professional norms and work routines of online journalists in the United States. *Journalism, 16*(3), 376–391. https://doi.org/10.1177/1464884913511565

Anderson, C. J. (1998). When in doubt use proxies: Attitudes to domestic politics and support for the EU. *Comparative Political Studies, 31*(5), 569–601.

References

Anderson, P. J., & McLeod, A. (2004). The great non-communicator? The mass communicator deficit of the European Parliament and its Press Directorate. *Journal of Common Market Studies, 42*(5), 897–917.

Anderson, P. J., & Weymouth, T. (1999). *Insulting the public? The British Press and the European Union*. Longman.

Archontaki, I. (2012). *The framing of the EU by the Greek press and the role of journalistic sources*. Master Study in Graduate School of Communication. Universiteit van Amsterdam.

Balcytiene, A., Raeymaeckers, K., De Bens, E., Vincuniene, A., & Schroder, R. (2007). Understanding the complexity of EU Communication: The spokespersons' perspective. In *AIM research consortium, understanding the logic of EU reporting from Brussels: Analysis of the interviews with EU correspondents and spokespersons. Adequate Information Management in Europe-Working Papers*, Vol. 2. Bochum, Project Verlag, pp 151–162.

Bee, C. (2008). The institutionally constructed European identity: Public sphere and citizenship narrated by the Commission. *Perspectives on European Politics and Society, 9*(4), 431–450.

Beyers, H. (2006). What constitutes a good online news site? A comparative analysis of American and European awards. *Communications: The European Journal of Communication Research, 31*(2), 215–240.

Bijsmans, P., & Altides, C. (2007). Bridging the gap between EU politics and citizens? The European Commission, national media and EU affairs in the public sphere. *Journal of European Integration, 29*(3), 323–340.

Blondel, J., Sinnott, R., & Svensson, P. (1998). *People and parliament in the European Union: Participation, democracy, and legitimacy*. Oxford University Press.

Boczkowski, P. J., & De Santos, M. (2007). When more media equals less news: Patterns of content homogenization in Argentina's leading print and online newspapers. *Political Communication, 24*(2), 167–180.

Boomgaarden, H., de Vreese, C. H., Schuck, A., Azrout, A., Elenbaas, M., Van Spanje, J. H. P., & Vliegenthart, R. (2013). Across time and space: Explaining variation in news coverage of the European Union. *European Journal of Political Research, 52*(5), 608–629.

Brettschneider, F., Maier, M., & Maier, J. (2003). From D-mark to euro: the impact of mass media on public opinion in Germany. *German Politics, 12*(2), 45–64.

Broersma, M. J., & Graham, T. (2012). Social media as beat: Tweets as a news source during the 2010 British and Dutch elections. *Journalism Practice, 6*(3), 403–419.

Brüggemann, M. (2005). How the EU constructs the European public sphere: Seven strategies of information policy. *Javnost/The Public, 12*(2), 57–74.

Carpenter, S. (2010). A study of content diversity in online citizen journalism and online newspaper articles. *New Media and Society, 12*(7), 1064–1084.

Cassidy, W. P. (2005). Variations on a theme: The professional role conceptions of print and online newspaper journalists. *Journalism and Mass Communication Quarterly, 82*(2), 264–280.

Chang, T. K., Southwell, B. G., Lee, H. M., & Hong, Y. (2012). Jurisdictional protectionism in online news: American journalists and their perceptions of hyperlinks. *New Media and Society, 14*(4), 684–700.

Colson, V., & Heinderyckx, F. (2008). Do online journalists belong in the newsroom? A Belgian case of convergence. In C. Paterson & D. Domingo (Eds.), *Making online news. The ethnography of news media production* (pp. 143–154). Peter Lang.

Corbett, R., Jacobs, F., & Shackleton, M. (2011). *The European Parliament* (8th ed.). John Harper Publishing.

Cover, R. (2006). Audience inter/active: Interactive media, narrative control and reconceiving audience history. *New Media and Society, 8*(1), 139–158.

Dahlgren, P. (1996). Media logic in cyberspace: Repositioning journalism and its publics. *Javnost/The Public, 3*(3), 59–72.

De Vreese, C. H. (2001a). Europe in the news: A cross-national comparative study of the news coverage of key EU events. *European Union Politics, 2*(3), 283–307.

De Vreese, C. H. (2001b). Election coverage – New directions for public broadcasting: The Netherlands and beyond. *European Journal of Communication, 16*(2), 155–179.
De Vreese, C. H. (2003). Television reporting of second-order elections. *Journalism Studies, 4*(2), 183–198.
De Vreese, C. H., & Boomgaarden, H. G. (2006a). Media effects on public opinion about the enlargement of the European Union. *Journal of Common Market Studies, 44*(2), 419–436.
De Vreese, C. H., & Boomgaarden, H. G. (2006b). Media message flows and interpersonal communication: The conditional nature of effects on public opinion. *Communication Research, 33*(1), 1–19.
De Vreese, C. H., & Kandyla, A. (2009). News framing and public support for a common foreign and security policy. *Journal of Common Market Studies, 47*(3), 453–481.
De Vreese, C. H., & Semetko, H. A. (2004). News Matters: Influences on the vote in the Danish 2000 Euro referendum campaign. *European Journal of Political Research, 43*(5), 699–722.
De Vreese, C. H., Peter, J., & Semetko, H. A. (2001). Framing politics at the launch of the euro: A cross-national comparative study of frames in the news. *Political Communication, 18*(2), 107–122.
De Vreese, C. H., Banducci, S., Semetko, H., & Boomgaarden, H. (2005). Off-line: The 2004 European Parliamentary elections on television news in the enlarged Europe. *Information Polity, 10*(3), 177–188.
De Vreese, C. H., Banducci, S., Semetko, H. A., & Boomgaarden, H. A. (2006). The news coverage of the 2004 European Parliamentary election campaign in 25 countries. *European Union Politics, 7*(4), 477–504.
Demertzis, N. (2006). Europe on the agenda? The Greek case. In M. Maier & J. Tenscher (Eds.), *Campaigning in Europe – Campaigning for Europe* (pp. 277–293). Lit Verlag.
Deuze, M. (2003). The web and its journalisms: considering the consequences of different types of newsmedia online. *New Media and Society, 5*(2), 203–230.
Deuze, M. (2004). What is multimedia journalism? *Journalism Studies, 5*(2), 139–152.
Deuze, M. (2005). What is journalism? Professional identity and ideology of journalists reconsidered. *Journalism, 6*(4), 442–464.
Dibean, W., & Garrison, B. (2001). How six online newspapers use web technologies. *Newspaper Research Journal, 22*(2), 79–94.
Dimitrova, D., & Neznanski, M. (2006). Online journalism and the war in cyberspace: A comparison between U.S. and international newspapers. *Journal of Computer-Mediated Communication, 12*(1), 248–263.
Dimitrova, D. V., Connolly-Ahern, C., Williams, A. P., Kaid, L. L., & Reid, A. (2003). Hyperlinking as gatekeeping: Online newspaper coverage of the execution of an American terrorist. *Journalism Studies, 4*(3), 401–414.
Elenbaas, M., de Vreese, C. H., Boomgaarden, H. G., & Schuck, A. R. T. (2012). The impact of information acquisition on EU performance judgments. *European Journal of Political Research, 51*(6), 728–755.
Engebretsen, M. (2006). Shallow and static or deep and dynamic? Studying the state of online journalism in Scandinavia. *Nordicom Review, 27*(1), 3–16.
Esser, F. (1999). Tabloidization of news. A comparative analysis of Anglo American and German press journalism. *European Journal of Communication, 14*(3), 291–324.
European Commission. (2001). *Communication from the Commission to the Council, European Parliament, Economic and Social Committee, the Committee of the Regions on "A new framework for co-operation on activities concerning the information and communication policy of the European Union"*. 27.06.2001 COM/2001/0354 final. Available at: https://eur-lex.europa.eu/legal-content/EN/TXT/PDF/?uri=CELEX:52001DC0354&from=bg
European Commission. (2002). *Communication from the Commission, to the Council, the European Parliament, the Economic and Social Committee and the Committee of the Regions on "An Information and Communication Strategy for the European Union"*, 02.10.2002. COM

References

(2002) 350 final. Available at: https://eur-lex.europa.eu/LexUriServ/LexUriServ.do?uri=COM:2002:0350:FIN:EN:PDF

European Commission. (2004). *Communication from the Commission, to the Council, the European Parliament, the European Economic and Social Committee and the Committee of the Regions on "Implementing the information and communication strategy for the European Union", 20.04.2004. COM (2004) 196 final*. Available at: https://eur-lex.europa.eu/LexUriServ/LexUriServ.do?uri=COM:2004:0196:FIN:EN:PDF

European Commission. (2005a). *"Action Plan to improve communicating Europe by the Commission" 20.7.2005, SEC (2005) 985 final*. Available at: https://eur-lex.europa.eu/legal-content/EN/TXT/HTML/?uri=LEGISSUM:l10102&from=MT

European Commission. (2005b). *Communication from the Commission, to the Council, the European Parliament, the European Economic and Social Committee and the Committee of the Regions "The Commission's contribution to the period of reflection and beyond: Plan-D for Democracy, Dialogue and Debate" 13.10.2005, COM(2005) 494 final*. Available at: https://eur-lex.europa.eu/LexUriServ/LexUriServ.do?uri=COM:2005:0494:FIN:en:PDF

European Commission. (2006). *White Paper on a European Communication policy. 01.02.2006, COM (2006) 35 final*. Available at: https://eur-lex.europa.eu/legal-content/EN/TXT/PDF/?uri=CELEX:52006DC0035&from=EN

European Commission. (2007). *Communication from the Commission, to the Council, the European Parliament, the European Economic and Social Committee and the Committee of the Regions "Communicating Europe in Partnership". 03.10.2007, COM (2007) 568 final*. Available at: https://eur-lex.europa.eu/legal-content/EN/TXT/HTML/?uri=LEGISSUM:l11017

European Parliament. (1998). Resolution on the information and communication policy in the European Union. 01.06.1998. Official Journal C 167, P.0230 (A4-0115/98). Available at: https://eur-lex.europa.eu/legal-content/EN/TXT/HTML/?uri=CELEX:51998IP0115&rid=1

European Parliament. (2002). *Resolution on the Commission communication on a new framework for cooperation on activities concerning the information and communication policy of the European Union*. COM (2001) 354. P5_TA (2002) 0109. Available at: https://www.europarl.europa.eu/sides/getDoc.do?reference=P5-TA-2002-0109&type=TA&language=EN&redirect

European Parliament. (2005). *Resolution on the implementation of the European Union's information and communication strategy*. 12.05.2005. (2004/2238(INI)) P6_TA0183. Available at: https://op.europa.eu/el/publication-detail/-/publication/51c7df33-f656-4c25-a8f2-f985f4671c93/language-en

European Parliament. (2006). *Resolution on the White Paper on a European Communication policy, 16.11.2006 (2006/2087(INI)) P6_TA (2006) 0500*. Available at: https://eur-lex.europa.eu/legal-content/EN/TXT/?uri=CELEX%3A52006IP0500

European Parliament. (2010). *Resolution on journalism and new media – creating a public sphere in Europe*. 07.09.2010 (2010/2015(INI)) OJ C 308E, 20.10.2011, p. 55–61. Available at: https://eur-lex.europa.eu/legal-content/EN/TXT/PDF/?uri=CELEX:52010IP0307&from=GA

European Parliament. (2018). *About Parliament/Organisation and rules/Organisation/Delegations*. Retrieved February 7, 2018, from: http://www.europarl.europa.eu/aboutparliament/en/20150201PVL00010/Organisation

Franklin, M., Marsh, M., & Wlezien, C. (1994). Attitudes towards Europe and referendum votes: A response to Siune and Svensson. *Electoral Studies, 13*(2), 117–121.

Gabel, M. (1998). Public support for European Integration: An empirical test of five theories. *Journal of Politics, 60*(2), 333–354.

Gabel, M., & Palmer, H. (1995). Understanding variation in public support for European integration. *European Journal of Political Research, 27*(1), 3–19.

Gattermann, K. (2013). News about the European Parliament: Patterns and external drivers of broadsheet coverage. *European Union Politics, 14*(3), 436–457.

Gavin, N. T. (2000). Imagining Europe: Political identity and British television coverage of the European economy. *British Journal of Politics and International Relations, 2*(3), 352–373.

Gavin, N. T. (2001). British journalists in the spotlight: Europe and media research. *Journalism, 2*(3), 299–314.

Gleissner, M., & De Vreese, C. H. (2005). News about the EU Constitution: Journalistic challenges and media portrayal of the European Union Constitution. *Journalism, 6*(2), 221–242.

Gulyas, A. (2013). The influence of professional variables on journalists' uses and views of social media: A comparative study of Finland, Germany, Sweden and the United Kingdom. *Digital Journalism, 1*(2), 270–285.

Habermas, J. (2012). *The crisis of the European Union: A response*. Polity.

Hall, J. (2001). *Online journalism: A critical primer*. Pluto Press.

Harrison, J., & Pukallus, S. (2015). The European community's public communication policy (1951-1967). *Contemporary European History, 24*(2), 233–251.

Inglehart, R. (1970). Cognitive mobilization and European identity. *Comparative Politics, 3*(1), 45–70.

Inglehart, R. (1977). *The silent revolution*. Princeton University Press.

Kandyla, A., & De Vreese, C. (2011). News media representations of a common EU foreign and security policy: A cross-national content analysis of CFSP coverage in national news media. *Comparative European Politics, 9*(1), 52–75.

Karlsson, M. (2012). Charting the liquidity of online news: Moving towards a method for content analysis of online news. *International Communication Gazette, 74*(4), 385–402.

Karlsson, M., & Strömbäck, J. (2010). Freezing the flow of online news: Exploring approaches to the study of the liquidity of online news. *Journalism Studies, 11*(1), 2–19.

Karp, J., Banducci, S., & Bowler, S. (2003). To know it is to love it? Satisfaction with democracy in the European Union. *Comparative Political Studies, 36*(3), 271–292.

Kevin, D. (2001). Coverage of the European Parliament elections of 1999: National public spheres and European debates. *Javnost/The Public, 8*(1), 21–38.

Klinenberg, E. (2005). Convergence: News production in a digital age. *The Annals of the American Academy of Political and Social Science, 597*(1), 48–64.

Kontochristou, M., & Mascha, E. (2014). The Euro crisis and the question of solidarity in the European Union: Disclosures and manifestations in the European press. *Review of European Studies, 6*(2), 50–62.

Larsson, A. O. (2012). Interactivity on Swedish newspaper websites: What kind, how much and why? *Convergence: The International Journal of Research into New Media Technologies, 18*(2), 195–213.

Larsson, A. O. (2013). Staying in or going out? *Journalism Practice, 7*(6), 738–754.

Laursen, B. (2012). Transparency in the Council of the European Union: Why journalists don't get the full picture. *Journalism, 14*(6), 771–789.

Laursen, B., & Valentini, C. (2013). Media relations in the Council of the European Union: Insights into the Council press officers' professional practices. *Journal of Public Affairs, 13*(3), 230–238.

Lecheler, S. S. (2008). EU membership and the press: An analysis of the Brussels correspondents from the new member states. *Journalism, 9*(4), 443–464.

Leroy, P., & Siune, K. (1994). The role of television in European elections: The cases of Belgium and Denmark. *European Journal of Communication, 9*(1), 47–69.

Lewis, J., & Cushion, S. (2009). The thirst to be first. An analysis of breaking news stories and their impact on the quality of 24-hour news coverage in the UK. *Journalism Practice, 3*(3), 304–318.

Lewis, J., Stephen, C., & James, T. (2005). Immediacy, convenience or engagement? An analysis of 24-hour news channels in the UK. *Journalism Studies, 6*(4), 461–477.

Lilleker, D., Koc-Michalska, K., Zajac, J., & Michalski, T. (2016). Social media actions and interactions: The role of the Facebook and Twitter during the 2014 European Parliament elections in the 28 EU nations. In: *Digital media, power, and democracy in election campaigns*, 2–3 July 2015, Washington, DC (Unpublished), Retrieved May 30, 2016, from: http://eprints.bournemouth.ac.uk/22484/1/KKM-DGL-TM-JZ-Washington2015-FINAL.pdf

Lloyd, J., & Marconi, C. (2014). *Reporting the EU: News, media and the European institutions*. Reuters Institute for the Study of Journalism, University of Oxford, I.B. Tauris & Co. Ltd.

Lubbers, M., & Scheepers, P. (2010). Divergent trends of Euroscepticism in countries and regions of the European Union. *European Journal of Political Research, 49*(6), 787–817.

Machill, M., Beiler, M., & Fischer, C. (2006). Europe-topics in Europe's media: The debate about the European public sphere: A meta-analysis of media content analysis. *European Journal of Communication, 21*(1), 57–88.

MacLeod, A. (2003). *An analysis of the impact of the United Kingdom print and broadcast media upon the legitimacy of the European Parliament in Britain.* PhD Dissertation, University of Central Lancashire.

Maier, J., & Rittberger, B. (2008). Shifting Europe's boundaries: Mass media, public opinion and the enlargement of the EU. *European Union Politics, 9*(2), 243–267.

Martins, A. I., Lecheler, S., & de Vreese, C. H. (2012). Information flow and communication deficit: Perceptions of Brussels-based correspondents and EU officials. *Journal of European Integration, 34*(4), 305–322.

Massey, B. L., & Levy, R. M. (1999). Interactivity, online journalism and English-language web newspapers in Asia. *Journalism and Mass Communication Quarterly, 76*(1), 138–151.

Meyer, C. (1999). Political legitimacy and the invisibility of politics: Exploring the European Union's communication deficit. *Journal of Common Market Studies, 37*(4), 617–639.

Michailidou, A. (2006). *The role of the Internet in the European Union's public communication strategy and the emerging European public sphere.* Doctoral Thesis. Loughborough University.

Michailidou, A. (2012). "Second Order" elections and online journalism. *Journalism Practice, 6*(3), 366–383.

Mitchelstein, E., & Boczkwoski, P. (2009). Between tradition and change: A review of recent research on online news production. *Journalism, 10*(5), 562–586.

Morgan, D. (1995). British news and European Union news: The Brussels news beat and its problems. *European Journal of Communication, 10*(3), 321–343.

Neuberger, C., Tonnemacher, J., Biebl, M., & Duck, A. (1998). Online: The future of newspapers? Germany's dailies on the World Wide Web. *Journal of Computer-Mediated Communication, 4*(1). https://doi.org/10.1111/j.1083-6101.1998.tb00087.x

Norris, P. (2000). *A virtuous circle: Political communications in postindustrial societies.* Cambridge University Press.

O'Sullivan, J. (2005). Delivering Ireland: Journalism's search for a role online. *Gazette, 67*(1), 45–68.

O'Sullivan, J., & Heinonen, A. (2008). Old values, new media: Journalism role perceptions in a changing world. *Journalism Practice, 2*(3), 357–371.

Palacios, M. & Diaz Noci, J. (Eds.) (2007). *Online journalism: Research methods. A multidisciplinary approach in comparative perspective.* Servicio Editorial. Universidad del Pais Vasco.

Pătruț, M. (2015). Blog role in consolidating the image of the candidate for European Parliament Elections. *European Journal of Science and Theology, 11*(4), 117–130.

Paulussen, S. (2004). Online news production in Flanders: How Flemish online journalists perceive and explore the Internet's potential. *Journal of Computer-Mediated Communication, 9*(4). https://doi.org/10.1111/j.1083-6101.2004.tb00300.x

Peter, J., & de Vreese, C. H. (2004). In search of Europe – A cross-national comparative study of the European Union in national television news. *Harvard Journal of Press/Politics, 9*(4), 3–24.

Peter, J., Semetko, H. A., & de Vreese, C. H. (2003). EU Politics on television news. A cross-national comparative study. *EU Politics, 4*(3), 305–327.

Quandt, T. (2008). Old and new routines in German online newsrooms. In C. Paterson & D. Domingo (Eds.), *Making online news. The ethnography of new media production* (pp. 77–97). Peter Lang.

Quandt, T., Löffelholz, M., Weaver, D. H., Hanitzsch, T., & Altmeppen, K. D. (2006). American and German online journalists at the beginning of the 21st century: A bi-national survey. *Journalism Studies, 7*(2), 171–186.

Ryfe, D., Mensing, D. & Ceker, H. (2012). Popularity is not the same thing as influence: A study of the bay area news system. Paper presented at the *International Symposium on Online Journalism*, Austin, TX, April, 2012. https://isoj.org/wp-content/uploads/2018/01/Mensing.pdf

Saltzis, K. (2012). Breaking news online: How news stories are updated and maintained around-the-clock. *Journalism Practice, 6*(5–6), 702–710.

Schroeder, R. (2004). Online review: Interactive info graphics in Europe –added value to online mass media: a preliminary survey. *Journalism Studies, 5*(4), 563–570.

Schuck, A. R. T., & de Vreese, C. H. (2006). Between risk and opportunity: News framing and its effects on public support for EU enlargement. *European Journal of Communication, 21*(1), 5–32.

Schweitzer, E. J. (2009). Europeanisation on the internet? The role of German party websites in the 2004 European Parliamentary elections. *Observatorio (OBS) Journal, 3*(3), 20–40. https://doi.org/10.15847/obsOBS332009262

Schweitzer, E. J. (2012). The mediatization of e-campaigning: Evidence from German party websites in state, national, and European Parliamentary elections 2002–2009. *Journal of Computer-Mediated Communication, 17*(3), 283–302. https://doi.org/10.1111/j.1083-6101.2012.01577.x

Semetko, H. A., & Valkenburg, P. M. (2000). Framing European politics: A content analysis of press and television news. *Journal of Communication, 50*(2), 93–109.

Semetko, H. A., de Vreese, C. H., & Peter, J. (2000). Europeanised politics – Europeanised media? European integration and political communication. *West European Politics, 23*(4), 121–141.

Sifft, S., Brüggemann, M., Kleinen, V., Königslöw, K., Peters, B., & Wimmel, A. (2007). Segmented Europeanization: Exploring the legitimacy of the European Union from a public discourse perspective. *Journal of Common Market Studies, 45*(1), 127–155.

Souliotis, D. (2013). The coverage of the economic crisis by the British and Greek press. Indications of a European public sphere? In G. Pleios (Ed.), *The media and the crisis* (pp. 227–269). Papazisis Publications. [In Greek].

Spanier, B. (2010). Trying to square the circle – The challenge of being an EU Commission spokesperson. In C. Valentini & G. Nesti (Eds.), *Public communication in the European Union. History, perspectives and challenges* (pp. 191–216). Cambridge Scholars Publishing.

Statham, P. (2010). Media performance and Europe's communication deficit: A study of journalists' perceptions. In C. Bee & E. Bozzini (Eds.), *Mapping the European public sphere. Institutions, media and civil society* (pp. 117–139). Ashgate.

Steensen, S. (2011). Online journalism and the promises of new technology. *Journalism Studies, 12*(3), 311–327.

Theodosiadou, S., Kostarella, I. & Tsantopoulos, G. (2004). Greek journalists reporting Europe. Paper presented at the *Conference of the European Sociological Association in Thessaloniki*. Greece, 5–7 November 2004.

Trenz, H. J. (2004). Media coverage on European governance: Exploring the European Public sphere in national quality newspapers. *European Journal of Communication, 19*(3), 291–319.

Ursell, G. (2001). Dumbing down or shaping up? New technologies, new media, new journalism. *Journalism, 2*(2), 175–196.

Valentini, C. (2007). EU media relations. Views of Finnish and Italian journalists. *GMJ Mediterranean edition, 2*(2), 82–96.

Van der Wurff, R. (2005). Impacts of the internet on newspapers in Europe: Conclusions. *International Communication Gazette, 67*(1), 107–120.

References

Van der Wurff, R., Lauf, E., Balcytiene, A., Fortunati, L., Holmberg, S., Paulussen, S., & Salaverria, R. (2008). Online and print newspapers in Europe in 2003 - Evolving towards complementarity. *Communications, 33*(4), 403–430.

Vliegenthart, R., Schuck, A. R. T., Boomgaarden, H. G., & de Vreese, C. H. (2008). News coverage and support for European integration 1990-2006. *International Journal of Public Opinion Research, 20*(4), 415–439.

Weber, M. S. (2012). Newspapers and the long-term implications of hyperlinking. *Journal of Computer-Mediated Communication, 17*(2), 187–201. https://doi.org/10.1111/j.1083-6101.2011.01563.x

Widholm, A. (2016). Tracing online news in motion: Time and duration in the study of liquid journalism. *Digital Journalism, 4*(1), 24–40.

Chapter 5
Content Analysis and Semi-Structured Interviews as Assessment Tools

The purpose of this chapter is to set out the key dimensions of the methodological approach that is used in this study. The first section focuses on content analysis, while the second explains how semi-structured interviews are used and how they are able to fill in some of the gaps in understanding, gaps that an application of content analysis on its own would leave. The selected research methods contribute to the examination and analysis of (a) the way in which the EP is covered in the selected news websites in the UK and Greece, (b) the problems that the EP is facing in communicating itself in the selected news websites in the UK and Greece, and (c) the potential solutions for the EP in order to overcome these problems.

5.1 Use of Content Analysis for Examining the Coverage of the EP in News Websites in the UK and Greece

Content analysis is one of the most popular research methods in the broad discipline area of media and communication. With content analysis, as implied by the definition, the content of something, in our case of the text of the news item, is analysed. A classic definition of content analysis as a research method is the following: "Content analysis is a research technique for the systematic classification and description of communication content according to certain usually predetermined categories. It may involve quantitative or qualitative analysis, or both. Technical objectivity requires that the categories of classification and analysis be clearly and operationally defined so that other researchers can follow them reliably" (Wright, 1986: 125, in Berger, 2014). In addition, Berger (2014) argues that with content analysis we analyse only the manifest content of a text, and not the things that are implied by this. Content analysis is by definition a quantitative method since through this method one tries to identify and count the occurrence of specific characteristics and dimensions of texts and through this to be able to say something about the messages, images, representations of such texts and their wider social significance (Hansen & Machin, 2013: 89). Thus, content analysis can provide some indication of relative prominences and absences of characteristics in media texts (Hansen and Machin, 2013).

Content analysis has been used as the main methodological tool in studies examining the EU and the EU institutions' media coverage and aspects such as the basic themes of the coverage, the visibility (the amount of news items), the tone of the news, the framing (Semetko et al., 2000; De Vreese, 2001; Peter and de Vreese, 2004; Gleissner and De Vreese, 2005). That is why content analysis is being selected as the most suitable research method to use here.

The process of conducting the content analysis has been broken down into the following steps, as proposed by Hansen & Machin (2013):

5.1.1 Defining the Research Problem

The book aims to identify and critically analyse the problems that the EP is facing in communicating itself to selected online news media in the UK and Greece and then to suggest potential solutions for the EP in order to overcome these problems. To this end, the specific research questions that will be addressed are the following:

RQ1: What is the coverage of the European Parliament's institutional powers and their output in selected news websites in the UK and Greece?

RQ2: What are the problems that the EP is facing in communicating its institutional powers and their output to the selected news websites in the UK and Greece?

RQ3: What solutions could be proposed to the EP to enhance its communication performance in relation to the news websites of the UK and Greece and which of these solutions could be applied with some potential for success?

5.1.2 Review of Relevant Literature and Research

The definition of the research problem, along with the formulation of the aforementioned Research Questions, has been anchored to the review of the relevant literature as seen in Chaps. 2–4.

5.1.3 Selection of the Media Sample

The process of the selection of media and sample involves (a) the selection of the mass communication medium for the analysis, (b) the selection of the specific media outlets for the analysis, (c) the sampling of issues or dates, and (d) the sampling of the relevant content for the analysis.

5.1 Use of Content Analysis for Examining the Coverage of the EP in News...

The Selection of News Websites for Content Analysis The selection of online news media has been made on the basis of the increasing use of the Internet, during the period under examination (2011–2013) in the EU and both in the UK and Greece, as a source for obtaining information both on European political matters and on the European Parliament. In autumn 2012, the Internet has gained ground (43%, +10 since November 2011) as a medium for obtaining information on the EP, following television (64%, −5) and ahead of the written press (33%, −2), and the radio (15%, −3) (European Parliament, 2013). During the same period, the news websites (31%) were mentioned, by the EU citizens, as the most preferred source for obtaining information on the EP, followed by the websites of the European Parliament (17%), the online social networks (8%), and blogs (3%) (European Parliament, 2013).

Regarding the UK, in autumn 2012, the Internet has gained ground as source of obtaining information on the EP. For example, in autumn 2012, 60% (+13) of the UK citizens said that they would use primarily the Internet as a source in order to look for information on the European Parliament, followed by the TV (49%, −7%), the press (25%, −2%), and the radio (8%, −1%) (European Parliament, 2013). The news websites (48%) were mentioned, by the UK citizens, as the most preferred source for obtaining information on the EP, followed by the websites of the European Parliament (22%), online social networks (7%), and blogs (4%) (European Parliament, 2013).

As far as Greece is concerned, in autumn 2012, the Internet gained ground (+7% since autumn 2011) as a medium for obtaining information on the EP by Greek citizens, following television (−19% since autumn 2011) and ahead of the press (−10% since autumn 2011), and the radio (−4% since autumn 2011) (European Parliament, 2013). However, during the same period, blogs (15%) were mentioned, by the Greek citizens, as the most preferred source for obtaining information on the EP, followed by the online social networks (14%), news websites (14%), and the websites of the European Parliament (12%) (European Parliament, 2013).

The Selection of the Specific Online Media for the Analysis The news websites in Greece and in the UK were selected according to the following criteria:

- Popularity: This criterion is based on the traffic ranking provided by www.alexa.com—a website providing traffic statistics for the most popular websites per country, and which is frequently used by many scholars as a web metric site (Kim et al., 2013; Rone, 2013; Beheshti-Kashi and Makki, 2013; Messner and DiStaso, 2013; Trilling and Schoenbach, 2013; Michailidou, 2012). According to Alexa.com "The country traffic rank is a measure of how a website is doing among internet users in a particular country relative to other sites over the past month. The rank by country is calculated using a combination of the estimated average daily unique visitors to a site and the estimated number of page views on that site from users in that country over the past month. The site with the highest combination of unique visitors and page views is ranked #1 in that country" (Alexa, 2013).

- Accessibility and availability of the research material: this criterion requires functional online archives for the collection of the news items for the period under examination.
- News websites having an online presence during the period under examination (2011–2013).

The news websites that met the aforementioned criteria were: (1) www.in.gr and www.protothema.gr for the case of Greece, and (2) www.bbc.co.uk and www.theguardian.co.uk for the case of the UK.

In addition to the aforementioned criteria, the websites that will be used as case studies for the content analysis have been selected because: (1) they are either required to be impartial as a result of regulatory requirements (that is the case for the BBC) or considered as a typical case of factual and detached style of reporting, as this is the case for the www.in.gr (Milioni et al., 2012), and (2) they are predominantly pro-EU as the existing literature has shown; this is the case for the Guardian website (Anderson and Weymouth, 1999) and www.protothema.gr (Milioni et al., 2012; Michailidou, 2012).

While this might at first sight seem to limit the value of this study in terms of its ability to identify problems in the EP's communication with its citizens via online news media, there are in fact key arguments in favour of this specific approach. In short, it would be expected that the EP would have problems in securing effective communication via pronouncedly Eurosceptic news sites as those of the Telegraph, Mail, or Express in the UK and tackling the EP's communications problems with these might well be virtually impossible given the entrenched attitudes that each of these sites reflects. However, the sites that offer the EP the best chance of communicating effectively are those that are near the centre and the Europhile end of the spectrum because these are the sites where improvements in the EP's communications performance should in theory be most achievable. If there are significant areas where the EP is performing weakly in relation to these ("more friendly to the EP") sites, then it is of real value if a study can both identify the areas where it is so doing together with the reasons for this and possible solutions.

The Selection of the UK and Greece as Case Studies As already seen in Sect. 3.7, Greece and the UK—during the period under examination—are the two member states in the EU with the highest scores of negative perceptions towards the EP. These negative feelings make the UK and Greece two of the most "difficult" states as far as the communication of the EP messages is concerned, and that is why they have been selected as relevant case studies.

The Sampling of Issues or Dates The time period that has been selected for the analysis of the relevant empirical data is a routine, non-EP elections period. In this way, the coverage of the EP in routine periods is not expected to be affected by the salience of the EP elections, since during EP elections the media coverage of the EP is increased due to the saliency of the specific event (De Vreese et al., 2005, 2006). In addition, a routine (non-election) period is selected for the analysis, since the need to research EU affairs in routine periods has also been identified by different scholars

(De Vreese, 2001; Michailidou, 2012; Gattermann, 2013). Thus, the chosen time period runs from 1st September 2011 to 1st September 2013, covering two annual cycles of the 7th Parliamentary term, and being the closest to the 2014 EP elections 2-year routine period. The selection of this period also takes into consideration the fact that the campaign for the 2014 EP elections was officially launched by the EP on 10th September 2013.

The Sampling of Relevant Content The unit of the content analysis is the news item. A news item in order to be selected had to mention European Parliament, or any equivalent (Member of the European Parliament, Committee of the European Parliament, President of the European Parliament, etc.) in the title, the highlight section, or in the first paragraph of the news item, plus twice independently (not in the same sentence) in the text. If the first paragraph is short, then the second one is used for the first reference. This is the so-called 1 + 2 rule that has been used by other scholars as well (Jasson, 2009; Gattermann, 2013) and ensures that the EP (or any equivalent) has a minimum reference in the news item.

The news items from the Greek websites have been retrieved from the available and accessible own online archives. For the retrieval of the news items the search terms "ΕυρωπαϊκόΚοινοβούλιο", "Ευρωβουλή", "Ευρωβουλευτής", "ΕυρωπαϊκήΒουλή", and "Ευρωκοινοβούλιο" have been used.

The news items from the UK websites have been retrieved as follows: For the case of www.theguardian.co.uk the relevant news items have been retrieved from the Nexis database which is a database including, inter alia, local, regional, and national newspapers, newsletters, magazines, and more. For the case of the www.bbc.co.uk the relevant news items have been retrieved with the use of the Advanced Search option offered by the Google Search engine. The relevant search terms, the period under examination, and the specific news website (bbc.co.uk) were selected in the respective fields of the Advanced Search option.

For the retrieval of the news items for both websites the search terms "European Parliament", "MEP", and "Members of the European Parliament" have been used.

For all the news items the website www.web.archive.org has been used in order to verify that the status of the news items (on the date of their retrieval) was the same as the status of the news items on the date of their publication. The website www.web.archive.org has been archiving the web for 20 years and has preserved billions of webpages from millions of websites in their first original status.

Totally 1051 news items (650 news items in the selected Greek news websites, and 401 news items in the selected UK news websites) relating to the European Parliament were collected, and analysed for the 2-year routine period under examination (01/09/2011–01/09/2013).

5.1.4 Defining Analytical Categories

In this part of the content analysis, the variables relating to the coverage of the EP have been defined. The analytical categories that have been created and used as variables for every news item, in the content analysis, are the following:

- The date of the posting of the news item.
- The time of the posting of the news item.
- The title of the news item.
- The author of the news item.
- The EP (or any equivalent actor's) activity that the news item emerged from.
- The EP institutional power (Legislative power/Budgetary power/Supervisory and scrutiny power/System development power) that the news item refers to.
- The tone (if any) of the coverage of the EP (or any equivalent) in the news item.
- The actors who evaluate the EP (or any equivalent) (in the case of a news items with tone).
- The output of the EP that the news item refers to (in the case of the news item with reference to the EP output).
- The tone towards the output of the EP in the news item (in the case of the news item with reference to the EP output).
- The actors who speak about the EP output (in the case of news item with reference to the EP impact).
- The online features (hyperlinks or videos) accompanying the relevant EP news item.
- The kind of information that the videos accompanying the EP news item provide to the reader.
- The material that the hyperlinks (embedded in the text of the news story) link to.

For every selected news item, the EP's (or any other equivalent actor's) activity that the news item emerged from, was identified. For example, some of the activities were the following: Domestic (or non-domestic) MEP's interviews, press releases, or statements, the EP's President's speech, European Political Party press conferences, the European Parliament's Committee visits, debate-discussions in the EP, etc.

In order to identify and examine the kind of the EP's institutional power that the news item referred to, the following guidelines were used: In cases where there was reference in the selected news items to the ordinary legislative procedure (the co-decision procedure), to the EP consultation role, to the EP being asked for its opinion on proposed legislation, to the EP giving its consent, approving or rejecting a legislative proposal, to the EP giving its opinion, adopting resolutions and voting on reports, or to the EP's right of legislative initiative (Corbett et al., 2011; European Parliament, 2014a), this was identified and coded as a news item referring to the EP's legislative power. In cases where there was a reference, in the selected news item, to the EP deciding (with the Council of the European Union) on the entire annual budget of the EU, or to the EP exercising budgetary control (Corbett et al., 2011;

European Parliament, 2014b; Staab, 2008), then this was identified and coded as a news item referring to the EP's budgetary powers. In cases where there was a reference, in the selected news items, to the EP exercising scrutiny and control over the EU executive through debates, questions and reports, or through MEPs' written questions, or through the right of the EP to approve or dismiss the European Commission, and the executive of other EU institutions and agencies (Corbett et al., 2011; European Parliament, 2014c) then this was identified and coded as a news item referring to the EP's scrutiny and control of the executive powers. In cases where there was a reference to the EP (or any equivalent actor) arguing for and trying to promote constitutional changes at the EU level (Corbett et al., 2011), then this was identified and coded as a news item referring to the EP's constitutional changes powers.

For the assessment of the tone of the coverage towards the EP (or any equivalent) or towards the EP's output, the analysis focused on whether this was presented in a negative, positive, neutral (both negative and positive) way, or whether the news items had no tone at all (in other words, that there was not any evaluative stance in the news item). A similar approach towards tone assessment has also been followed in studies by other scholars (Gleissner and De Vreese, 2005; Peter et al., 2003; Anderson and Weymouth, 1999; Esser, 1999; Norris, 2000; Menendez Alarcon, 2010).

It should be noted that tonal analysis, as used here, does not provide all of the nuances in the analysed coverage that would be identified through the use of critical discourse analysis (bias by omission, for example, as in Fairclough, 1995 or covert bias, as in Anderson and Weymouth, 1999), but it does provide us with significant information from a public relations (PR)/communication viewpoint. In terms of positive PR the EP needs to be aiming for as much coverage as possible that is either of a positive or "no tone" nature and the methodology applied here enables the key information as to the extent to which either of these is present to be identified. Critical discourse analysis would indeed give more information but, as Fairclough himself acknowledged in his 1995 study, as a methodological approach it is highly complex and time consuming and from the point of view of this study its application would have greatly restricted the number of news texts that it would have been practical to examine. Tonal analysis is a realistic and practical alternative approach; therefore, that, as was shown above, has already been successfully applied within the literature.

In order to examine and measure the presence within the selected coverage of actors who evaluate the EP (or any equivalent), these were identified as domestic or non-domestic politicians, domestic or non-domestic MEPs, etc., with an evaluative stance towards the EP (or any equivalent). This is again a similar approach that has been followed by other scholars as well (Gleissner and De Vreese, 2005; Peter et al., 2003; Anderson and Weymouth, 1999; Esser, 1999; Norris, 2000; Menendez Alarcon, 2010). In cases where there was a tone towards the EP (or any equivalent) in the news item, but there was not any actor identified in it, it was assumed that the actor evaluating the EP (or any equivalent actor) was the relevant journalist who wrote the specific news item.

In order to examine and measure the presence of the EP's output in the news items and following the example of the predefined questions developed by Semetko and Valkenburg (2000), a similar set of predefined questions was used. The set included the following questions: Does the story refer to the output of the EP's activity? If this kind of reference is present, what is the specific output that is being described? What is the tone, in the specific news item, regarding the EP output?

For the examination of the presence of online "add-ons" (such as hyperlinks and videos) in the relevant news items, the hyperlinks and video elements that were accompanying the news story were coded. In the coding process the basic distinctions were: (a) the hyperlinks that were embedded in the text of the news story and the ones that were not embedded in it, and (b) the internal hyperlinks (linking to relevant news items within the same news website) and external ones (linking to material outside the news website); these are distinctions that have been also used by other scholars (Dimitrova et al. 2003; Dimitrova and Neznanski, 2006; Van der Wurff, 2005; Larsson, 2013). In addition—with regard to the external hyperlinks—the kind of material that they link to (for example, other news websites, websites of campaign groups, websites of domestic or non-domestic MEPs, European Parliament websites, pdf documents, YouTube videos, etc.) was also examined and coded.

The same approach had been followed with regard to the videos accompanying the news story, where again a basic distinction was made between videos embedded in the text of the news item, and those videos not embedded in it. The basic themes of the information that the videos provided to the readers were also coded. In addition, in the cases where it could be identified, the origin of the video was also coded (e.g. whether the video was produced by the news website itself, or the video originated from an affiliated TV channel, etc.).

5.1.5 Constructing a Coding Schedule and Protocol

After the definition of the relevant analytical categories, these have been set out in a codeable form in a coding schedule, which serves as a guide in conducting the content analysis.

5.1.6 Piloting the Coding Schedule and Checking Reliability

Piloting the coding schedule of the content analysis is a necessary process before moving to the empirical analysis. An essential element of this phase is that it includes some necessary checks for ensuring the reliability of the coding process. Reliability in content analysis is essentially about consistency, either between different coders (inter-coder reliability) or of the individual coder's coding practice over time (intra-coder reliability) (Hansen & Machin, 2013). In our case, intra-coder reliability checks, and corrections, have been done over the piloting period in order to ensure the reliability of the coding process.

5.1.7 Data Preparation and Analysis

The relevant empirical data have been collected and analysed with the use of the Microsoft Excel spreadsheet software.

5.2 Use of Semi-Structured Interviews

The process of the interview, as a research method, could be described as a conversation between the researcher and the informant, where the goal of the researcher is to obtain information (Berger, 2000). The specific format of semi-structured interviews, where the researcher (interviewer) has prepared a list of questions to ask the informant, allows the interviewer to have the flexibility to go beyond the answers and thus enters into a dialogue with the interviewee; at the same time, it helps the interviewer to understand how interviewees generate and deploy meaning in social life, and the interviewees to answer more freely to the questions than in the case of the standardized interviews (Berger, 2000; May, 2011). Last but not least, semi-structured interviews provide a more suitable structure for comparability (meaningful comparison) of the data coming from them, in comparison, for example, to the unstructured interview (Berger, 2000; May, 2011).

These types of interviews have been used by scholars in previous studies, for examining political journalism (Baisnée, 2000; Pfetsch, 2001), EU journalism (Gleissner and de Vreese, 2005; Statham, 2008, 2010), the EU's media relations performance (Anderson and McLeod, 2004), or the EU press officers' tasks and communication activities (Laursen, 2012; Laursen & Valentini, 2013).

The use of in-depth semi-structured interviews with online journalists and with European Parliament Liaison Office (EPLO) officers in Greece and in the UK, seemed the most appropriate method for (a) examining the problems that the EP is facing in communicating its institutional powers and their output to the selected news websites in the UK and Greece and (b) for the identification and critical analysis of potential ways for the EP to communicate itself more effectively to the EU citizens in Greece and in the UK, through the news websites.

5.2.1 Building the Set of Themes and Questions

Following the semi-structured interview methodologies of the aforementioned studies, the first step of the empirical investigation was to build the set of themes and questions to be used in the interview questionnaire.

For the interviews with the online journalists in Greece and the UK, these were built mainly upon the literature regarding the EU media relations performance as seen in Sect. 4.8. Thus, the main themes discussed in the relevant interviews with the online journalists in both countries were related to:

- The evaluation (both in quantitative and qualitative terms) of the information material (written or oral) provided by the EPLO, where issues such as the EP and EPLO website, the press releases, the existence of the element of output in the information material provided by the EPLO, or the extent of customization of the information material were discussed.
- The evaluation of the EPLO's facilitation role, where issues such as the EPLO's support to journalists, or the speed of EPLO's response to journalists' enquiries, were discussed.
- The evaluation of EPLO's source strategies, where issues such as the frequency with which online journalists are contacted by EPLO officers who want to get their message across and try to penetrate their information resource pool, the extent to which online journalists want a more aggressive source strategy, or the extent to which such practice might jeopardize the EPLO's credibility were discussed.
- The evaluation of the extent to which the EPLO's media relations activities overall take into consideration the changes in the journalistic practices and working routines of online journalists, where subordinate issues such as the acknowledgment by the EPLO's of the increased workload and pressure that online journalists face to immediately write and upload news stories, or of the alterations in the news gathering practices of the online journalists, or the evaluation of the provision of online elements such as hyperlinks or multimedia, were discussed.

Apart from the aforementioned themes, the interviews with the online journalists in both countries under examination also included the following interview themes, which seemed necessary for the identification of the problems that the EPLOs face in their media relations performance, and for the identification and critical analysis of potential ways for the EP to communicate more effectively to the citizens of Greece and the UK:

- Problems that online journalists encounter in their media relations with the EPLOs in both countries.
- Suggestions proposed by the online journalists for further improvements in the media relations performance of the EPLOs.
- The EP news production process, where subordinate issues such as the news selection criteria for EP news stories, the sources used when writing EP

news stories and for stories about the EP's impact, the use of social media in news gathering practice, the sources and the selection criteria used for the online "add-on" elements—such as hyperlinks and multimedia—of the news stories were discussed.

In the case of the EPLO officers in the UK and Greece, the semi-structured interviews included themes that were related to the examination of the EP's online media coverage and the EPLO's media relations performance. In particular, the set of themes in the relevant interviews with the EPLO officers was the following:

- The objectives of the EPLO officers regarding the EP's online media coverage.
- The objectives of the EPLO officers regarding the EPLO's media relations performance.
- The working routines of the EPLO officers, where subordinate issues such as the daily routine of the EPLO officers, the use of social media for online media relations, production, customization, and dissemination of the information material, the provision of online elements—such as hyperlinks or multimedia, and the source strategy were discussed.
- The problems that the EPLO officers identify in their media relations performance.

5.2.2 Sampling of the Online Journalists

Regarding the sampling of the online journalists for the interviews, the criteria used for their selection were the following:

- The journalists had to work in popular news websites.
- The journalists had to be home-based journalists (not Brussels-based correspondents).
- The journalists should have dealt on a regular basis (even if not exclusively) with EU and EP affairs (whether they were EU affairs editors or political editors).

Taking into account the above criteria, the sample eventually comprised of 16 journalists working online, 10 online journalists from Greece, and 6 online journalists from the UK. In order to make the sample more representative, online journalists working in the news websites under examination and online journalists working in 5 other popular quality news websites (4 other news websites for the case of Greece and 1 other news website for the case of the UK) were included. It should be mentioned that in the case of the UK, and despite the efforts made to approach as many online journalists as possible, the heavy workload that the journalists had in their news organizations and their limited time availability did not allow for a larger sample. In addition, the reason for the selection of journalists from other news websites as well, is that they also work in news websites which are rather pro-European; meaning that they do not face any constraints and negative anti-European attitude in their newsrooms. Thus, it is assumed that these sites offer the EP the best chance of communicating effectively and at the same time these sites are the place where improvements in the EP's communications performance should in theory be most achievable. In addition, the specific news websites journalists work in the most popular news websites both in Greece and in the UK, and thus they are the most likely to express journalism's dominant professional ideas, cultures, and practices within their national media system (Benson et al., 2012).

The preliminary and follow-up interviews with the online journalists in the UK and Greece, were anonymized, and took place during the period 2013–2016 in Greece and in the UK.

In the case of Greece, journalists from the following news websites were interviewed: (Table 5.1)

The sample of the Greek online journalists that were interviewed includes: 5 EU affairs editors, 3 political editors, and 2 political affairs chief editors.

In the case of the UK, journalists from the following news websites were interviewed: (Table 5.2)

The sample of the UK online journalists that were interviewed includes: 2 EU affairs editors and 4 political reporters.

Table 5.1 Greek news websites and journalists interviewed

Number	Name/Code of Journalist	Name of news website
1	JOUR.GR.1	www.zougla.gr
2	JOUR.GR.2	www.zougla.gr
3	JOUR.GR.3	www.zougla.gr
4	JOUR.GR.4	www.in.gr
5	JOUR.GR.5	www.skai.gr
6	JOUR.GR.6	www.in.gr
7	JOUR.GR.7	www.protothema.gr
8	JOUR.GR.8	www.protothema.gr
9	JOUR.GR.9	www.news247.gr
10	JOUR.GR.10	www.efsyn.gr

Table 5.2 UK news websites and journalists interviewed

Number	Name/Code of Journalist	Name of news website
1	JOUR.UK.1	www.theguardian.com
2	JOUR.UK.2	www.theguardian.com
3	JOUR.UK.3	www.bbc.com
4	JOUR.UK.4	www.bbc.com
5	JOUR.UK.5	www.bbc.com
6	JOUR.UK.6	www.independent.co.uk

5.2.3 Sampling of the EPLO Officers

Regarding the sampling of the EPLO officers, the criteria for their selection were the following:

- The EPLO officers had to be full-time EP civil servants in permanent positions in the EPLO in Greece (Athens) or in the UK (London),
- The EPLO officers should be dealing (or have previous experience) with the handling of the press and media relations of the EPLO.

Taking into account the above criteria, the sample for the interviews eventually comprised of 3 EPLO officers, 2 EPLO officers from Greece, and 1 from the UK. The preliminary and the follow-up interviews with them, were anonymized, and took place during the period 2013–2016 in Greece and in the UK.

The details are set out below in Table 5.3.

5.2.4 Data Analysis

After the semi-structured interviews had been conducted (each interview lasted approximately 1 h) and recorded, the transcription of the interviews was done. A very important part of this process was to make sense of the information in the transcribed interviews (Berger, 2000; May, 2011). Based on the initial readings of the transcripts, statements were extracted, paraphrased, and set into context. Then the available information was categorized and classified manually according to the interview themes, in order to find common patterns, and make comparisons among the data.

The findings emerging from the in-depth semi-structured interviews with the online journalists in Greece and in the UK concerning the assessment of the EPLO's media relations performance are presented in Chap. 7, while the findings which are related to the identification and critical analysis of potential ways for the EP to communicate itself more effectively to EU citizens in Greece and in the UK are included in Chaps. 8–10.

Table 5.3 EPLO's officers interviewed

Number	Name/Code	EPLO Office
1	EPLO.GR.1	Athens EPLO
2	EPLO.GR.2	Athens EPLO
3	EPLO.UK.1	London EPLO

References

Alexa, The Web Information Company. (2013). *What is Alexa traffic rank in country*. Retrieved September 10, 2013, from http://www.alexa.com/help/traffic-learn-more

Anderson, P. J., & McLeod, A. (2004). The great non-communicator? The mass communicator deficit of the European Parliament and its Press Directorate. *Journal of Common Market Studies, 42*(5), 897–917.

Anderson, P. J., & Weymouth, T. (1999). *Insulting the public? The British Press and the European Union*. Longman.

Baisnée, O. (2000). Can Political journalism exist at the EU level? Paper presented at the *workshop (no. 17) on 'Political journalism: New Challenges, New Practices' at ECPR joint sessions*, Copenhagen, April 14–19.

Beheshti-Kashi, S., & Makki, B. (2013). Social media news: Motivation, purpose and usage. *International Journal of Computer Science and Information Technology, 5*(2), 97–105.

Benson, R., Blach-Ørsten, M., Powers, M., Willig, I., & Zambrano, S. (2012). Media systems online and off: Comparing the form of news in the United States, Denmark, and France. *Journal of Communication, 62*(1), 21–38.

Berger, A. (2000). *Media and communication research methods: An introduction to qualitative and quantitative approaches*. Sage.

Berger, A. (2014). *Media and communication research methods. An introduction to qualitative and quantitative approaches* (3rd ed.). Sage.

Corbett, R., Jacobs, F., & Shackleton, M. (2011). *The European Parliament* (8th ed.). John Harper Publishing.

De Vreese, C. H. (2001). Europe in the news: A cross-national comparative study of the news coverage of key EU events. *European Union Politics, 2*(3), 283–307.

De Vreese, C. H., Banducci, S., Semetko, H., & Boomgaarden, H. (2005). Off-line: The 2004 European Parliamentary elections on television news in the enlarged Europe. *Information Polity, 10*(3), 177–188.

De Vreese, C. H., Banducci, S., Semetko, H. A., & Boomgaarden, H. A. (2006). The news coverage of the 2004 European Parliamentary election campaign in 25 countries. *European Union Politics, 7*(4), 477–504.

Dimitrova, D., & Neznanski, M. (2006). Online journalism and the war in cyberspace: A comparison between U.S. and international newspapers. *Journal of Computer-Mediated Communication, 12*(1), 248–263.

Dimitrova, D. V., Connolly-Ahern, C., Williams, A. P., Kaid, L. L., & Reid, A. (2003). Hyperlinking as gatekeeping: Online newspaper coverage of the execution of an American terrorist. *Journalism Studies, 4*(3), 401–414.

Esser, F. (1999). Tabloidization of news. A comparative analysis of Anglo American and German press journalism. *European Journal of Communication, 14*(3), 291–324.

European Parliament. (2013). *European Parliament Eurobarometer (EB/EP 78.2, November 2012)*. Directorate -General for Communication.

European Parliament. (2014a). *About Parliament/Powers and Procedures – Legislative powers*. Retrieved November 27, 2014, from: http://www.europarl.europa.eu/aboutparliament/en/0081f4b3c7/Law-making-procedures-in-detail.html

European Parliament. (2014b). *About Parliament. Powers and procedures-budgetary powers*. Retrieved November 27, 2014, from: http://www.europarl.europa.eu/aboutparliament/en/003dcd4001/The-budget-procedure-explained.html

European Parliament. (2014c). *About Parliament. Powers and procedures-supervisory powers*. Retrieved November 27, 2014, from: http://www.europarl.europa.eu/aboutparliament/en/00b9de8689/Oversight-and-control-functions.html

Fairclough, N. (1995). *Media discourse*. Edward Arnold.

Gattermann, K. (2013). News about the European Parliament: Patterns and external drivers of broadsheet coverage. *European Union Politics, 14*(3), 436–457.

References

Gleissner, M., & De Vreese, C. H. (2005). News about the EU Constitution-Journalistic challenges and media portrayal of the European Union Constitution. *Journalism, 6*(2), 221–242.

Hansen, A., & Machin, D. (2013). *Media and communication research methods*. Palgrave Macmillan.

Jasson, C. (2009). *Developing discourse? National referendums and news coverage of the European constitutional process*. London School of Economics and Political Science.

Kim, J. Y., Painter, D. L., & Miles, M. D. (2013). Campaign agenda-building online: The effects of online information source and interactivity on affective evaluations and the salience of the election. *Journal of Information Technology and Politics, 10*(3), 326–340.

Larsson, A. O. (2013). Staying in or going out? *Journalism Practice, 7*(6), 738–754.

Laursen, B. (2012). Transparency in the Council of the European Union: Why journalists don't get the full picture. *Journalism, 14*(6), 771–789.

Laursen, B., & Valentini, C. (2013). Media relations in the Council of the European Union: Insights into the Council press officers' professional practices. *Journal of Public Affairs, 13*(3), 230–238.

May, T. (2011). *Social research: issues, methods and process* (4th ed.). Open University Press.

Menendez Alarcon, A. V. (2010). Media representation of the European Union: Comparing newspaper coverage in France, Spain, and the United Kingdom. *International Journal of Communication, 4*, 398–415.

Messner, M., & DiStaso, M. W. (2013). Wikipedia versus Encyclopedia Britannica: A longitudinal analysis to identify the impact of social media on the standards of knowledge. *Mass Communication and Society, 16*(4), 465–486.

Michailidou, A. (2012). "Second Order" elections and online journalism. *Journalism Practice, 6*(3), 366–383.

Milioni, D., Vadratsikas, K., & Papa, V. (2012). Their two cents worth: Exploring user agency in readers' comments in online news media. *Observatorio(OBS) Journal, 6*(3), 21–47.

Norris, P. (2000). *A virtuous circle. Political communications in postindustrial societies*. Cambridge University Press.

Peter, J., & de Vreese, C. H. (2004). In search of Europe – A cross-national comparative study of the European Union in national television news. *Harvard Journal of Press/Politics, 9*(4), 3–24.

Peter, J., Semetko, H. A., & de Vreese, C. H. (2003). EU Politics on television news. A cross-national comparative study. *EU Politics, 4*(3), 305–327.

Pfetsch, B. (2001). Political communication culture in the United States and Germany. *The International Journal of Press/Politics, 6*(1), 46–67.

Rone, J. (2013). Bulgarian pirates: At the world's end. *Cultural Trends, 22*(1), 2–13.

Semetko, H. A., & Valkenburg, P. M. (2000). Framing European politics: A content analysis of press and television news. *Journal of Communication, 50*(2), 93–109.

Semetko, H. A., de Vreese, C. H., & Peter, J. (2000). Europeanised politics – Europeanised media? European integration and political communication. *West European Politics, 23*(4), 121–141.

Staab, A. (2008). *European Union explained: Institutions, actors, global impact*. Indiana University Press.

Statham, P. (2008). Making Europe news: How journalists view their role and performance. *Journalism: Theory, Practice and Criticism, 9*(4), 398–422.

Statham, P. (2010). Media performance and Europe's communication deficit: A study of journalists' perceptions. In C. Bee & E. Bozzini (Eds.), *Mapping the European public sphere. Institutions, media and civil society* (pp. 117–139). Ashgate.

Trilling, D., & Schoenbach, K. (2013). Skipping current affairs: The non-users of online and offline news. *European Journal of Communication, 28*(1), 35–51.

Van der Wurff, R. (2005). Impacts of the internet on newspapers in Europe: Conclusions. *International Communication Gazette, 67*(1), 107–120.

Chapter 6
European Parliament's Media Coverage in the News Websites

This chapter presents the research findings from the content analysis of the EP coverage in the selected news websites in the UK and Greece, regarding the visibility of the European Parliament's institutional powers, the tone towards the EP (or any equivalent) and its institutional powers, the visibility and the patterns of visibility of the European Parliament's output, the tone of the coverage of the European Parliament's powers output, and the extent to which there is additional Internet-facilitated information provided in the coverage of the EP (hyperlinks, audiovisual material) in both countries.

6.1 European Parliament's Media Coverage in the Selected News Websites in Greece

6.1.1 The Visibility of the European Parliament's Institutional Powers in Greece

In the case of the selected Greek news websites, 650 news items related to the European Parliament were collected in total, according to the selection criteria (see Chap. 5), and content analysed for the 2-year routine period under examination (01/09/2011–01/09/2013).

As seen in Fig. 6.1, the majority of them (405 news items or else 62.3% of the total EP news items in the two Greek websites) did not have any reference to the EP institutional powers (legislative powers, budgetary powers, supervisory and scrutiny powers, EU system development powers). They rather referred, for example, to activities undertaken by domestic or non-domestic members of the European Parliament, by the President of the European Parliament, or by European Political Parties (e.g. interviews, statements, visits, and conferences) or to debates held in

6 European Parliament's Media Coverage in the News Websites

[Bar chart showing classification of EP news items:
- News items referring to the EP legislative power: 96
- News items referring to the EP budgetary power: 34
- News items referring to the EP supervisory and scrutiny power: 111
- News items referring to the EU system development power: 4
- Other EP news items: 405]

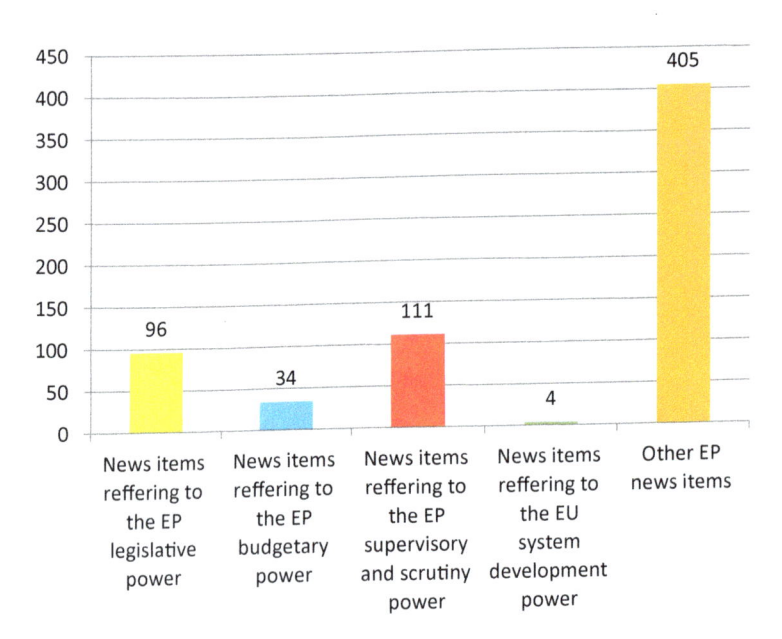

Fig. 6.1 Classification of EP news items in Greek news websites

the EP, or to the EP awarding prizes and organizing exhibitions, etc., without however any reference to the aforementioned EP powers.

A significant number of EP news items (111 news items or else 17.07% of the total news items) referred to the EP's supervisory and scrutiny powers. The vast majority of these items were related to domestic MEP's parliamentary questions, or non-domestic MEP's parliamentary questions (which had however a domestic interest), while a smaller amount of news items in this category referred to the EP exercising its appointment and dismissal powers (e.g. the appointment of members of the Board of the European Central Bank), or to debates held in the European Parliament within its supervisory and control function.

Following that, 96 news items (or else 14.7% of the total news items) referred to the EP's legislative powers. These news items referred to the EP adopting legislation through the ordinary legislative procedure, while a smaller number of news items referred to the other dimensions of the EP's legislative power, such as the EP giving its opinion on proposed legislation, the EP adopting resolutions, the EP voting on reports, or the EP approving or rejecting proposed legislation.

As far as the EP's budgetary powers are concerned, 34 news items (or else 5.23% of the total news items) referred to the power of the EP in deciding and negotiating, along with the European Council and the European Commission, on the EU budget.

Finally, only 4 news items (or else 0.61% of the total news items) referred to the EP system development powers, for example, a non-domestic member of the European Parliament raising the issue of EU federalism and a more powerful

6.1 European Parliament's Media Coverage in the Selected News Websites in...

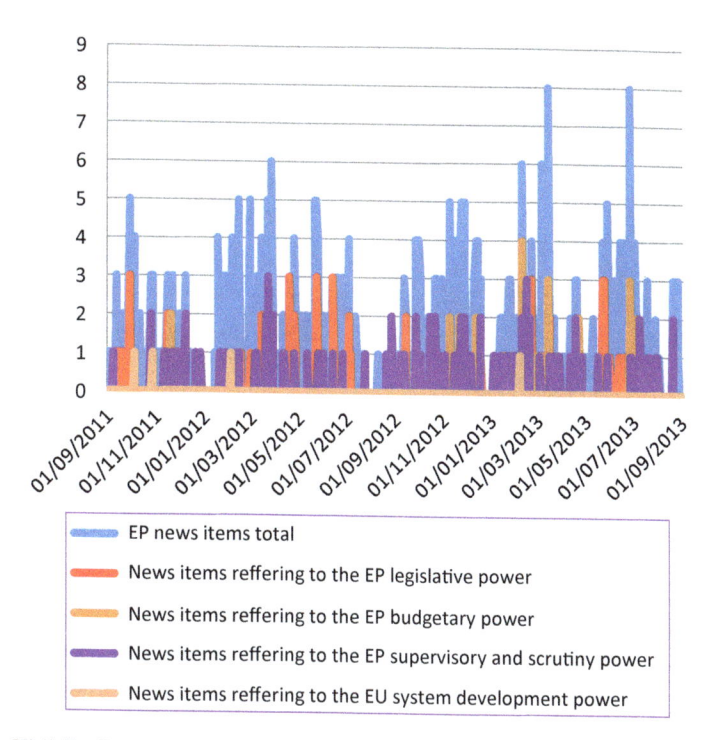

Fig. 6.2 Visibility Patterns of the EP's powers in the Greek news websites

European Parliament, or in another news item, the President of the EP demanding more powers for the EP.

The aforementioned data indicate that, during the 2-year routine period under examination, the EP institutional powers are significantly less visible in the selected news websites in Greece in comparison to the amount of EP new items which is irrelevant to its specific institutional powers. (As seen above 62.3% of the total EP coverage had no reference to the EP's powers, while 37.7% had reference to them.)

As far as the visibility patterns of the European Parliament's institutional powers during this period are concerned, as seen in Fig. 6.2, despite the fact that there is a regular provision of EP news items by the two Greek sites under examination, this regular provision concerns, in the significant majority of cases, the EP news which is not related to the EP's powers. These visibility patterns demonstrate once more the significantly lower levels of visibility of the EP's powers in comparison to the visibility of the EP's "other news" items.

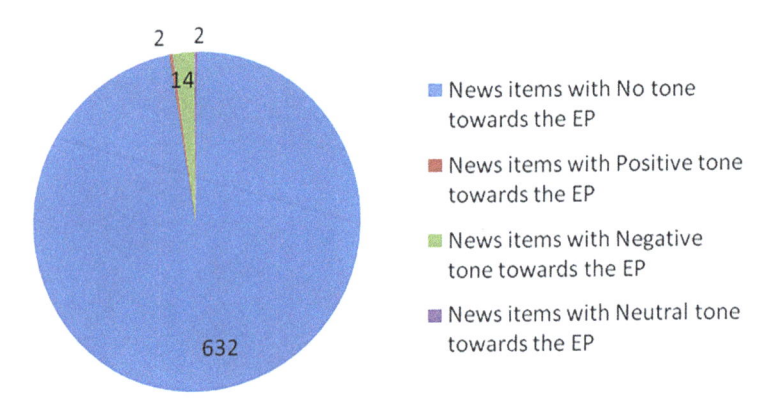

Fig. 6.3 Tone of the coverage of the EP in the selected Greek news websites

6.1.2 The Tone Towards the EP (or any Equivalent)

The vast majority of the EP news items in the Greek news websites during the routine period under examination have no evaluative stance (no tone) towards the EP or any equivalent (e.g. MEPs), as seen in Fig. 6.3. More specifically, 632 news items (or else 97.2% of the total news items) do not have any evaluative stance, 14 news items (or else 2.1% of the news items in total) have a negative tone, and 2 news items (0.6% of the news items in total) have a positive tone, while 2 news items (0.3% of the total news items) have a neutral tone (both positive and negative tone) towards the EP or any equivalent.

Thus, the EP as an institution (or equivalent actors such as MEPs) is obtaining, to a significant extent, online media coverage for itself and its institutional powers in the Greek websites under examination that does not have any evaluative stance. This means that there is great potential for the EP to improve its positive image, through the news websites, in the Greek audience.

6.1.3 The Visibility and the Patterns of Visibility of the European Parliament's Output

From the total of 650 news items that have been collected and analysed, only 56 news items (8.6% of the total number of EP news items) referred to the output of the EP's institutional powers whether this is an amendment of a legislative text, an approval of a directive, the rejection of EU budget, etc. As seen in Fig. 6.4, 34 news items (5.2% of the total number of EP news items) referred to the output of the EP's legislative powers, 13 news items (2% of the total number of EP news items) referred to the output of the EP's budgetary powers, 6 news items (0.9% of the total number of EP news items) referred to the output of the EP supervisory and scrutiny powers,

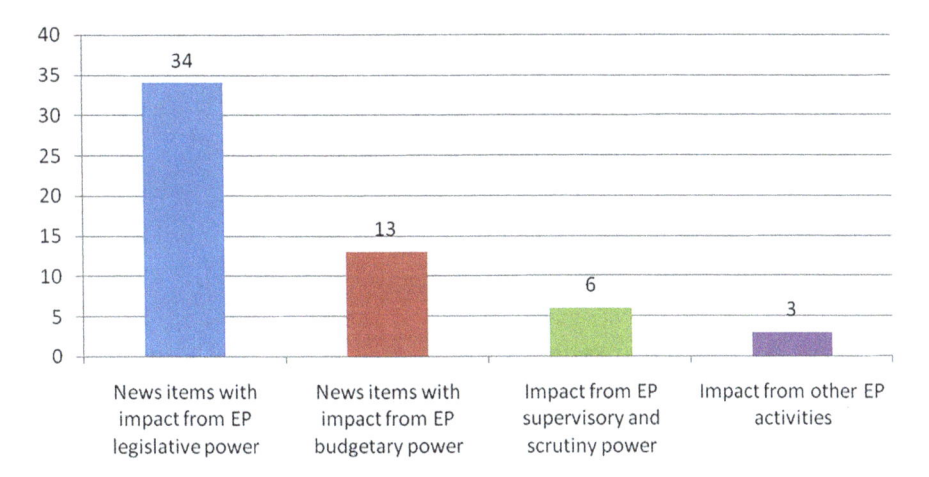

6.1 European Parliament's Media Coverage in the Selected News Websites in... 105

Fig. 6.4 News items referring to the output of the EP's powers in Greek news websites

and 3 news items (or else 0.46% of the total number of EP news items) referred to the output of other EP activities.

In another perspective, one can see that out of 245 news items referring to the EP's institutional powers, 53 of them had a reference to the parliament's output (that is to say that 21.6% of the news items referring to the EP's institutional powers had a reference to their output).

Thus, in quantitative terms the EP is not receiving adequate coverage for its output, since the number of news items referring to the output of its activities is to a significant extent lower than both the total amount of EP news items (8.6% of the total amount of news items refer to EP output) and the amount of EP news referring to the EP's institutional powers (21.6% of the amount of news items referring to the EP's institutional powers had a reference to its output).

As seen in Fig. 6.5, which portrays the visibility patterns of the news items referring to the EP's output, the visibility of the EP's output is to a significant extent limited during the 2-year routine period under examination, compared to the total amount of EP news items.

6.1.4 The Tone of the Coverage of the European Parliament's Powers Output

From the total amount of 56 news items that refer to the EP's powers output, 26 news items have a positive tone, or in other words, they have a positive evaluative stance towards the output of the EP (that is a percentage of 46.4% of the total number of the news items that refer to the output of the EP's powers), while 1 news item has a negative tone (that is to say 1.78% of the total number of the news items that refer to the impact of the EP). The majority of the relevant news items, 29 news items

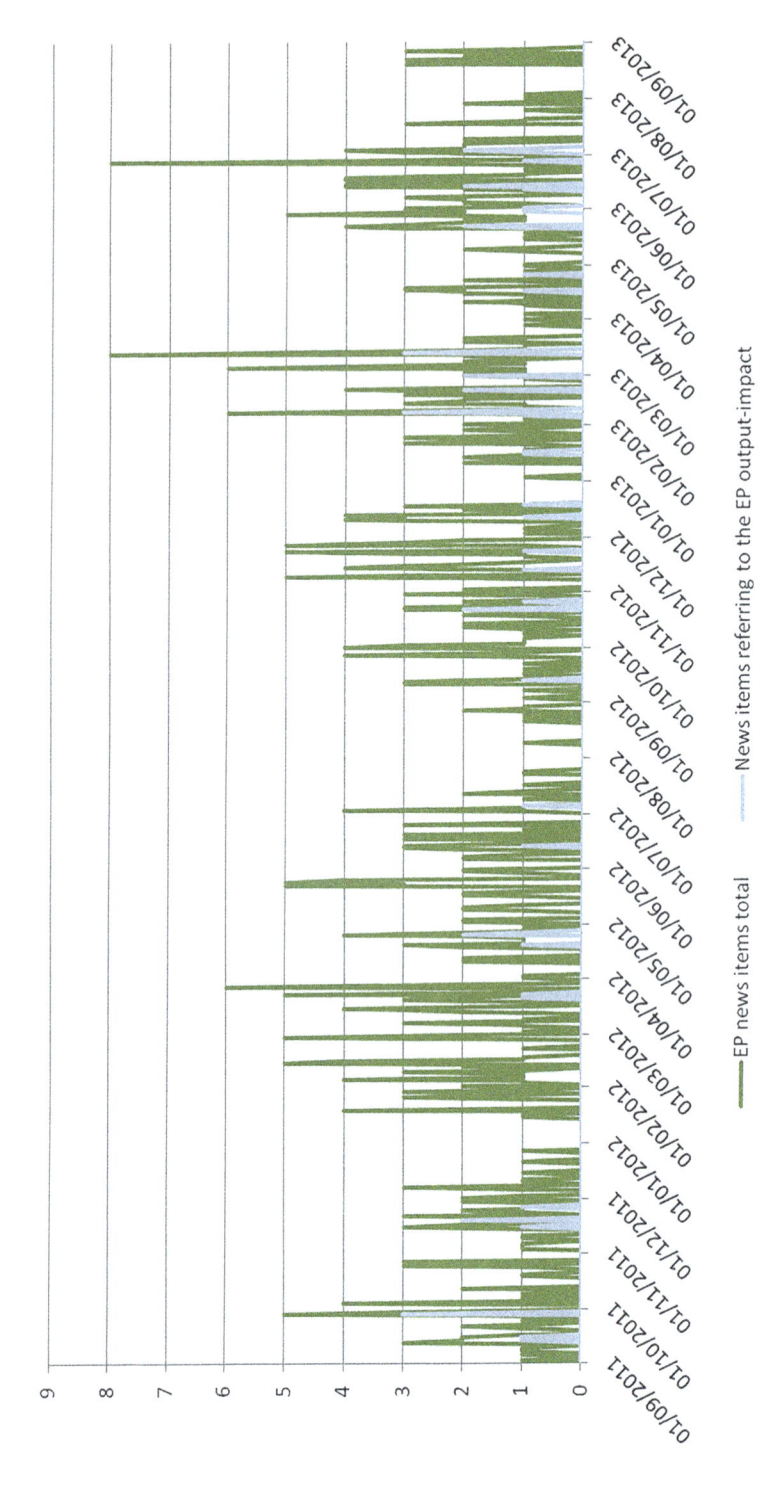

Fig. 6.5 Visibility patterns of news items referring to the output of the EP's powers in Greek website

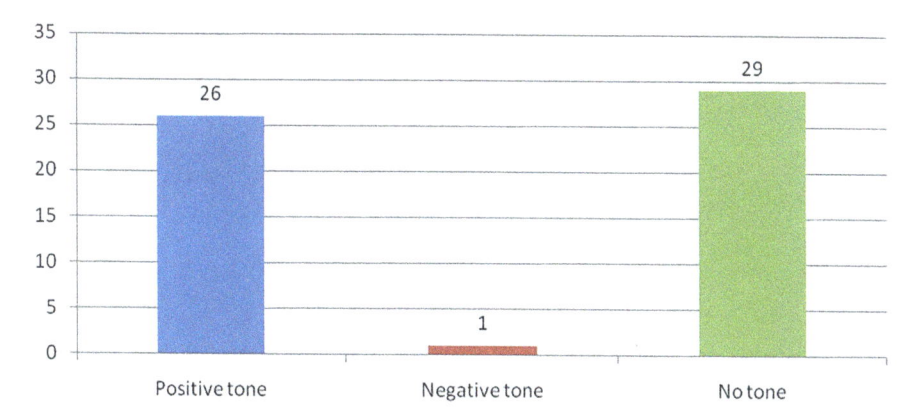

6.1 European Parliament's Media Coverage in the Selected News Websites in... 107

Fig. 6.6 The tone of the coverage of the EP's powers output in the Greek news websites

(51.7% of the total number of relevant news items), did not have any evaluative stance (thus, there was no tone) in the coverage of the European Parliament's powers output. The aforementioned data are also depicted in Fig. 6.6.

Thus, the EP output is visible in the selected Greek news websites either with no evaluative stance or with positive tone; however, it should be kept in mind that the overall number of news items that referred to the parliament's output, which has been used as the yardstick against which the tone of the coverage has been measured, is relatively modest.

6.1.5 The Existence of Additional Internet-Facilitated Information Provided in the Coverage of the EP

From the total number of 650 EP news items in the two Greek news websites under examination, the majority of them (364 news items) did not have any hyperlinks or multimedia features accompanying the EP news story.

Video Elements in the EP News Stories in the Greek News Websites

In 55 relevant news items (out of the 650 news items in total, or 8.4% of the total number of EP news items), there was a video element, accompanying the EP online news story. The kind of information that these video elements provided to the readers of the news websites and the extent to which there was additional information provided for the EP are further elaborated in the following paragraphs.

The majority of the relevant videos (Fig. 6.7) embedded in the online news stories (in 7 news items) showed non-domestic MEPs speaking in the European Parliament about the EU and the Greek crisis and criticizing the European Commission for its handling of the crisis. In 5 news items, the videos portrayed domestic politicians

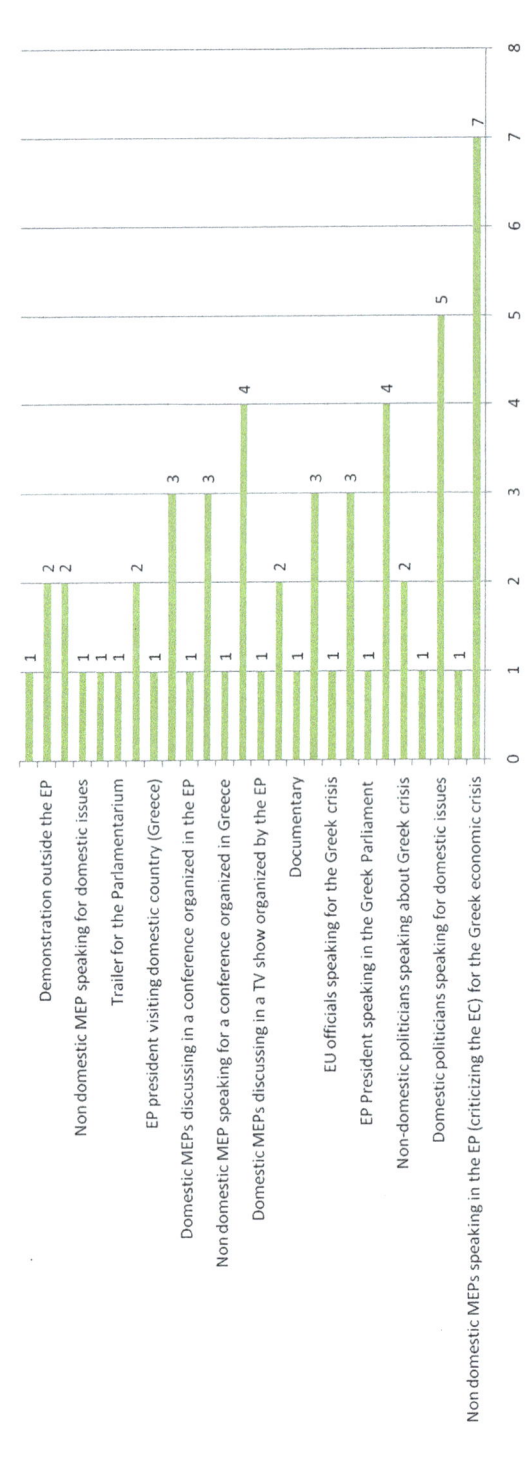

Fig. 6.7 Analysis of the online video features accompanying the news story in the Greek news websites

Category	Count
Demonstration outside the EP	1
Non domestic MEP speaking for domestic issues	2
Trailer for the Parlamentarium	2
EP president visiting domestic country (Greece)	1
Domestic MEPs discussing in a conference organized in the EP	1
Non domestic MEP speaking for a conference organized in Greece	2
Domestic MEPs discussing in a TV show organized by the EP	1
Documentary	3
EU officials speaking for the Greek crisis	3
EP President speaking in the Greek Parliament	3
Non-domestic politicians speaking about Greek crisis	4
Domestic politicians speaking for domestic issues	2
Non domestic MEPs speaking in the EP (criticizing the EC) for the Greek economic crisis	4

speaking about domestic issues, with no direct relevance to the EP dimension of the news story. In 4 news items, the video elements augmented the information in the news item by showing the EP (members of the EP) scrutinizing the externally involved actors ("Troika") for its activities concerning the Greek sovereign debt crisis.

In a few cases, the video elements showed (1) MEPs from a European Political Group (Social Democrats) supporting a domestic political party for the forthcoming Greek elections (in 3 news items), (2) the EP President speaking in a conference organized by the EPLO in Greece (in 3 news items), (3) information relevant to domestic MEPs' personal issues (3 news items), or information about domestic issues in general (3 news items). In addition, the video elements showed non-domestic politicians speaking about the Greek debt crisis (2 news items), the EP president meeting with domestic politicians (2 news items), non-domestic MEP activity (3 news items) and domestic MEP activity (2 news items), and demonstrations outside the EP building (2 news items). Last but not least, there were also video elements in the Greek news websites under examination showing, inter alia, a domestic MEP parliamentary question (1 news item), a non-domestic MEP speaking about domestic issues (1 news item), domestic and non-domestic MEPs speaking in a conference organized by the EP (2 news items), the EP President visiting Greece and speaking in the Greek Parliament (2 news items), or the European Commission answering a domestic MEP's parliamentary question (1 news item).

These few video elements (compared to the total amount of EP news items), which augmented the content of the news items, provided to a significant extent information which was not related to the institutional powers and output of the European Parliament; the sole exception was the case of the EP's supervisory and scrutiny powers, where a fifth (23.6%) of the relevant video elements showed MEPs (mainly non-domestic), in the framework of their supervisory and scrutiny role, criticizing the European Commission, or the "Troika", for their activities in handling the EU/Greek economic crisis (in total 11 news items), or the Commission answering domestic MEPs' parliamentary questions (2 news items).

Hyperlinks in the EP News Stories in the Greek News Websites

A significant amount of EP news items (216) provided hyperlinks (not embedded in the text of the news story) to relevant news stories in the same news website. In 22 news items, there was a hyperlink (embedded in the text of the story) to relevant news stories in the same news website, while in fewer cases (14 news items) there were links (embedded in the text of the story) to other news websites (Fig. 6.8).

In 29 news items, out of the total of 650 news items, there was a hyperlink (not embedded in the text of the news story) provided to the EU/EP website. In 5 news items (out of the total of 650 news items, or 0.7% of the EP news items in total) there were hyperlinks (embedded in the text of the news story) to EP reports or documents. In 4 news items (0.6% of the EP news items in total), there were links (embedded in

110   6 European Parliament's Media Coverage in the News Websites

- News items with Video: 55
- News items with No online feature: 364
- News items with Link (outside news story) to relevant news story in the same...: 216
- News items with Link (outside news story) to relevant news story in other...: 2
- News items with Link (inside news story) to relevant news story in the same...: 22
- News items with Link (inside news story) to relevant news story in other...: 14
- News items with Link (inside news story) to EP report/document: 5
- News items with Link (inside news story) to the EP / EU Audiovisual Service: 4
- News items with Infographics, etc.: 0
- News items with Other online features: 3

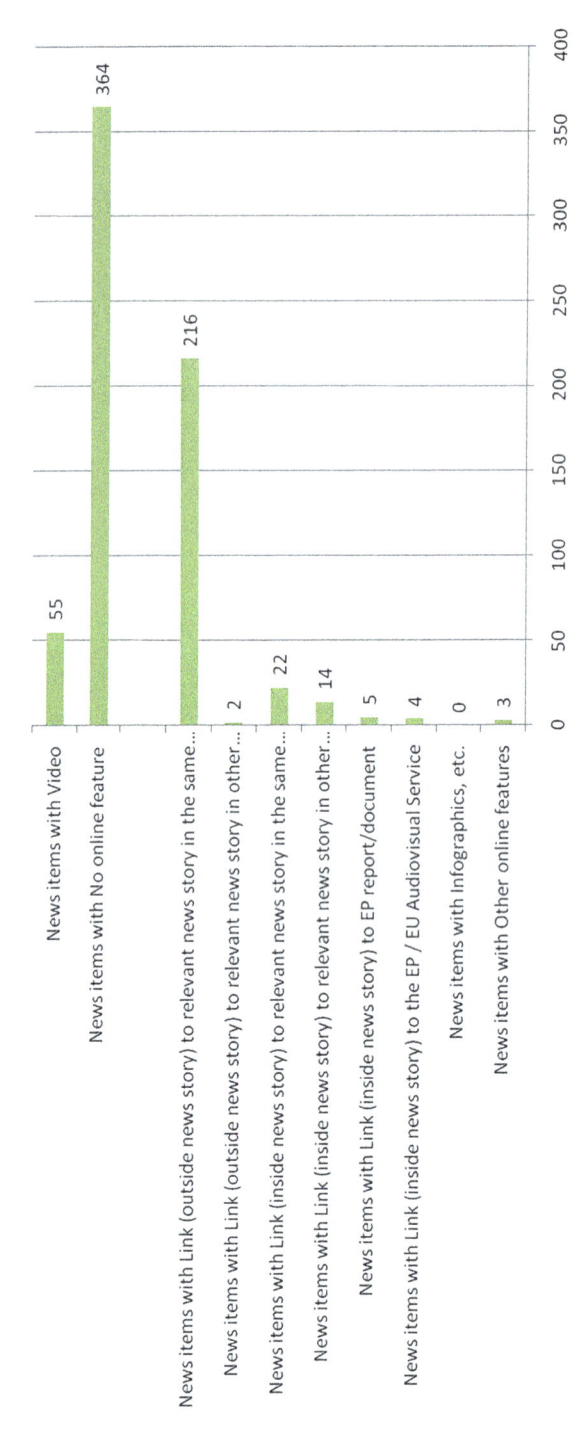

Fig. 6.8 Hypertextuality and multimediality in the EP news items in the Greek news websites

the text of the news story) to the EP/EU Audiovisual Service. Last but not least, there were 3 news items with other online features.

The additional information that is provided by the news websites under examination in the relevant EP news items, relating to the EP's powers and output (or even to the EP in general), through online elements such as hyperlinks to EP material, to the EP's website, or to the EP's Audiovisual Service or multimedia, is very limited, especially if we take into consideration the total amount of the EP-relevant news items (650 news items), or even in comparison to the amount of EP news items referring to the EP's institutional powers (245 news items).

6.1.6 Conclusions from the Examination of the EP Media Coverage in the Selected Greek News Websites

Based on the analysis of the empirical data concerning the examination of the EP media coverage in the selected Greek news websites during the specific routine period, the following conclusions are drawn:

The EP's institutional powers (legislative powers, budgetary powers, supervisory and scrutiny powers, EU system development powers) do not receive significant coverage since the majority of EP news items (62.3% of the total EP news items in the two Greek websites under examination) did not refer to them, but rather referred to other EP news, which had nothing to do with the EP's aforementioned institutional powers. In addition, the EP does not receive any significant coverage for its output, since the number of news items referring to the output of its powers is to a significant extent lower than both the total amount of EP news items (8.6% of the total amount of news items referred to the output of the EP) and the amount of EP news referring to the EP's institutional powers (21.6% of the amount of news items referring to the EP's institutional powers had a reference to their output).

These findings are in accordance with relevant research, which shows that in routine periods the daily European Parliament debates and workings remain largely invisible to the public (Anderson & Weymouth, 1999; Norris, 2000). In addition, the specific findings provide insights into an under-researched topic, which is the news coverage of the EP's output in the Greek context (De Vreese, 2001, 2003; McLeod, 2003; De Vreese et al., 2005, 2006; Michailidou, 2012; Anderson & Weymouth, 1999; Norris, 2000; Gattermann, 2013).

As far as the tone of the coverage is concerned, the EP obtains, in the vast majority of the news items, coverage with no evaluative stance (or in other words no tone), while regarding its output it obtains coverage which has either no evaluative stance, in the significant majority of the cases, or a positive tone (in a few cases). These findings are explained by the fact that the selected news websites have a rather pro-European or impartial attitude in reporting EP new stories; however, seeing it from a PR/communication approach, this also means that there is great potential for the EP to increase its positive coverage in the specific websites.

The additional information that is provided in the relevant EP news items about the EP's institutional powers and impact (or even about the EP in general), through elements such as external hyperlinks to EP material, to the EP website, or to the EP Audiovisual Service or multimedia, is very limited, compared to the total amount of EP-relevant news items (650 news items), or even compared to the amount of EP news items referring to the EP's institutional powers (245 news items). These findings can be interpreted either from the side of the news websites, and thus be in line with the majority of previous relevant research, which shows that news websites do not take advantage of the hyperlinking and multimedia potential offered (Dimitrova et al., 2003; Dimitrova & Neznanski, 2006; Van der Wurff, 2005; Larsson, 2013; Schroeder, 2004; Van der Wurff et al., 2008), or from the EP public relations/communication side, and thus indicating the poor relationship between the news websites, or the journalists themselves, and the EP as a content provider (Weber, 2012).

The limited coverage of the EP institutional powers and output in the selected news websites in Greece has negative implications for its relevant recognition and consequently its social legitimacy. The fact that there are more numerous EP items which however have nothing to do with the EP institutional powers and output in comparison to the EP news items referring to them limits to a significant extent the visibility of the performance and the output of the EP. As seen in Sect. 3.4, the performance and the output of a political institution is a crucial determinant that shapes public perceptions towards the institution and influences its social legitimacy as well. In addition, the fact that the limited visibility of the EP's institutional powers and output is found in news websites that are considered to have a pro-European or impartial stance should be considered a flaw in the EP's communication and media relations performance, since these sites are supposed to offer the EP the best chance of communicating effectively. Thus, from the EP PR/communication point of view this limited coverage might also imply some inadequacies in the EP communication performance. The situation is the same, regarding the limited provision of elements such as external hyperlinks to EP material, to the EP website, or to the EP Audiovisual Service or multimedia, since it indicates, to an extent, the poor relationship between the news websites, or the journalists themselves, and the EP as a content provider.

6.2 European Parliament's Media Coverage in the Selected News Websites in the UK

6.2.1 *The Visibility of the European Parliament's Institutional Powers in the UK*

In the case of the UK, in total 401 news items related to the European Parliament were collected from the selected websites (www.theguardian.co.uk and www.bbc.

6.2 European Parliament's Media Coverage in the Selected News Websites in the... 113

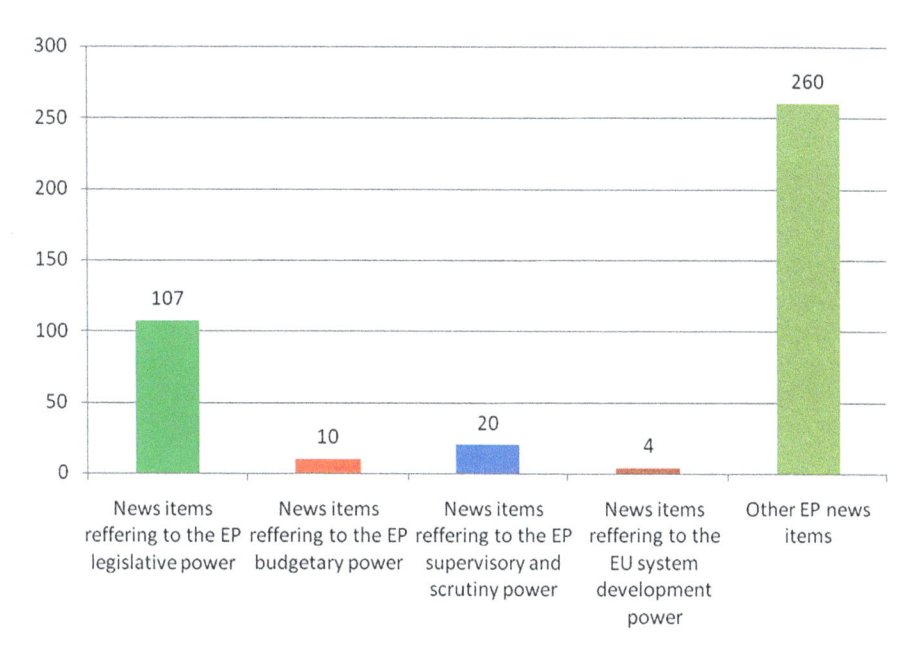

Fig. 6.9 Classification of EP news items in the UK news websites

co.uk) and analysed for the 2-year routine period under examination (01/09/2011–01/09/2013).

As seen in Fig. 6.9, the significant majority of them (260 news items, or 64.8% of the total EP news items in the two UK websites under examination) did not have any reference to the EP's institutional powers. Instead, they referred, for example, to different activities undertaken by domestic or non-domestic MEPs, by the President of the European Parliament, or by European Political Parties (e.g. interviews, statements, visits, and conferences) or to debates held in the EP and to the EP awarding prizes and organizing exhibitions, without however these activities having any reference or relation to the aforementioned EP powers.

A fifth of the total number of EP news items (107 news items or 26.6% of the total) referred to the EP's legislative powers. The majority of these news items referred to the EP's process of adopting legislation through the ordinary legislative procedure, while a smaller number of news items referred to other dimensions of the EP's legislative power such as the EP giving its opinion on proposed legislation, the EP adopting resolutions, the EP voting on reports, or the EP approving or rejecting proposed legislation.

Following that, 20 news items (or 4.9% of the total) referred to the EP's supervisory and scrutiny powers, the majority of which were mainly related to debates held in the European Parliament within its supervisory and control function, and to the EP exercising its appointment and dismissal powers. Very few items were related to parliamentary questions asked by domestic or non-domestic MEPs.

As far as the EP's budgetary powers are concerned, 10 news items (or 2.4% of the total) referred to the power of the EP in deciding and negotiating, along with the European Council and the European Commission, on the EU budget. Finally, only 4 news items (or 1% of the total EP news items) referred to the EP's system development powers (e.g. to the alleged need for further EU integration with more powers for the EP in the EU governance system).

According to above, it can be claimed that the EP's institutional powers visibility in the UK news websites under examination is significantly smaller in comparison to the amount of EP coverage which is irrelevant to its specific powers. From the total amount of 401 EP news items there were 260 "other EP news items" in comparison to 141 news items referring to the EP's powers. In other words, 64.8% of the total EP coverage had no reference to the EP's powers, while 35.2% was relevant to them.

As far as the visibility patterns of the European Parliament's powers during this period are concerned, as seen in Fig. 6.10, despite the fact that there is a regular provision of EP news items in the two UK news websites under examination, this regular provision concerns to a greater extent EP news which is not related to the EP's powers (that is the category "other EP" news items).

6.2.2 The Tone Towards the EP (or any Equivalent)

As seen in Fig. 6.11 in the vast majority of the EP news items in the selected UK news websites during the routine period under examination, there is no evaluative stance (they had no tone) towards the EP or any equivalent. More specifically, 358 news items (or 89.2% of the total news items) had no tone, 28 news items (or 6.9% of the news items in total) had a negative tone, and 5 news items (1.24% of the news items in total) have a positive tone, while 10 news items (2.49% of the total news items) had a neutral tone (both positive and negative) towards the EP or any equivalent.

The specific findings show that the EP is as an institution which is obtaining, to a significant extent, an online media coverage for itself and its powers, in the UK news websites under examination, with no evaluative stance/spin; however, this also means that there is great potential for the EP to improve its positive image, through the news websites, in the UK.

6.2 European Parliament's Media Coverage in the Selected News Websites in the... 115

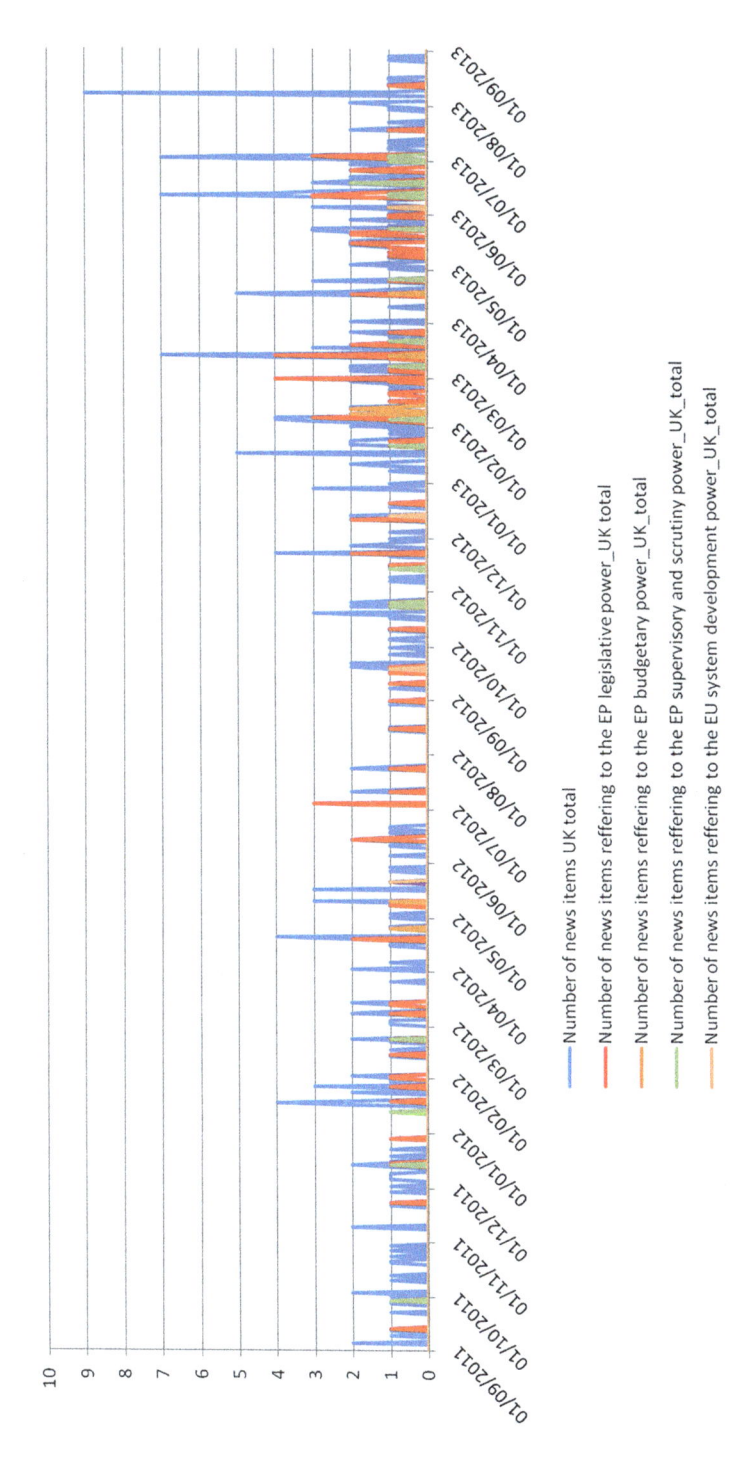

Fig. 6.10 Visibility patterns of the EP powers in the UK news websites

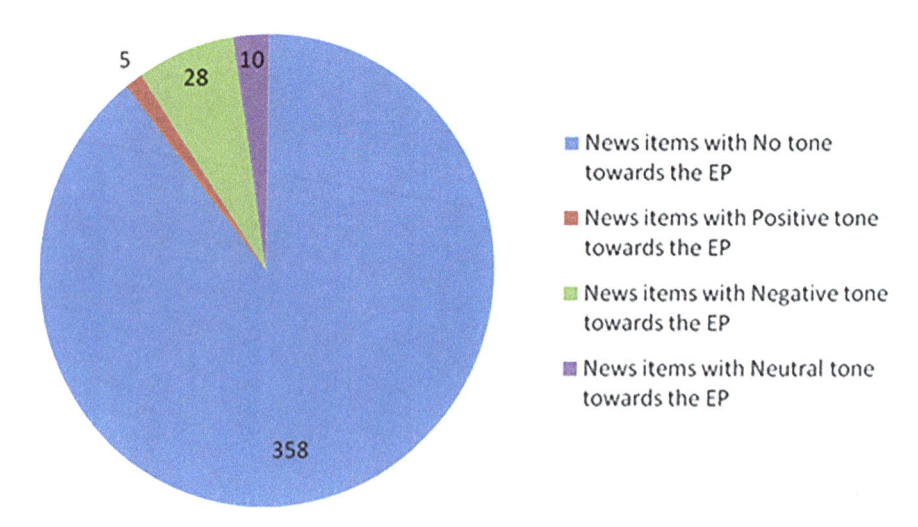

Fig. 6.11 Tone of the coverage of the EP in the selected UK news websites

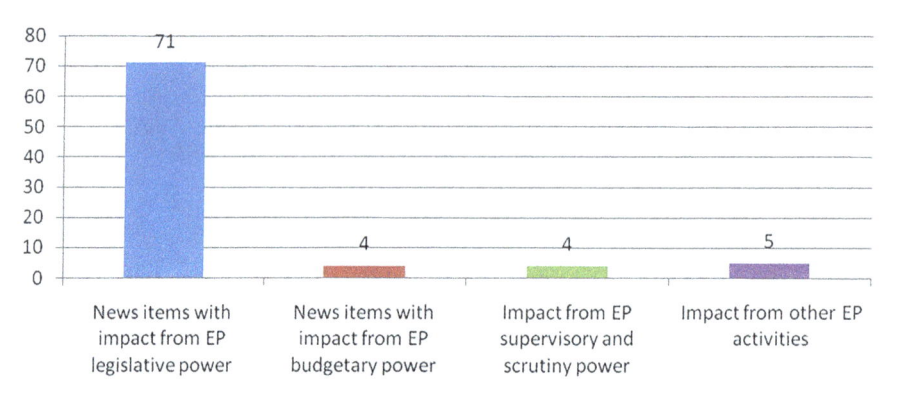

Fig. 6.12 News items referring to the output of the EP's powers in the UK news website

6.2.3 The Visibility and the Patterns of Visibility of the European Parliament's Output

From the total of 401 news items that have been collected and analysed in the UK news websites, 84 news items (or 20.94% of the total number of EP news items) referred to the output of the EP's institutional powers.

As seen in Fig. 6.12, 71 news items (or 17.7% of the total number of EP news items) referred to the output of the EP's legislative powers, 4 news items (or else 0.99% of the total number of the news items) referred to the output of the EP's budgetary powers, and 4 news items (or else 0.99% of the total number of the news items) referred to the output of the EP's supervisory and scrutiny powers, while

5 news items (or else 1.24% of the total number of the news items) referred to the output of other EP activities. In another perspective, one can observe that from the 141 news items referring to the EP's institutional powers in the UK news websites under examination, 84 news items had a reference to the EP's output (that is to say that 59.7% of the amount of news items referring to the EP's institutional powers had a reference to its impact).

According to the aforementioned, the number of news items referring to the output of the EP's powers is to a significant extent lower than the total amount of EP news items (20.94% of the total amount of news items), and lower than the amount of EP news referring to the EP's institutional powers (59.7% of the news items referring to the EP's institutional powers had a reference to its impact).

As seen in Fig. 6.13, which portrays the visibility patterns of news items referring to the EP's output, in comparison to the total amount of EP news items, the visibility of the EP output is rather limited during the 2-year routine period under examination in the selected UK news websites.

6.2.4 *The Tone of the Coverage of the European Parliament's Powers Output*

From the total amount of 84 news items that refer to the EP's powers output, 50 news items have a positive tone, or in other words refer positively to the output of the EP (that is a percentage of 59.2% of the total number of the news items that refer to the output of the EP's powers), while 14 news items have a negative tone (that is to say 16.6% of the total number of news items that refer to the output of the EP). In addition, 20 news items (or 23.8% of the total number of the relevant news items) did not have any evaluative stance in the coverage of the European Parliament's powers output (see Fig. 6.14).

Thus, the EP is gaining a reasonably positive online media coverage in the UK websites under examination, for its output within the context of the overall number of news items on its output. The picture is much less impressive when the number of items containing positive coverage is contrasted with the overall number of news items covering the EP during the case study period.

6.2.5 *The Existence of Additional Internet-Facilitated Information Provided in the Coverage of the EP*

The relevant analysis of the total number of 401 EP news items in the two UK news websites under examination during the specific routine period, as seen in Fig. 6.15, has led to the following results: In 95 EP news items there were no online features at all. The majority of the relevant EP news items (260 news items) had hyperlinks, not

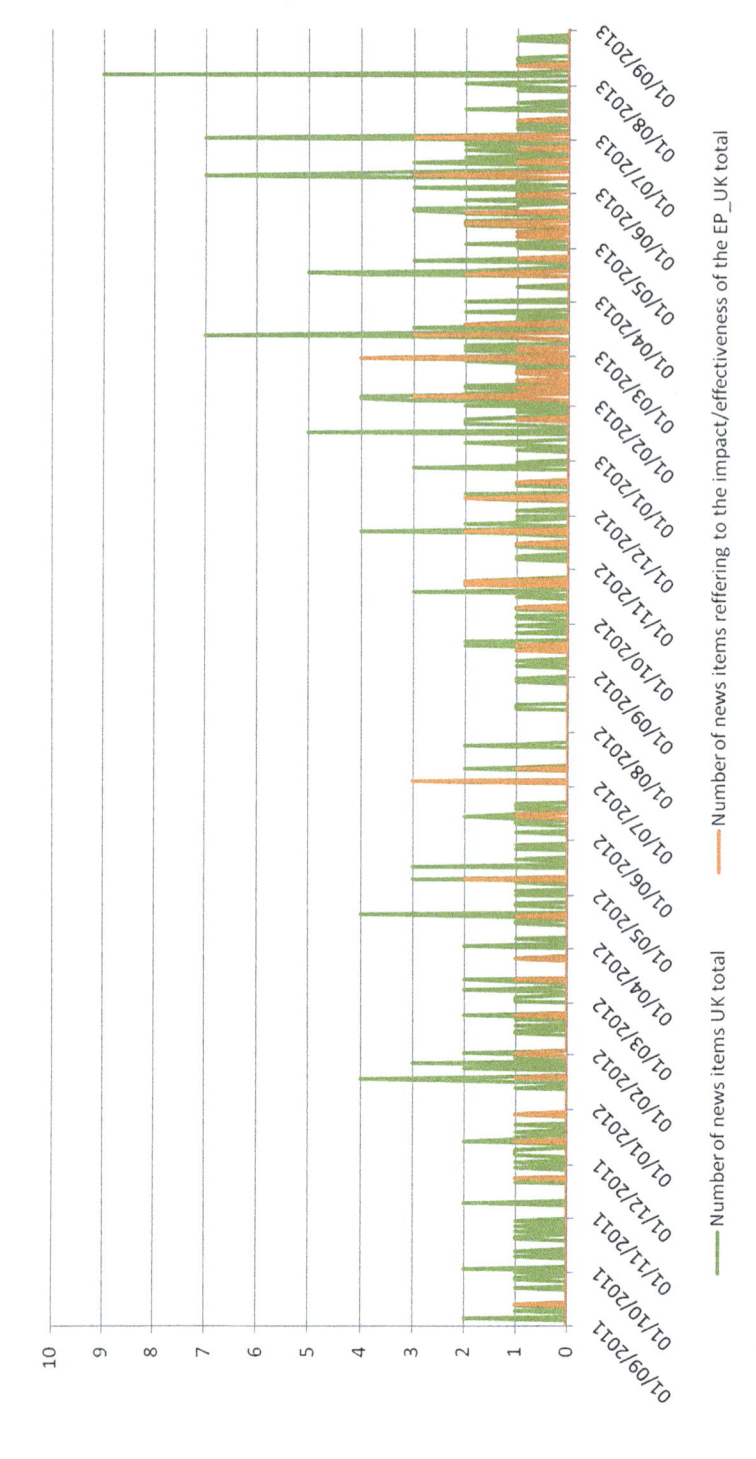

Fig. 6.13 Visibility patterns of the news items referring to the output of the EP's powers in the UK news websites

6.2 European Parliament's Media Coverage in the Selected News Websites in the... 119

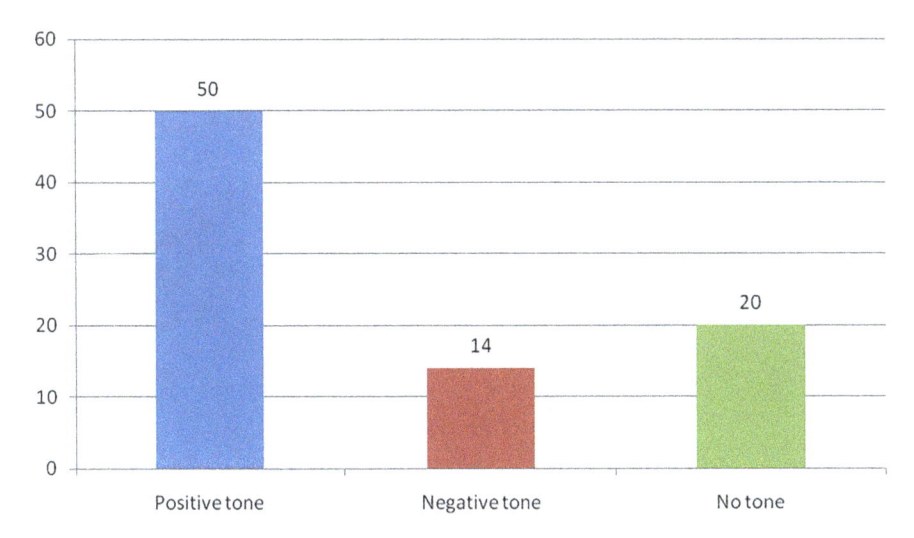

Fig. 6.14 The tone of the coverage of the EP's powers output in the UK news websites

embedded in the main text of the news story, to relevant news stories in the same website, while in fewer cases, news items (73) had hyperlinks, again not embedded in the main text of the news story, to other external websites. However, there were more EP news items (127 news items), with hyperlinks, embedded in the text of the news story, to external websites (material), than EP news items (75 news items) with hyperlinks, embedded in the text of the news story, to relevant news stories in the same website.

Video Elements in the EP News Items in the UK News Websites Under Examination

The results of the analysis of the 96 news items in the UK news websites under examination, which had a video element accompanying the online news story, are summarized in Fig. 6.16.

The majority of the videos were showing European Parliament sessions (and more specifically debates on legislative issues or proposals), while a number of news items (9 news items) were accompanied by videos that were showing personal stories of citizens with a small reference to the EP (or any equivalent). There were also videos showing domestic politicians speaking about EU issues (in 8 news items) and showing EP debates on non-EU countries' progress reports (again in 8 news items, all of them in the BBC news website).

Fewer videos have been showing domestic MEPs criticizing EU activities (in 7 news items), the European Parliament scrutinizing other EU institutions (in 4 news items), presentations of non-legislative reports by EP Committees (in 4 news items), or non-domestic politicians speaking in the European Parliament (in 4 news items).

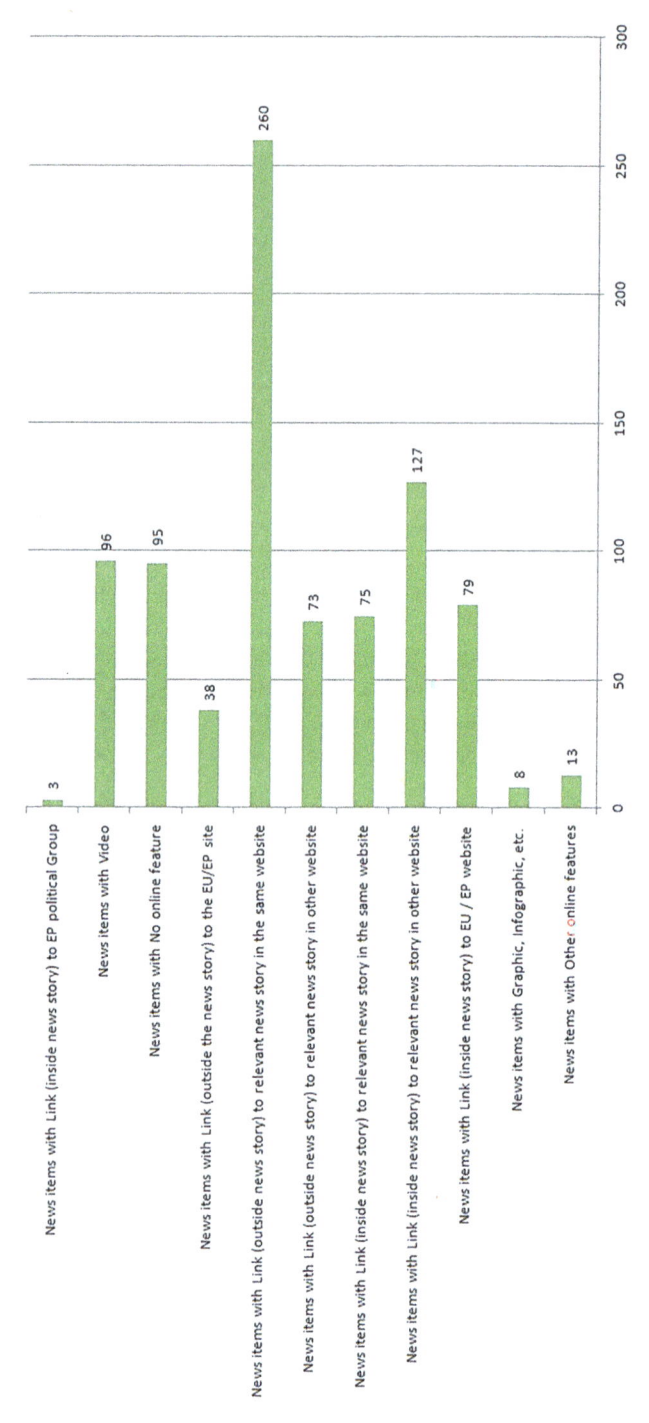

Fig. 6.15 Hypertextuality and multimediality in the EP news items in the UK news websites

- News items with Link (inside news story) to EP political Group: 3
- News items with Video: 96
- News items with No online feature: 95
- News items with Link (outside the news story) to the EU/EP site: 38
- News items with Link (outside news story) to relevant news story in the same website: 260
- News items with Link (outside news story) to relevant news story in other website: 73
- News items with Link (inside news story) to relevant news story in the same website: 75
- News items with Link (inside news story) to relevant news story in other website: 127
- News items with Link (inside news story) to EU / EP website: 79
- News items with Graphic, Infographic, etc.: 8
- News items with Other online features: 13

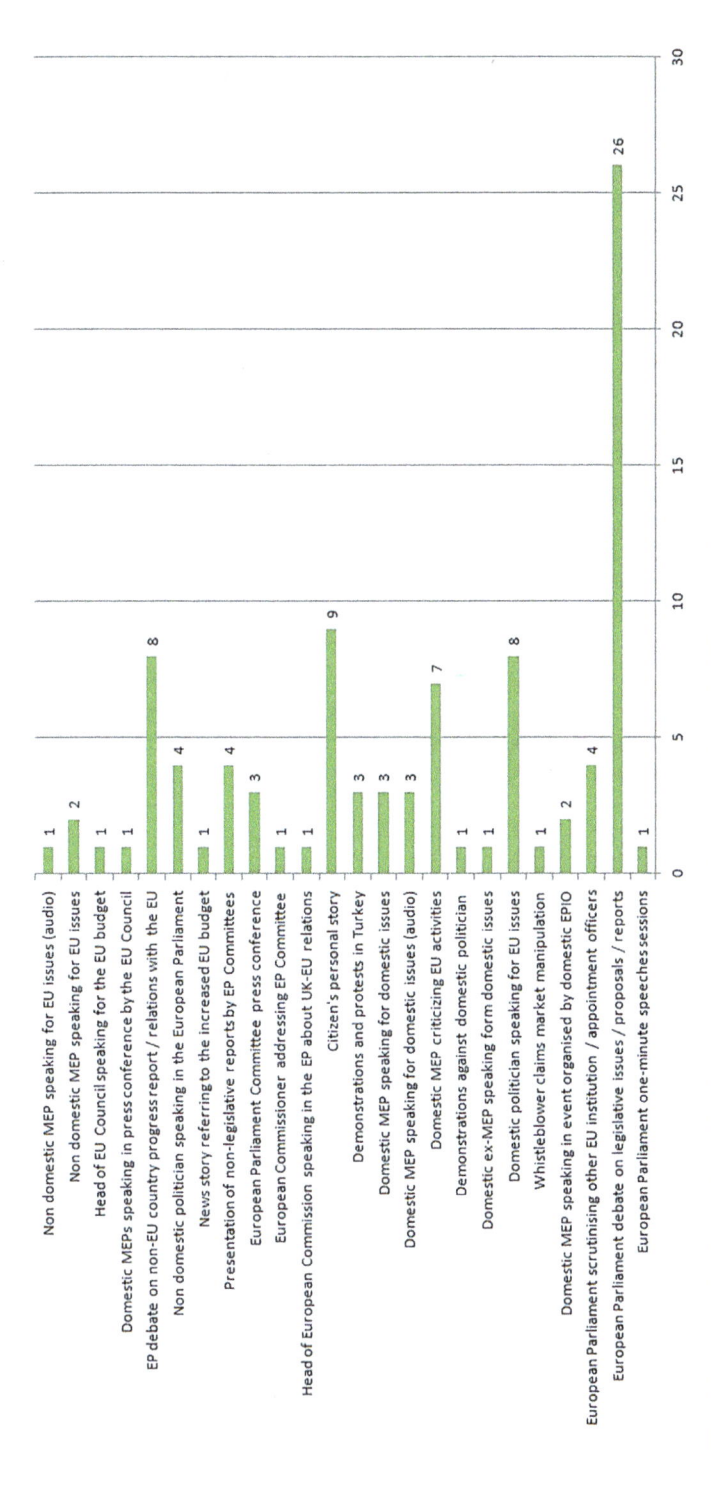

6.2 European Parliament's Media Coverage in the Selected News Websites in the... 121

Fig. 6.16 Analysis of the online video features accompanying the news stories in the UK news websites

Category	Count
Non domestic MEP speaking for EU issues (audio)	1
Non domestic MEP speaking for EU issues	2
Head of EU Council speaking for the EU budget	1
Domestic MEPs speaking in press conference by the EU Council	1
EP debate on non-EU country progress report / relations with the EU	8
Non domestic politician speaking in the European Parliament	4
News story referring to the increased EU budget	1
Presentation of non-legislative reports by EP Committees	4
European Parliament Committee press conference	3
European Commissioner addressing EP Committee	1
Head of European Commission speaking in the EP about UK-EU relations	1
Citizen's personal story	9
Demonstrations and protests in Turkey	3
Domestic MEP speaking for domestic issues	3
Domestic MEP speaking for domestic issues (audio)	3
Domestic MEP criticizing EU activities	7
Demonstrations against domestic politician	1
Domestic ex-MEP speaking form domestic issues	1
Domestic politician speaking for EU issues	8
Whistleblower claims market manipulation	1
Domestic MEP speaking in event organised by domestic EPIO	2
European Parliament scrutinising other EU institution / appointment officers	4
European Parliament debate on legislative issues / proposals / reports	26
European Parliament one-minute speeches sessions	1

Fewer videos showed domestic MEPs speaking for domestic issues (3 new items), European Parliament Committees' press conferences (3 news items), domestic MEPs speaking in events organized by the UK EPLO (2 news items), non-domestic MEPs speaking for EU issues (2 news items), European Parliament one-minute speech sessions (1 news item), EU officials speaking in the EP (1 news item), and domestic MEPs speaking in a press conference organized by the EU Council (1 news item).

The video elements in the news items of the UK websites under examination (96 video-enhanced news items out of 401), which augmented the content of the news items, provided to an extent further information which was related to the powers of the EP and in most of the cases related to the EP's legislative and scrutiny/supervisory powers. More specifically, in 44 news items out of the 96 items accompanied by a video element (thus in 45.8% of the EP news items accompanied by video element), there were video elements showing European Parliament sessions (debates on legislative issues or proposals), domestic MEPs criticizing EU activities, the European Parliament scrutinizing other EU institutions, presentations of reports by EP Committees, or European Parliament Committees' press conferences. However, no video element was found accompanying an EP news item related to the output of the European Parliament.

Based on these findings, the extent to which the video elements accompanying the online EP news stories provided additional information about the EP's institutional powers is very limited, particularly when it is remembered that most of the 401 EP news items overall do not contain any video. In the case of the EP's output, there is no video-enhanced coverage at all.

Hyperlinks and Other Online Features Accompanying EP News Items in the UK News Websites

In 72 news items there were hyperlinks, embedded in the text of the news story, to the EP/EU website. More specifically, in 14 news items there was a hyperlink to the European Parliament website and more specifically to proposed or voted on legislative texts, in 7 news items there was a hyperlink to European Parliament press releases, in 5 news items there was a hyperlink to the European Parliament homepage website, in 3 news items there was a hyperlink to the European Parliament Committee homepage website, in 5 news items there was a hyperlink to European Parliament text of reports, in 1 news item there was a hyperlink to 1 MEP profile in the EP website, and in 1 news item, there was a hyperlink to the European Parliament website, to the calendar of the EP plenary sessions.

Out of the total amount of 401 EP news items in the UK news websites under examination and during the specific 2-year routine period, there are 36 news items with relevant hyperlinks, embedded in the online news text, leading to the EP website (different sections of it) and providing in that way additional information to the reader. In other words, within the total amount of EP online news items, a percentage of 8.9% provides this kind of information with relevant hyperlinks embedded in the online news text.

Apart from that, in 38 news items, there were links (not embedded in the text of the news story) to the EU/EP website. More specifically, in 22 news items there was a hyperlink to the EP website homepage, in 3 news items there was a hyperlink to domestic MEPs' websites, in 2 news items there was a hyperlink to the website of European political groups, in 1 news item there was a hyperlink to the text of an EP recommendation, in 1 news item there was a hyperlink to the website of a European Parliament Intergroup, in 1 news item there was a hyperlink to the European Parliament Committee website, and in 2 news items there were hyperlinks to the website of the European Parliament Sakharov Prize.

In the same sample and during the specific 2-year routine period, there are 30 news items with relevant hyperlinks, not embedded in the online news text, leading to the EP website (or to different sections of it) and providing in that way additional information for the reader. In other words, from the total amount of EP online news items in the case studies, only a percentage of 7.4% provides this kind of information with relevant hyperlinks not embedded in the online news text.

In addition, in 8 EP news items there were graphic features. More specifically, in 3 news items there was a statistic graphic sourced by the European Parliament concerning statistical figures for the EP elections turnout, in 2 news items there were graphics, sourced by the European Commission, concerning data on the EU fisheries policy, in 1 news item there was a graphic portraying the levels of gas price (this graphic was produced by the Guardian website itself), in 1 news item there was a graphic for the contribution of each member state to the EU budget sourced by the European Commission, and in 1 news item there was a statistical graphic concerning the allocations of the EU budget sourced by the European Council.

Thus, out of 401 EP news items in the UK news websites under examination and during the specific 2-year routine period, there are only 3 news items with a graphic sourced by the European Parliament which provided in that way additional information for the reader. In other words, as regards the total amount of EP online news items, only a percentage of 0.74% provides this kind of information.

According to the above analysis, the additional information provided by the UK news websites under examination in the relevant EP news items, about the EP's powers and impact (or even for the EP in general), through online elements such as hyperlinks to EP material or to the EP website or multimedia such as graphics, is rather limited in comparison to the total amount of EP-relevant news items (401 news items), or even in comparison to the amount of news items referring to the EP's institutional powers (141 news items). In addition, the extent to which the video elements, accompanying the online EP news stories, provide additional information about the EP's institutional powers is also limited (there is video only in 96 news items out of a total of 401 news items), while in the case of the EP's output there is no video at all.

6.2.6 Conclusions from the Examination of the EP Media Coverage in the Selected UK News Websites

Based on the analysis of the data concerning the examination of the EP media coverage in the selected UK news websites during the specific routine period, the following conclusions are drawn:

The EP's institutional powers do not gain significant coverage in the UK news websites under examination in comparison to the amount of EP coverage which is irrelevant to its specific powers. As it was seen, out of the total amount of 401 EP news items there were 260 "other EP news items" in comparison to 141 news items referring to the EP's powers (in other words, 64.8% of the total EP coverage had no reference to the EP's powers, while 35.2% was relevant to them). In addition, the EP is not receiving significant coverage for its output in the UK news websites under examination, since the number of news items referring to the output of the EP's institutional powers is to a significant extent lower than the total amount of EP news items (20.94% of the total amount of news items), and lower than the amount of news referring to the EP's institutional powers (59.7% of the amount of news items referring to the EP's institutional powers had a reference to their impact).

These findings are in accordance with relevant research which shows that in routine periods the daily European Parliament debates and workings remain largely invisible to the public (Anderson & Weymouth, 1999; Norris, 2000). Regarding the news coverage of the EP's output, this has not been researched previously in the UK context (De Vreese, 2001, 2003; McLeod, 2003; De Vreese et al., 2005, 2006; Michailidou, 2012; Anderson & Weymouth, 1999; Norris, 2000; Gattermann, 2013), and the fact that the specific findings here cannot fit in an existing research corpus emphasizes their original contribution to the literature.

The EP is obtaining, to a significant extent, online media coverage for itself and its powers in the UK news websites under examination that has no evaluative stance/spin (there are very few cases of news items with an evaluative stance towards the EP where the tone is predominantly negative). In addition, the EP's institutional powers output is gaining rather positive coverage since 59.2% of the total number of news items that refer to the output have a positive tone. However, the degree of success is rather less impressive when the number of items in which positive coverage is secured is compared with the overall number of EP news items in the case studies. The above findings are explained, as in the case of Greece, by the fact that the selected news websites have a rather pro-European or impartial attitude in reporting EP new stories; yet, seeing it from a PR/communication approach, and considering the negative tone of the coverage in very few items, this also means that there is great potential (meaning that it would be rather easier) for the EP to increase its positive coverage in the specific websites.

The additional information that is provided by the UK news websites under examination in the relevant EP news items, about the EP's powers and output (or even about the EP in general), through online elements such as hyperlinks to EP material or to the EP website or multimedia such as graphics, is very limited in comparison to the total amount of EP-relevant news items, or even in comparison to the amount of EP news items referring to the EP's institutional powers. In addition, the extent to which the video elements, accompanying online EP news stories, provide additional information about the EP's institutional powers is limited, while in the case of the EP's output there is no video. These findings can be interpreted, similar to the case of Greece, either from the side of the news websites, and thus be in line with the majority of previous relevant research which shows that news websites do not take advantage of the hyperlinking and multimedia potential offered (Dimitrova et al., 2003; Dimitrova & Neznanski, 2006; Van der Wurff, 2005; Larsson, 2013; Schroeder, 2004; Van der Wurff et al., 2008), or from the EP public relations/communication side, and thus indicating the poor relationship between the news websites, or the journalists themselves, and the EP as a content provider (Weber, 2012).

In general, the limited coverage of the EP institutional powers and output in the selected news websites in the UK has negative implications for its relevant recognition and consequently its social legitimacy. (This is the case in Greece as well.) The fact that there are more numerous EP items which however have nothing to do with the EP institutional powers and output in comparison to the EP news items referring to them limits to a significant extent the visibility of the performance and the output of the EP.

As seen in Chap. 3, the performance and the output of a political institution is a crucial determinant that shapes public perceptions towards the institution and influences its social legitimacy as well. In addition, the fact that the limited visibility of the EP's institutional powers and output is found in news websites that are considered in the UK to have a pro-European or impartial stance should be considered a flaw in the EP's communication and media relations performance, since these sites are supposed to offer the EP the best chance of communicating effectively. Thus, from the EP PR/communication point of view this limited coverage might also indicate some inadequacies in the EP communication performance. Similar is the case regarding the limited provision of elements such as external hyperlinks to EP material, to the EP website, or to the EP Audiovisual Service or multimedia, since it indicates, to an extent, the poor relationship between the news websites, or the journalists themselves, and the EP as a content provider.

6.3 Conclusions for the Greek and the UK Case

This chapter presented the research findings of the examination of the media coverage of the EP's institutional powers and its output in the selected news websites in Greece and in the UK, for the 2-year routine period under examination (September 2011–September 2013).

Concerning the visibility of the European Parliament's institutional powers and impact in both countries, this was examined, through content analysis, by measuring the proportion of the EP news stories (which had a reference either to the parliament's institutional powers or to its output) in comparison to the total amount of EP news reporting in the specific media outlets during specific routine periods. Visibility was also assessed by examining the frequency and patterns of the relevant EP news media coverage over the routine periods under examination.

The conclusion drawn from the examination of the coverage in both the UK and Greece is that the European Parliament's institutional powers and output are not visible in the selected Greek and UK news websites in the 2-year routine period (2011–2013). However, when the EP gains this kind of visibility it is rather successful in both countries, in securing online media coverage with no tone, while in the cases where there is an evaluative stance the tone is mainly negative towards MEPs, but positive towards the output of the EP. In addition, the very limited information that is provided in the EP news stories through online elements such as external hyperlinks to EP material or multimedia is an indicator, inter alia, of the rather poor relationship between the news websites, or the journalists themselves, and the EP as a content provider.

These research findings fit well with the majority of the relevant literature, which shows that there is low visibility of EU news in routine periods with the daily EP debates, Commission business, or presidential initiatives remaining largely invisible to the public, both in the UK and Greek context (Anderson & Weymouth, 1999; Norris, 2000; Peter et al., 2003; Gleissner & De Vreese, 2005; Kandyla & De Vreese, 2011; Peter & de Vreese, 2004; Kontochristou & Mascha, 2014). Apparently, the aforementioned research findings are not in line with the findings of previous studies on the media coverage of the EU's output or policies, which in both countries tends to be significantly negative (Anderson & Weymouth, 1999; Semetko et al., 2000; de Vreese et al., 2001; Gleissner & de Vreese, 2005; Kandyla & de Vreese, 2011; Souliotis, 2013). However, the nuanced research within some studies shows that the Guardian is predominantly in favour of the EU, with a small number of significant disagreements over (for example) social and business policies (Anderson & Weymouth, 1999); thus, given that the Guardian website is one of the key case studies, here the results should not be a surprise. Equally, the BBC is charged with being impartial across the range of its coverage as part of the regulatory conditions that it is required to meet, so, once again, it should come as no surprise that its coverage includes positive as well as negatively toned coverage.

What is of interest here is the extent to which the EP is able to gain positive coverage in such websites where it has in theory a much better chance of so doing than in the determinedly Eurosceptic sites like those of the Telegraph, Mail, or Express in the UK. Again, the EP apparently seems to be doing well in both Greece and the UK with regard to the selected websites when the coverage with no evaluative stance and that with a positive tone is added together in percentage terms. The problems seem rather to lie with the visibility of coverage of the EP's powers and output overall, because the significant failings in that respect greatly dilute the impact of the positive coverage.

The aforementioned research findings also fit well with the relevant literature which shows that websites do not employ in full either the potential of hyperlinking, especially to external links material (Neuberger et al., 1998; Massey & Levy, 1999;

Dibean & Garrison, 2001; Dimitrova et al., 2003; Dimitrova & Neznanski, 2006; Van der Wurff, 2005; Larsson, 2013), or their multimedia potential (Van der Wurff et al., 2008; Schroeder, 2004). However, the fact that there is limited presence of the EP's hyperlinks and multimedia in the relevant news items also serves as an indicator of the poor relationship between the news websites, or the journalists themselves, and the EP as a content provider (Weber, 2012). Given that there are only a few studies concerning the coverage of the EU or the EP in news websites and the relevant visibility of hyperlinks or multimedia within them (Kevin, 2001; Michailidou, 2012), the above research findings make a contribution to the relevant literature corpus.

At this point it has to be mentioned that the more numerous and more general (in the sense that that they do not have any reference to any of the EP institutional powers and output) references to the EP in the selected news websites in both the UK and Greece are considered irrelevant for the scope of the analysis. As it has been mentioned in Chap. 3, the public perceptions towards the EU and the EU institutions, which form their relevant social legitimacy, are shaped, inter alia, by the media coverage of the performance of these institutions and their output. Thus, the focus is just on these specific news items. In addition, the fact that there are much more numerous and general references to the EP (or any equivalent) in comparison to the limited number of the EP news items with reference to its institutional powers indicates the gap that the EP needs to cover regarding its communication and media relations performance in the member states under examination.

References

Anderson, P. J., & Weymouth, T. (1999). *Insulting the public? The British press and the European Union*. Longman.
De Vreese, C. H. (2001). Election coverage – New directions for public broadcasting: The Netherlands and beyond. *European Journal of Communication, 16*(2), 155–179.
De Vreese, C. H. (2003). Television reporting of second-order elections. *Journalism Studies, 4*(2), 183–198.
De Vreese, C. H., Banducci, S., Semetko, H., & Boomgaarden, H. (2005). Off-line: The 2004 European Parliamentary elections on television news in the enlarged Europe. *Information Polity, 10*(3), 177–188.
De Vreese, C. H., Banducci, S., Semetko, H. A., & Boomgaarden, H. A. (2006). The news coverage of the 2004 European parliamentary election campaign in 25 countries. *European Union Politics, 7*(4), 477–504.
De Vreese, C. H., Peter, J., & Semetko, H. A. (2001). Framing politics at the launch of the euro: A cross-national comparative study of frames in the news. *Political Communication, 18*(2), 107–122.
Dibean, W., & Garrison, B. (2001). How six online newspapers use web technologies. *Newspaper Research Journal, 22*(2), 79–94.
Dimitrova, D. V., Connolly-Ahern, C., Williams, A. P., Kaid, L. L., & Reid, A. (2003). Hyperlinking as gatekeeping: Online newspaper coverage of the execution of an American terrorist. *Journalism Studies, 4*(3), 401–414.

Dimitrova, D., & Neznanski, M. (2006). Online journalism and the war in cyberspace: A comparison between U.S. and international newspapers. *Journal of Computer-Mediated Communication, 12*(1), 248–263.

Gattermann, K. (2013). News about the European Parliament: Patterns and external drivers of broadsheet coverage. *European Union Politics, 14*(3), 436–457.

Gleissner, M., & De Vreese, C. H. (2005). News about the EU constitution-journalistic challenges and media portrayal of the European Union constitution. *Journalism, 6*(2), 221–242.

Kandyla, A., & De Vreese, C. (2011). News media representations of a common EU foreign and security policy. A cross-national content analysis of CFSP coverage in national news media. *Comparative European Politics, 9*(1), 52–75.

Kevin, D. (2001). Coverage of the European Parliament elections of 1999: National public spheres and European debates. *Javnost/The Public, 8*(1), 21–38.

Kontochristou, M., & Mascha, E. (2014). The Euro crisis and the question of solidarity in the European Union: Disclosures and manifestations in the European press. *Review of European Studies, 6*(2), 50–62.

Larsson, A. O. (2013). Staying in or going out? *Journalism Practice, 7*(6), 738–754.

Massey, B. L., & Levy, R. M. (1999). Interactivity, online journalism and English- language web newspapers in Asia. *Journalism & Mass Communication Quarterly, 76*(1), 138–151.

McLeod, A. (2003). An analysis of the impact of the United Kingdom print and broadcast media upon the legitimacy of the European Parliament in Britain. PhD study. University of Central Lancashire.

Michailidou, A. (2012). "Second order" elections and online journalism. *Journalism Practice, 6*(3), 366–383.

Neuberger, C., Tonnemacher, J., Biebl, M., & Duck, A. (1998). Online: The future of newspapers? Germany's dailies on the World Wide Web. *Journal of Computer-Mediated Communication, 4*(1). https://doi.org/10.1111/j.1083-6101.1998.tb00087.x

Norris, P. (2000). *A virtuous circle. Political communications in postindustrial societies*. Cambridge University Press.

Peter, J., & de Vreese, C. H. (2004). In search of Europe – A cross-national comparative study of the European Union in national television news. *Harvard Journal of Press/Politics, 9*(4), 3–24.

Peter, J., Semetko, H. A., & de Vreese, C. H. (2003). EU politics on television news. A cross-national comparative study. *EU Politics, 4*(3), 305–327.

Schroeder, R. (2004). Online review. Interactive info graphics in Europe –added value to online mass media: A preliminary survey. *Journalism Studies, 5*(4), 563–570.

Semetko, H. A., de Vreese, C. H., & Peter, J. (2000). Europeanised politics – Europeanised media? European integration and political communication. *West European Politics, 23*(4), 121–141.

Souliotis, D. (2013). The coverage of the economic crisis by the British and Greek press. Indications of a European public sphere? In G. Pleios (Ed.), *The media and the crisis* (pp. 227–269). Papazisis publications. [In Greek].

Van der Wurff, R. (2005). Impacts of the internet on newspapers in Europe: Conclusions. *International Communication Gazette, 67*(1), 107–120.

Van der Wurff, R., Lauf, E., Balcytiene, A., Fortunati, L., Holmberg, S., Paulussen, S., & Salaverria, R. (2008). Online and print newspapers in Europe in 2003 – evolving towards complementarity. *Communications, 33*(4), 403–430.

Weber, M. S. (2012). Newspapers and the long-term implications of hyperlinking. *Journal of Computer-Mediated Communication, 17*(2), 187–201. https://doi.org/10.1111/j.1083-6101.2011.01563.x

Chapter 7
Assessment of the Media Relations Performance of the EPLOs

This chapter presents the research findings from the semi-structured interviews conducted with online news journalists in the UK and Greece, regarding the assessment of the communication and media relations performance of the European Parliament Liaison Offices (EPLOs) in Greece and in the UK. The assessment focuses on the extent to which the EPLO's communication material either in written or in oral form meets online journalist's needs and expectations, the extent to which the EPLO's media relations activities facilitate online journalists' work when producing EP news stories, the extent to which the EPLO implements an adequate "source strategy" towards journalists, and the extent to which the EPLO media relations activities overall take into consideration the changes in the journalistic practices of the online journalists.

In the previous chapter (Chap. 6), the characteristics of the coverage of the EP institutional powers and output in the selected news websites in the UK and Greece for a specific 2-year routine period (2011–2013) were examined. The research findings that seem to be the most problematic regarding the communication performance of the EP are the ones which indicate that the European Parliament's institutional powers and output in both countries are not visible in the selected news websites, while the very limited information that is provided in the EP news stories through online elements, such as external hyperlinks to EP material or multimedia, could be considered as an indicator, inter alia, of the rather poor relationship between the news websites, or the journalists themselves, and the EP as a content provider.

Based on the aforementioned findings and in line with the rationale developed in Chap. 4 that the media coverage of the EU institutions is affected, inter alia, by the communication and media relations performance of the institutions themselves, this chapter presents the research findings concerning the assessment of the communication and media relations performance of the European Parliament Liaison Offices (EPLOs) in Greece and in the UK. The findings are based on in-depth semi-structured interviews conducted with 10 online journalists in Greece and 6 online journalists in the UK (working in the sites under examination and in other popular sites in both countries). The journalists who are not working in the websites under examination come from other popular, rather pro-European or of impartial stance, news websites, which means that they do not face any constraints or strong anti-European attitudes in their newsrooms when covering EU or EP news stories. The inclusion of them in the research sample gives a further added value in this book, since these journalists originate from sites where improvements in the EP's communications performance should in theory be most achievable. If there are significant areas where the EP communication and media relations performance is weak in relation to these journalists and sites, then it is of real value to identify these areas, the underlying reasons, and possible solutions. At the same time, the specific online journalists work in the most popular news websites both in Greece and in the UK; thus, they are most likely to express journalism's dominant professional ideas, cultures, and practices within their national media system (Benson et al., 2012).

The questions asked in the semi-structured interviews and consequently the assessment of the EPLO's performance were based on the literature on EU communication/media relations and the literature on online journalism as these were developed in Chap. 4 (see also Methodology in Chap. 5).

7.1 Assessment of the Media Relations Performance of the EPLO in Greece

7.1.1 The Extent to which the EPLO's Communication Material Either in Written or in Oral Form Fits Online Journalist's Needs and Expectations

The findings of the interviews as regards the assessment of the EP and the EPLO website content by 10 online journalists in Greece are summarized in Table 7.1.

Table 7.1 Assessment, by the Greek online journalists, of the EP and the EPLO website content and material

- The majority of the online journalists (6 journalists) characterized both the EP and the EPLO websites as a complete source of information for their job, thus a journalistic tool, with much content there; however, for some of them (4 journalists) it is difficult sometimes to navigate through them and find, for example, information on how the discussions have gone in the committees or in the plenary sessions.
- A number of online journalists (3 journalists) found that the EP and the EPLO websites have a bureaucratic language, with the information given in a non-journalistic way.
- 4 journalists said that they cannot consider the EP and the EPLO websites a useful tool (source) for their job and they do not use them very much.
- 1 journalist argued in favour of the live streaming option provided by the EP and the EPLO websites.
- 1 journalist assessed the EP/EPLO websites as very useful just for confirmation. Purposes during the writing of an EP news story.

7.1 Assessment of the Media Relations Performance of the EPLO in Greece

Table 7.2 Assessment, by the Greek online journalists, of the press releases and the information material provided by the EPLO

- The significant majority of online journalists (8 journalists) assessed the information material as general in nature, institutional, with technical and bureaucratic language, and with the content not helping them to go deeper in a story, but being just the basic starting point upon which they build their story.
- Some journalists (4 journalists) actually assessed the information provided by the EPLO as non-journalistic, compared to the information provided by the members of the European Parliament (MEPs) or by the European political parties.
- 2 journalists also raised the issue that the information material provided by the EPLO is not customized for the Greek reality and audience.
- 1 journalist said that the information included in the press releases is helpful and is written in a journalistic way with useful short historical background concerning the specific issue.
- A number of online journalists (4 journalists) assessed the provision of press and information material by the EPLO as poor (in quantitative terms) and said that they would like to receive more of it.
- 1 journalist said that sometimes the information material provided by the EPLO is outdated since the EPLO is a bit slow, in journalistic terms, in issuing and providing information material.

Based on the above data, regarding websites of the EP and EPLO in Greece, the majority of the online journalists considered them useful journalistic tools and complete sources of information. However, some of them face difficulties when they navigate through them (they find it a bit complicated). Last but not least, some of the online journalists that have been interviewed have said that the information provided in the websites is not always "in a journalistic way" (e.g. technical language) and thus not really useful for them. For example, one of the journalists said: *"As far as the EPLO website is concerned, it is not fast, direct and journalistic...I would like to go to a site and see what actually happened in the EP in a more journalistic way...the EPLO website it is typical, you just see the programme, an agenda for events, etc.... I wish it could become a little bit more journalistic"* (JOUR.GR.3).

As far as the press releases and the information material provided by the EPLO are concerned, the findings are presented in Table 7.2.

According to the above findings, the information and communication material available and provided to the online journalists (in written form) does not cover significantly their needs and expectations, since it is of general nature, with institutional, technical, and bureaucratic language; thus, it is not helpful for them to go deeper in a story. In addition, according to some journalists, the information material is sometimes a bit outdated, poor in quantitative terms, and most importantly not customized to the Greek audience. An interesting point to stress is that some journalists actually assessed the information provided by the EPLO as non-journalistic compared to the information provided by the MEPs or by the European political parties. For example, one of the journalists said: *"In contrast to the European political parties, the EP press officers will focus on a more general and less targeted presentation... thus for a journalist who wants to have the political or micro-political news story from a press release, it is of his interest to use the press releases from the political parties... it helps the journalist more to have the more political news story" (JOUR.GR.7).*

With reference to the oral communication of the Greek online journalists with the EPLO officers, the findings are presented in Table 7.3.

According to the findings above, half of the journalists have not managed to get or initiate, through oral communication with EPLO officers, news stories for the EP, and some of them characterized the oral communication as being very institutional and thus useless for them. Some journalists said that there have been cases when the EPLO officers told them something more (off the record) orally, and this has led to the initiation of EP news stories. Fewer journalists said that they did not have any oral contact with EPLO officers at all, despite the fact that they would like to have one.

7.1.2 The Extent to which the EPLO's Media Relations Activities Facilitate Online Journalists' Work when Producing EP News Stories

The findings of the conducted interviews with the online journalists as far as the facilitation role of the EPLO towards journalists is concerned are presented in Table 7.4.

Table 7.3 Assessment, by the Greek online journalists, of the oral communication with EPLO officers

- Half of the online journalists (5 journalists) said that they have never got (or initiated) news stories through oral communication from the EP's people either in the EPLO or in Brussels.
- 2 journalists also characterized the information provided orally by the EPLO and EP officers as very institutional and thus useless for them.
- A number of journalists (3 journalists) said that sometimes the EPLO officers told them something more (off the record) orally and this has led to the initiation of EP news stories.
- 2 journalists said that they did not have any contact and thus oral communication with the EPLO officers and said that they would like to have it since it would help them in their job.

Table 7.4 Assessment, by the Greek online journalists, of the facilitation role of the EPLO

- 7 journalists were satisfied with the support provided by the EPLO.
- 3 journalists supported that the EPLO can help them upon a specific point.
- 1 journalist raised the issue of speed in the response of the EPLO, by saying that sometimes the EPLO officers are a bit slow in their responses.
- 2 journalists said that they have never contacted the EPLO when they needed something for a story and that is why they cannot assess its facilitation role.

According to the findings, the vast majority of the online journalists were satisfied with the facilitation role of the EPLO and the support provided to them, while fewer journalists stated that the EPLO has a limited role and can help them upon a specific point. Last but not least, the issue of slow speed in the responses of the EPLO was also identified as a problem. For example, one journalist characteristically said: *"There is an issue concerning the speed and the immediacy when you need more information and explanations" (JOUR.GR.7)*.

7.1.3 The Extent to which the EPLO Implements an Adequate "Source Strategy"

With reference to the assessment by the online journalists of the implementation by the EPLO of a successful source strategy, the findings are presented in Table 7.5.

According to these findings, the source strategy of the EPLO has been assessed by the journalists as rather inadequate, since the EPLO contacts and informs them about relevant news and events either not often or very rarely or, in fewer cases, not at all. The significant majority of journalists said that they would like a more aggressive source strategy by the EPLO, without considering it an intervention in their job. Some indicative quotes coming from the interviews as regards the implementation of a successful source strategy by the EPLO are the following: *"The EPLO has never called us...if it is something important, it would be nice to have this kind of contact.... they could just say us...guys this happened just have a look...we would want such kind of information and contact...we would not consider it an intervention in our job" (JOUR.GR.3)*. Another journalist said: *"It happens (they contact us) but not so often...and not under, as far as I can understand, a specific organized source strategy approach (...). I would like a more aggressive approach from their side" (JOUR.GR.10)*.

Table 7.5 Assessment, by the Greek online journalists, of the "source strategy" of the EPLO

- 1 journalist said that he has never been contacted by the EPLO in order to be given any relevant information, and he said that he would like to be contacted more often by the EPLO in order to be aware of any news or forthcoming events.
- 5 journalists said that the EPLO sends them relevant material information and they have been contacted by EPLO officers in order to be informed of any relevant news and events that might be of importance, not regularly or often though.
- 4 journalists said that the EPLO officers very rarely contact them and let them know of forthcoming news, issues, and events that might be of interest/importance.
- 9 journalists said that they would like a more aggressive source strategy by the EPLO, without considering it an intervention in their job.

7.1.4 The Extent to which the EPLO Media Relations Activities Take into Consideration the Changes in the Journalistic Practices of the Online Journalists

As regards the question of whether the EPLO media relations activities overall take into consideration the changes in the journalistic practices of the online journalists, the findings are summarized in Table 7.6.

According to the relevant findings, the EPLO is not taking adequately into consideration the fact that online journalists face increased workload and pressure in their job (higher pressure and tighter deadlines than journalists in the so-called traditional media). Journalists overall have also referred to the inability of the EPLO to follow the speed needed for immediate response to journalists' requests, for publishing press releases and information material in general, and for regular and continuous provision of information material. For example, a journalist has pointed out that: *"As far as the timing issue is concerned, if something important happens in the EP, the Greek News Agency will issue the news...the EPLO here will publish something after 5-6 hours...and in this case it will be again a simple press release, so in many cases we don't expect something from them"(JOUR.GR.2)*. Similarly, another journalist said: *"There have been cases when they send me material and I had already published it 5 hours before...In terms of timing I think that they are already slow when sending the news releases...I don't expect from the EPLO to get the news quick and in a more journalistic way" (JOUR.GR.3)*.

Table 7.7 summarizes the findings of the interviews with the online journalists in Greece as regards the extent to which the EPLO media relations activities overall take into consideration possible alterations in the news gathering practices of the online journalists.

According to the findings, the significant majority of online journalists believe that the EPLO acknowledges the importance of the Internet and e-mail as news gathering tools and sends all the information material through e-mails. The majority of the online journalists follow the EPLO social media accounts; however, most of them have not been contacted—via messages or tags in posts—by the EPLO through the relevant social media accounts. The majority of journalists who follow the EPLO social media account assessed the relevant content as institutional (reflecting the way

Table 7.6 Assessment, by the Greek online journalists, of the extent to which the EPLO takes into consideration their increased workload and pressure

• 3 journalists said that in many cases the EPLO media relations activities do not take into consideration the fact that online journalists work under high pressure and very tight deadlines (higher pressure and tighter deadlines than journalists in traditional media) since in many cases they are very slow in their responses to journalist requests.

• 4 journalists also referred to inadequacies of the EPLO generally in timing issues, since they consider the EPLO very slow and late in publishing press releases or other relevant information material for things that happen in the EP.

• 3 journalists also said that the EP does not have a regular provision of news and material, something that it is really important for news websites that operate at a 24/7 level.

7.1 Assessment of the Media Relations Performance of the EPLO in Greece   135

Table 7.7 Assessment, by the Greek online journalists, of the extent to which the EPLO takes into consideration possible alterations in the news gathering practices of the online journalists

- The vast majority of the online journalists (9 journalists) said that the EPLO sends them through e-mail all the relevant press releases and the information material.
- A number of online journalists (4 journalists) are not following the EP and the EPLO in social media and thus they cannot assess the social media policy of the EP.
- The majority of the online journalists (6 journalists) follow the EP/EPLO social media accounts.
- From a total of 6 online journalists who follow EP/EPLO social media accounts, 5 of them said that they have never been contacted through social media by the EPLO nor have they ever initiated an EP news story from the relevant social media accounts.
- 1 journalist, who follows the EPLO in social media, said that when they want to make him see something (e.g. an event or something similar) they usually tag him in a post or in a tweet, which he thinks that is a useful strategy; however, he said that this policy is more targeted for the EPLO activities, events, etc. and not for the case of an EP power or EP activity.
- A number of journalists (3 journalists) assessed the EPLO social media content as institutional and thus reflecting the way that the EPLO operates itself.
- A number of journalists (3 journalists) said that the EP/EPLO social media accounts do not have interesting things to say in comparison to the MEP's social media accounts.
- 1 journalist assessed the EPLO social media as good in saving him time from searching videos when he uses the videos uploaded in the social media accounts of the EP/EPLO.

that the EPLO operates) and not newsworthy in comparison, for example, to the social media accounts of the MEPs. However, very few journalists assessed the social media accounts as useful in terms of quickly finding videos to upload in the news stories, or in terms of being informed of events that the EPLO is holding.

With reference to the assessment by the online journalists of the provision, by the EPLO, of relevant online information enhancements (videos, hyperlinks, multimedia), the findings are presented in Table 7.8.

According to the findings of the interviews, the videos provided by the EPLO are characterized by the journalists as institutional and of little use. Some of the problems that might emerge concerning the videos are attributed for instance to the fact that in some cases there might not be a Greek translation in the videos, which will make it then difficult to be uploaded. As far as the provision of hyperlinks in the EPLO information material is concerned, half of the journalists interviewed assessed the hyperlinks as good and leading to material with added value for the EP news story. Fewer journalists characterized hyperlinks as being of little use. For example, a journalist said: *"The videos are a press service that is rapidly improving...but they are also institutional as well...for example you might have a statement from Junker or Schulz that is really important and because the EP has to be more institutional, they have in the same video every representative from the EP political parties... in journalistic terms this is actually making the video useless...however, in many cases they produce videos that are useful, have useful information and they are also short, so that we can actually have them in the website..for example what is the status for the movement of EU students in the EU...this adds value in the news story...and in some cases the video itself creates the news story..." (JOUR.GR.6).*

Table 7.8 Assessment, by the Greek online journalists, of the provision, by the EPLO, of relevant online information enhancements

• 1 journalist does not receive from the EPLO any online information enhancements, such as videos or hyperlinks.
• 2 journalists say that the EPLO material is, in most cases, without any online "add-on" elements (videos, links, multimedia).
• 2 journalists said that when they receive such material from the EPLO sometimes the hyperlinks do not lead to interesting links (e.g. a whole speech in the EP is of little use either for the journalist or for the audience).
• 5 journalists said that the hyperlinks in the information material provided by the EPLO are good, are useful (since they save time instead of searching for them), and provide an added value to the news story.
• 3 journalists said that when they receive such material from the EPLO, sometimes in the videos or in the live events there is not a Greek translation which is a problem.
• 4 journalists said that the EPLO information material in most cases has useful videos, edited and ready to be uploaded in the news website.
• 5 journalists said that in most cases the videos in the information material provided by the EPLO are of little use for journalistic purposes, since in many cases they are institutional and not well edited.

7.1.5 Conclusions of the Assessment of the EPLO Media Relations Performance in Greece

In general, the websites of the EP and the EPLO in Greece are characterized as useful journalistic tools and complete sources of information by the online journalists in Greece. However, sometimes navigation through them is a bit difficult due to their complicated site design, while the information provided in the websites is not always presented in a way that it could grab journalist's attention. The communication material (in written form) has been characterized by the Greek journalists as being of general nature, with institutional, technical, and bureaucratic language, while an issue which emerges is that the relevant material is not customized for the Greek audience; oral communication has also been characterized as being very institutional and thus useless for journalists.

Regarding the facilitation role of the EPLO and the support provided towards journalists, they have been characterized as satisfactory, despite the limited role of the EPLO in helping journalists up to a specific point. A more aggressive source strategy on behalf of the EPLO is also desirable, as this has been characterized as rather inadequate. With reference to the specific nature of online journalism, the EPLO is not taking adequately into consideration the fact that online journalists face increased workload and pressure in their job (higher pressure and tighter deadlines than journalists in the so-called traditional media). However, it acknowledges the importance of the Internet and e-mail as news gathering tools. The social media strategy could be improved (through personal contacts), with the relevant social media content being characterized as institutional and not newsworthy. The EP videos (provided by the EPLO) are also characterized, by the journalists, as institutional and of little use, while the hyperlinks provided in EP news stories have been characterized as good and leading to material with added value for the EP news story.

7.2 Assessment of the Media Relations Performance of the EPLO in the UK

7.2.1 The Extent to which the EP Communication Material Either in Written or Oral Form Fits Online Journalist's Needs and Expectations

The results of the assessment, by the 6 online journalists in the UK, of the EP and the EPLO websites are summarized in Table 7.9.

The vast majority of online journalists in the UK assessed both the EP and the EPLO websites as quite informative and useful for their jobs. However, some inadequacies, found by the journalists, concern the bureaucratic tone of the language, difficulties to find information on the websites, and sometimes the non-detailed content provided in the websites.

As far as the assessment by the online journalists in the UK of press releases and the information material provided is concerned, the findings are presented in Table 7.10.

The interviewed UK online journalists assessed the press releases and the information material provided by the EPLO as bureaucratic, apolitical, formal, and technical. However, they use the press releases and the information material by the EPLO as a starting point when writing EP news stories. For example, one journalist said: *"It is not the kind of thing that instantly proves to be interesting to journalists or indeed to many people I think (...) the press releases are there to do a*

Table 7.9 Assessment, by the online journalists in the UK, of the EP and the EPLO websites

- 2 journalists assessed as good and useful the EP and EPLO websites' option of watching the debates live.
- 1 journalist said that the parliament website has limitations due to the tone of the language and the bureaucratic terminology.
- 1 journalist said that the EP website is a useful tool, but it might be difficult to find some information on it sometimes; the same journalist said that he does not use the EPLO website as a source.
- 4 journalists assessed the EP/EPLO websites as quite informative and useful.
- 1 journalist said the EP/EPLO website is not detailed as he would like it to be.

Table 7.10 Assessment, by the online journalists in the UK, of the press releases and the information material provided by the EPLO

- 3 journalists use the press release as a starting point when writing his EP news story.
- 3 journalists believe that the press releases are formal and technical, with institutional language.

Table 7.11 Assessment, by the online journalists in the UK, of the oral communication provided by the EPLO officials

• All the journalists (6 journalists) said that they very rarely had oral communication with the EPLO officers in London, and from this communication they had never initiated any news story for the EP.

Table 7.12 Assessment, by the online journalists in the UK, of the facilitation role of the EPLO officials

• 5 journalists characterized the EPLO as professional and helpful in facilitating their work.
• 1 journalist said that he is not much in oral contact with the EPLO and thus he cannot assess its facilitation role.

particular job and that's not necessarily the job that journalists want...the press release is very rarely what we want as journalists...but just this is in the nature of the press releases you know...I use it as a starting point to write my story...I might take one or two sentences, that is unlikely to be the basis for the story" (JOUR. UK.1).

As regards the oral communication provided by the EPLO officials, the findings of the assessment by the online journalists in the UK are presented in Table 7.11.

According to the above findings, all the UK journalists assessed the oral communication provided by the EPLO officers (that rarely got) as not useful for them in initiating news stories, while one journalist supported that it would be helpful to have both kinds of information (both written and oral).

7.2.2 The Extent to which the EPLO's Media Relations Activities Facilitate Online Journalists' Work when Producing EP News Stories

With reference to the facilitation role of the EPLO officials, the findings of the assessment by the online journalists in the UK are summarized in Table 7.12.

The significant majority of the online journalists assessed the facilitation role of the EPLO as professional and helpful while doing their job.

7.2.3 The Extent to which the EPLO Implements an Adequate "Source Strategy"

Table 7.13 presents the findings of the assessment, by the 6 online journalists in the UK, of the "source strategy" of the EPLO.

The source strategy by the EPLO has been assessed by all journalists as inadequate, since they had been contacted by the EPLO either very rarely or in fewer cases

7.2 Assessment of the Media Relations Performance of the EPLO in the UK

Table 7.13 Assessment, by the online journalists in the UK, of the "source strategy" of the EPLO

• 4 journalists said that they had been contacted by the EPLO very few times in the framework of an EPLO source strategy policy.
• 2 journalists said that they have never been contacted by the EPLO in the framework of an EPLO sources strategy.
• All journalists said that they would like to be contacted more often since it would help them in doing their job better.
• 1 journalist said that he would prefer proactive source strategy by mail and not in an oral way.

Table 7.14 Assessment, by the online journalists in the UK, of the extent to which the EPLO takes into consideration their increased workloads and pressure

• 4 journalists raised the issue of the slow response of the EPLO officers to their requests.

not at all. All journalists expressed their need for a more aggressive source strategy and for being contacted more often by the EPLO officers since this would help them to do their job better. For example, one journalist said: *"No, they have never contacted me in order to let me know of news and events, and I think they could be more proactive...I would welcome such kind of suggestions...they would be doing a kind of PR job as well, but I would like that...it helps me to do my job better (...) I think journalists would welcome a more proactive approach...more informal contact" (JOUR.UK.1).*

7.2.4 The Extent to which the EPLO Media Relations Activities Take into Consideration the Changes in the Journalistic Practices of the Online Journalists

The findings of the assessment by the online journalists in the UK of the extent to which the EPLO media relations activities overall take into consideration journalistic practices of the online journalists are presented in Table 7.14.

The majority of the journalists assessed the extent to which the EPLO media relations activities overall take into consideration the fact that they face increased workload and pressure to immediately write and upload a news story as inadequate. Most of them said that they sometimes face delays in receiving their responses.

As regards the assessment by the online journalists in the UK of the extent to which the EPLO takes into consideration possible alterations in the news gathering practices of the online journalists (e.g. use of the Internet as a news gathering tool and use of social media in the daily practice of the online journalists), the findings are presented in Table 7.15.

According to the findings, the majority of journalists consider the extent to which the EPLO takes into consideration the use of the Internet and e-mails as a news gathering tool by the online journalists as adequate. The social media strategy is characterized as inadequate, since they have never been contacted through social

Table 7.15 Assessment by the online journalists in the UK, of the extent to which the EPLO takes into consideration possible alterations in the news gathering practices of the online journalists

- 4 journalists said that they receive the press releases and the information material sent by the EPLO through e-mails.
- 4 journalists said that they follow EPLO social media and that they have never been contacted by the EPLO through social media.
- 3 journalists assessed the social media policy of the EP/EPLO as inadequate mainly because of the apolitical language in the content.
- 1 journalist assessed the social media policy of the EP/EPLO as useful for verification purposes in news stories.

Table 7.16 Assessment, by the online journalists in the UK, of the provision by the EPLO of relevant online information enhancements

- 3 journalists said that they find hyperlinks provided by the EPLO as useful since they add value to the story and since they are credible.
- 4 journalists find the videos of the EP press service to be of little use.
- 1 journalist said that the links provided by the EPLO are of little use.

media (messages, tags, etc.) and because of the apolitical and non-journalistic language used in the posts of the social media accounts.

As far as the assessment of the provision by the EPLO of relevant online information enhancements (hyperlinks, videos) to the online journalists in UK is concerned, the findings are presented in Table 7.16.

The videos are characterized as of little use for journalistic purposes. In addition, half of the journalists assessed the hyperlinks provided by the EPLO as useful since they add value to the news story and they are credible.

7.2.5 Conclusions of the Assessment of the EPLO Media Relations Performance in the UK

The findings of the conducted interviews with the 6 journalists working in websites in the UK show that the communication material, either in written or in oral form, does not fit well with journalistic needs and expectations, since it is bureaucratic, apolitical, and formal. The EPLO is successful enough in its facilitation role; however, its source strategy has been assessed as inadequate, since online journalists had never been contacted (or they had been contacted only a few times) about relevant news and events. The EPLO media relations activities do not overall take into consideration the fact that online journalists face increased workload and pressure with a basic weakness being the delays in responses to journalists' inquiries. The extent to which the EPLO takes into consideration the use of the Internet and e-mails as a news gathering tool is adequate. However, the social media content is characterized as apolitical and non-journalistic.

The hyperlinks provided by the EPLO are useful enough since they add credibility and value to the news story. However, the videos provided by the EPLO are of little use for journalistic purposes.

7.3 Conclusions Concerning the Assessment of the EPLO's Media Relations Performance in Greece and in the UK

This chapter presented the research findings concerning the assessment of the communication and media relations performance of the European Parliament Liaison Offices (EPLOs) in Greece and in the UK. Based on the specific research findings, the following comparative conclusions can be drawn:

The information and communication material available and provided (either in written or in oral form) does not cover efficiently the needs and expectations of online journalists both in Greece and in the UK. Most of the interviewed online journalists characterize the provided information and communication material as general in nature, with institutional, technical, and bureaucratic (apolitical) language, and not helpful for going deeper into a story. In addition, the information material is sometimes a bit outdated, poor in quantitative terms, and not customized for the relevant audiences, whether these are in the UK or in Greece.

In the same vein, the oral communication provided by the EPLO officers in both countries does not seem to cover journalists' needs, since, on the occasions when it actually occurs, it is in institutional language and thus of little use. These research findings fit well with the existing research corpus which characterizes the EU information material as dull and overly complicated (Gleissner & De Vreese, 2005), bureaucratic, complex, and confused (Valentini, 2007; Lecheler, 2008), with technocratic language (Statham, 2010) and in a form that could not grab the media's attention (Anderson & McLeod, 2004).

The fact that the information and communication material (both in written and in oral form) seems to remain institutional, apolitical, and not newsworthy indicates that the EPLO officers cannot probably surpass the barriers of the bureaucratic nature of the EP and thus cannot provide material that could grab the journalists' attention. However, an important observation is that, according to journalists, the communication material is not adequately customized for the domestic audience, which is definitely a barrier that reduces the possibility of the material to be published or used in relevant EP news stories.

The facilitation role of both the EPLOs in Greece and the UK towards online journalists has been generally assessed as successful, since online journalists in both countries were generally satisfied with the support provided, and they have characterized it as professional and helpful while doing their job. An interesting point here is that these research findings are not in agreement with the relevant literature, which shows that journalists have characterized the institution's efforts as not being very supportive of their work (Gleissner & De Vreese, 2005) and the EU information officers as unwilling to help them (Morgan, 1995; Gavin, 2001). The findings here might be evidence that things have changed, concerning the specific element of the EPLO's media relations performance, although obviously a larger study would be necessary in order to confirm this hypothesis across the various member states.

The source strategy of the EPLOs in terms of the frequency with which online journalists are contacted in order to get their message across has been characterized as inadequate in both countries, since online journalists were respectively contacted either not often or very rarely. This finding is in accordance with the relevant research, which shows that European institutions make little effort to make themselves heard to national and sub-national journalists (Statham, 2010). However, it should be stressed that according to the current findings, journalists in both countries would like a more aggressive source strategy on behalf of the EPLOs, without considering it an intervention in their job. The fact that EPLO officers seem to make little effort to approach and make themselves heard to national and sub-national journalists also indicates an attitude that might be grounded to the institutional setting of the EP and to the fact that the EP should not probably spin stories. The inadequate source strategy of the EPLOs is in contrast to the more efficient source strategy of the MEPs and the more newsworthy material that they provide to journalists.

Regarding the extent to which the EPLO's media relations activities overall take into consideration the journalistic practices of the online journalists, the following conclusions can be drawn from the comparative analysis of the case studies: In both countries (Greece and the UK), the EPLOs seem not to take into consideration the fact that online journalists face increased workload and pressure in their job. The journalists who were interviewed referred to inadequacies of the EPLOs in the speed of response to journalists' requests, in the delayed publishing of press releases and information material in general, and in the lack of regular and continuous provision of information material. However, the EPLOs are successful in acknowledging the importance of the Internet and e-mail as news gathering tools for journalists, since they (the EPLOs) send all the information material through e-mails. As far as the social media strategy of the EPLOs is concerned, in both countries (Greece and the UK) this was characterized as inadequate (in terms of a news gathering tool) and not newsworthy in terms of content. The case is similar for the videos provided by the EPLOs, which were assessed as not newsworthy. However, in both countries, the hyperlinks provided in the relevant information material have been evaluated as useful, credible, and leading to material with added value for the EP news story.

Since the relevant literature on the extent to which the EP or the EU institutions media relations activities take into consideration the journalistic practices of the online journalists seems to be scarce, the specific research findings are important. The fact that the EPLOs do not take into consideration the increased workload and high pressure that online journalists face in their job, especially in terms of speed and timing, indicates that the EPLOs have not been able to adjust their communication and media relations activities to the working routines of online journalists. The online journalists are (or should be) an important target group for EPLOs, and the inability to adjust to their needs and the working routines seem to hinder the media relations performance of the EPLOs. Last but not least, the inadequate social media strategy and the not newsworthy social media content indicate, once more, the barrier that the bureaucratic nature of the EP and the EPLOs sets in the job of EPLO's officers.

At this point it should be mentioned that, despite the limited sample of the journalists interviewed (especially as regards the case of the UK journalists, for the reasons outlined in Chap. 5), the representativeness and the quality of the sampled journalists give to the findings a significant indicative value. As it has already been explained, the online journalists that have been interviewed (both in the UK and in Greece) come from sites with a pro-European or rather impartial stance towards the EU; thus, it is where improvements in the EP's communications performance—in theory—should be most achievable. If there are critical areas where the EP communication and media relations performance is weak in relation to these journalists and sites, then it is of real value to identify these areas, the underlying reasons, and possible solutions.

References

Anderson, P. J., & McLeod, A. (2004). The great non-communicator? The mass communicator deficit of the European Parliament and its Press Directorate. *Journal of Common Market Studies, 42*(5), 897–917.

Benson, R., Blach-Ørsten, M., Powers, M., Willig, I., & Zambrano, S. V. (2012). Media systems online and off: Comparing the form of news in the United States, Denmark, and France. *Journal of Communication, 62*(1), 21–38.

Gavin, N. T. (2001). British journalists in the spotlight: Europe and media research. *Journalism, 2*(3), 299–314.

Gleissner, M., & De Vreese, C. H. (2005). News about the EU Constitution-Journalistic challenges and media portrayal of the European Union Constitution. *Journalism, 6*(2), 221–242.

Lecheler, S. S. (2008). EU membership and the press: An analysis of the Brussels correspondents from the new member states. *Journalism, 9*(4), 443–464.

Morgan, D. (1995). British news and European Union news. The Brussels news beat and its problems. *European Journal of Communication, 10*(3), 321–343.

Statham, P. (2010). Media performance and Europe's communication deficit: A study of journalists' perceptions. In C. Bee & E. Bozzini (Eds.), *Mapping the European public sphere. Institutions, media and civil society* (pp. 117–139). Ashgate.

Valentini, C. (2007). EU media relations. Views of Finnish and Italian journalists. *GMJ Mediterranean Edition, 2*(2), 82–96.

Chapter 8
Identification and Critical Analysis of the Problems in the Online Media Coverage and Media Relations Performance of the EP in Greece and in the UK

This chapter presents a synthesis of the research findings of the examination of the EP online media coverage in the selected news websites in the UK and Greece and the results of the assessment of the EPLO's media relations performance. The aim of this synthesis is to identify and critically analyse the reasons behind the problems in both the EP online media coverage and the EPLO's media relations performance.

In other words, the small amount of coverage that the EP institutional powers and output has been getting in the Greek and British news websites is brought together with the journalists' evaluations of the problems with the service provided by the EPLOs in a detailed critical analysis of what all of this collectively reveals about the reasons for the low levels of coverage of the EP in online news media in the two countries. In the specific discussion the findings of the semi-structured interviews with Communication Officers in the EPLO's in the UK and Greece (presented in each of the following sections) will also be of great value, since they will reveal their view on the communication and media relation activities of the EPLOs.

According to the relevant research findings the identified problems are the following:

8.1 Lack of Collective Representation or Voice for the EP in the Media and Co-Existence of Different News Management Policies Between the EP and the MEPs

The research findings show that in both countries the coverage of the European Parliament institutional powers and output is very limited in comparison to the total amount of EP news items. As seen in Chap. 6, in the Greek news websites under examination 37.7% of the total amount of the EP news items referred to the EP institutional powers, while only 8.6% of the total amount of EP news items referred to the EP's output. In the UK news websites, 35.2% of the total amount of the EP news items referred to the EP institutional powers, while 20.94% of the total amount of EP news items referred to the EP output.

One of the reasons that could partially explain the limited visibility of the EP's institutional powers and output is that in both countries MEPs' (domestic or non-domestic) activities, not related to the EP institutional powers and output, are far more visible. More specifically, according to the research findings, in the selected Greek news websites the majority of the EP news items (405 news items, or 62.3% of the sample) did not have any reference to the EP institutional powers and they were rather related to domestic MEPs activities (e.g. interviews, statements, events for domestic issues, events or visits organized by domestic MEPs), non-domestic MEPs activities (events in the EP organized by non-domestic MEPs, interviews, statements by non-domestic MEPs for domestic issues), and leaders' of European political group activities (such as Martin Schulz and Pavel Svoboda who gave interviews and made statements for domestic issues). The situation is similar regarding the limited visibility of the EP output in the Greek news websites under examination since only 8.6% (56 news items out of 650 news items) of the total amount of EP news items referred to the EP's output.

In the case of the selected UK news websites, the majority of the EP news items (260 news items out of 401 news items or 64.8% of the total EP news items) did not have any reference to the EP institutional powers and were rather related to: domestic MEP's activities (interviews, statements, items regarding domestic issues) or non-domestic MEP's activities (interview, statements, events, etc.). The situation is similar with regard to the limited visibility of the EP output in the UK news websites; out of a total of 401 news items that have been collected and analysed, only 84 news items (20.94% of the total number of the EP news items) referred to the output of the EP.

The higher visibility of MEPs' activities in both countries could be partially explained (as it is revealed by the in-depth semi-structured interviews with the online journalists in Greece and in the UK) by the fact that: (a) MEPs are used predominantly as sources when online journalists write EP news stories and (b) MEPs have more efficient media relations in comparison to the media relations of the EP (through the EPLOs) as an institution (that is to say that MEPs provide more newsworthy information material, are more aware of the media logics, and have more aggressive source strategies). For example, one journalist said: *"Our sources are mainly the press releases of the MEPs" (JOUR.GR.6)* while as far as the more efficient media relations and source strategy deployed by the MEPs are concerned, one journalist characteristically said in the interview: *"The assistant of the MEPs are more helpful in this sense (media relations) (...) the real news stories come from the press officers of the European political parties or of the MEPs themselves...the MEPs have the stress to be re-elected and they care very much for their PR with the journalists...in journalistic terms the MEPs are better in that (...) the assistants of the MEPs have really strong source strategies...they will call me to let me know about the issues and try to persuade me to publish them...the EPLO here expects you to call it (...) the press officers of the European political parties are mostly in contact with the journalists, and not the EP officers who are*

8.1 Lack of Collective Representation or Voice for the EP in the Media and... 147

just in their institutional role, which is useless for the journalists (...) Yes their information material (of the MEPs) is more journalistic and that's because the press officers of the MEPs or of the political parties are usually journalists, media experts, and they know what journalists want" (JOUR.GR.6).

However, the important issue here that has to be noticed is that the MEPs' activities that are far more visible in the news websites are not related, in most cases, to the EP institutional powers and output. And this can be explained by the fact that: (a) either MEPs are not interested in relating themselves to the EP institutional powers and output, or/and (b) journalists are not interested in relating the MEPs so often to EP institutional powers and output, in their relevant coverage in both countries. Online journalists in both the UK and Greece have expressed their concerns on whether the MEPs are interested in their European Parliamentary role or they are just there in order to promote micro-political interests that have nothing to do with the institutional powers of the EP or its output. As one journalist characteristically said: *"It is the MEPs themselves that we have to blame...because they don't go there as European Members of the Parliament, they go there as representatives of their national Parliaments and they wait to return back to have a domestic political career (...) it (the EP) is an arena of national micro-political interest (...) they are not interested....even now the MEPs seem like they are representatives- ambassadors of their own countries (...) most of them promote themselves and the national micro-political interests (...) the MEPs...they see the EP as a step to return to their countries and have a career there...they think of it as a parenthesis (...) if the MEPs themselves wanted to see their role as MEPs of every European citizen and not as just ambassadors of their member state, then something could be improved... but for the time being it seems that they are not interested"* (JOUR.GR.7). In addition, journalists and newsrooms could also be partially blamed for not linking MEPs to their tasks and responsibilities in the European Parliament but rather linking them to domestic affairs. For example, one journalist from the UK said: *"I think it is fair to say that the Parliament is not taken very seriously in Britain by journalists...To the extent that the European Parliament does get coverage in the British media it has very often to do with the domestic activities of some of our MEPs like Nigel Farage and the other UKIP MEPs, I think it is fair to say unless the EP vote is absolutely crucial, which is very very rarely the case...it (the EP) won't get much press coverage"* (JOUR.UK.2).

This problem seems to be aggravated if one considers the EPLOs Communication Officers' view who support that one of the main responsibilities of the EPLOs is to facilitate and promote the publicization of the MEPs. For example, it was characteristically said: *"Well, it is not our priority to get ourselves (the EP personnel) in the media...because MEPs are those who have to express the political stance...so I am interested to have the MEP in the foreground...because MEPs have also a kind of legitimization"* (EPLO.GR.1).

Based on the above, the EP (as an actor of institutional communication) has to compete, to a large extent, the MEPs in order to publicize its institutional powers and output, while at the same time, the EP has to facilitate the publicization of the MEPs, whose visibility in the media—however—is not related, to a significant extent, to the

EP powers and output; in other words, the EP, paradoxically, facilitates the publicization of its "competitor" in the news media.

The aforementioned discussion reveals that the problem of the lack of collective representation or voice for the EP in the media, and the problem of the co-existence of different news management policies between the EP as an institution and the MEPs themselves, that have already been identified by other scholars as well (Morgan, 1995; Trenz, 2004; Anderson & McLeod, 2004), still exist and largely hinder the visibility of the EP in the news media.

8.2 Not Newsworthy Information Provided by the EP/EPLOs

Another reason that partially leads to the limited coverage of the EP institutional powers and output in the news websites in both countries is the fact that the EP information material provided to journalists is not newsworthy (in comparison to the more newsworthy information and communication material provided by the MEPs) and thus is not used by them, in the significant majority of cases.

As seen in Chap. 7, the EP information material has been characterized by the online journalists, as bureaucratic, not written in a journalistic way, technical, institutional, general, official and not having a political angle, which is useful and newsworthy for the journalists when producing EP news stories. This specific nature of the information provided by the EP exists, overall, in every kind of communication tool or material provided by the EP, such as: the website of the EP or of the EPLOs, the EP press releases, the oral communication that sometimes is provided by the EPLO officers, the hyperlinks and videos provided by the EP and the content of the social media accounts.

Due to these characteristics, the information provided by the EP is not helping journalists to go deeper into a story and in most cases, it is only the basis, the starting point, upon which journalists will try to develop their story. When journalists want to go a step further, they search it on their own, and they tend to communicate with the MEPs in order to get the political and the newsworthy side for their story. As one online journalist characteristically said regarding the press releases: *"The press releases is just a basis upon which I will try to develop my story...it is a basis that will make me afterwards to communicate with the EPLO here to ask probably for further explanations for the story...or to communicate with a MEP to have a political position as well" (JOUR.GR.5).*

The extremely technocratic and institutional character of the EP and consequently the EPLO information, along with the mix of the institutional and political information, has also been identified as a problem in the EP public communication by the EPLO officers themselves. The EPLO officers realize that they can help only to a specific point, especially in the cases of technocratic issues, when they forward journalists' request to specialized EP press officers. In addition, regarding the mix of the institutional and political information that they have to manage, one of the problems that they identify is that the guidelines they receive have in many cases bureaucratic rather than communicative character. And this co-existence of the institutional with the political level has some grey zones and some potential dangers in the EPLO communication. As it was characteristically said: *"Another potential difficult issue is the mix of the institutional with the political information...and sometimes you have to manage internal institutional problems...how you will manage a situation internally...with guidelines that have in many cases bureaucratic rather than communicative character...from the hierarchy...I would say that the mixed character of the EP where the institutional coexists with the political level has some grey zones and some potential dangers in our communication"* (EPLO. GR.2).

Another major dimension regarding the EP information provided to journalists, as this came out from the research findings, is related to the fact that this information is not adequately customized in order to be relevant to the domestic audience in the countries under examination. This dimension becomes even more problematic if we consider that the basic news selection criteria for journalists when writing EP stories are the domesticity (the relevance of the EP activity/output to the specific country) of the news in both countries. In addition, the research findings revealed that journalists in Greece and the UK consider that the material provided by the EP/EPLO does not usually include information concerning the output of the EP (thus not customized adequately for the relevant domestic audiences), which makes the EP information material not meeting their basic news selection criteria and thus being a reason for hindering to a great extent the visibility of the EP output. As it was characteristically mentioned in one interview: *"The impact of an EP decision, resolution, legislation for Greece is the very basic reason for an EP news story to be read by the readers (...) the press release usually will not have a reference to the impact of the EP...yes I try to find the impact and make the story more news worthy and more attractive"* (JOUR.GR.7).

According to the findings from the relevant interviews, the EPLO information and communication material is, to a large extent, produced and provided by the EP Secretariat mechanism in Brussels, and it is not customized to the needs of the domestic audience (there are not specific communication strategies and guidelines for the different member states). The EPLO officers cannot change the text coming from the Brussels communication mechanism, and their flexibility is limited to the point where they can make editorial decisions and select the information to which they will focus. However, the EPLO officers, according to the interviews, try to have an editorial logic and promote specific things both in the website and in their social media accounts.

Thus, the fact that the information and communication material is produced mainly by the EP Secretariat, combined with the limited role of the EPLOs in changing the text and customizing adequately the information to the interest of domestic audiences—and journalists—is also a major reason that explains why the EP information does not meet news selection criteria. As a result, as it has already been pointed out by other scholars (Valentini, 2008; Valentini & Laursen, 2012), this communication strategy of the EP, which is not sufficiently tailored to the individual communication needs of the countries, leads to potential communication problems and low visibility.

8.3 Inefficient Source Strategy by the EPLOs

A relevant issue, in addition to the not newsworthy information provided by the EP, is the inadequate source strategy of the EPLOs in both countries. The source strategy here is related to the frequency with which journalists are contacted by the EPLOs officers who want to get their message across and provide them with press statements, or other similar material. This inadequate source strategy could be considered, inter alia, as an explanatory factor for the low visibility of the EP in the news media, since a more aggressive source strategy by the EPLOs would make journalists publish EP news stories and would help them in doing their job better.

However, the findings of the interviews with the EPLO's officers reveal that the lack of an aggressive source strategy is something common in the tactics of the EPLO officers in both countries. According to them, the EPLO officers publish the information and consider that anyone who is interested in the relevant material will come and search it on his own. Interestingly enough, the EPLO officers do not adopt an aggressive source strategy because they believe that they have to maintain (secure) the credibility of the EP as an institution and because they believe that if they always seek journalists' attention, the EP will lose its credibility as a source. As it was characteristically mentioned by an interviewee: *"We don't work, and this is my view, by asking someone to publish us, as the politician's press offices do...I never do that because I believe that first of all I have to maintain (secure) the credibility of the institution (EP) and secondly I believe that on a long term basis the journalist, if you always ask for his attention, will underestimate you....what I am interested at is to produce materials and to make them attractive, and whoever is interested will take them..." (EPLO.GR.1).*

Based on the above, it can be argued that the EP institutional understanding of the function of the communication promotes a culture of impartiality and neutrality, an issue that has also been identified by other scholars studying the EP communication (Valentini, 2013). This non-aggressive source strategy seems to also contribute to the low visibility of the EP in the news websites in the specific countries under examination.

8.4 Communication Strategy Not Taking into Consideration Online Journalists' Needs

Another problem that could be considered a reason for the low visibility of the EP in the news websites (and for the low visibility of the EP online elements such as hyperlinks or videos) in the countries under examination stems from the fact that the EP's communication strategy does not take sufficiently into consideration some specific needs of online journalists such as: (a) the need for provision of online elements that could be used by the news websites such as videos or hyperlinks and (b) the need for timely and regular provision (regular flow) of material to the news websites that work with strict deadlines in a 24/7 news cycle, since the EPLOs are characterized as working with a newspaper mentality that, in most cases, does not fit with the online news media cycle.

This flaw in the media relations performance of the EP could be explained partially, based on the interviews with the EPLO officers both in Greece and in the UK, by the fact that there is not any specific news website strategy (a strategy that takes into consideration these specific online journalists' needs) and by the fact that the flow of information towards journalists follows mainly the legislative agenda. As it was characteristically said: *"Well the strategy (for news websites) is very much in line with our general communication strategy (...) news websites fall under press traditional...because in the UK, well I suppose this varies from country to country...in the UK the news websites are most of the time internet publication of press publications or broadcasters....so the editorial team will be very similar" (EPLO.UK.1).*

Thus, the fact that the communication strategy of the EPLOs is not in accordance with the media logic of the news websites seems to be another reason for the low visibility of the EP in news websites. However, regarding the issue of the efficient flow of information from the EP to the news media, and as scholars such as Raeymaeckers et al. (2007) argue, structural factors related to the organization and the programming of the legislative work of the EP, could be considered to impede the efficient flow of information from the EP to the news media.

8.5 Problems Related to the Operation: Function of the EPLOs

Last but not least, one of the problems that the EPLO's officers face, according to the findings of the interviews, is related to the difficulties they have in order to assess the effectiveness of some of their media relations activities; for example, assessing how many of the journalists that have participated in a press seminar or in a journalistic mission in Brussels or Strasbourg, have actually written (or have started writing) news stories about the EP. The EPLO officers claimed that (a) they do not have the tools to do that and (b) when they need to do such kind of assessment, they would have to sacrifice another activity (duty) which could be more important according to them. An interesting issue to notice here is that the same problem was also identified by journalists who suggested that the EPLO should assess better the impact of the journalistic missions in the EP sessions in Brussels or in Strasbourg and examine, for example, whether journalists, who have participated in them, actually produce EP news stories either in a short-term or in a longer-term perspective.

An additional factor that affects the efficiency of the Press Office of the EPLO is the limitations in the personnel in the press service of the EPLO, with the EPLO officers supporting that such kind of limitations do not allow them to face the pressure of the daily routine and be as effective as they would like to. Another kind of problem, relating mainly to the process of the dissemination of the EP information material to the journalists emerges from the fact that there are difficulties in updating and maintaining journalists' databases and contact details, because of the great mobility in the industry.

In addition, the EPLO officers acknowledge that they do not have adequate skills for the management of the EPLO's Internet and social media communication, in order to follow the developments in the relevant platforms, while they claim as a problem the fact that a large part of the daily routine is related to monitoring and reporting back to the EP Secretariat with the use of different tools, and probably there is not so much space within this routine for more communication activities.

In the same vein, problems that have been identified by the EPLO officers have to do with the fact that the EP faces competitive visibility in many cases by the Commission and the national players, while there is also a clash of the EPLO objective (increasing visibility of the EP) and the needs of the media (not interested in the EP). Last but not least, the EPLO officers consider that getting media interest—and fitting in the daily busy work schedules of the online journalists—is a great challenge in their job.

Similar problems such as under-resourced press and information offices in the member states, or insufficient media and public relations training for EPLO officers have also been identified by other scholars (Anderson & Weymouth, 1999; Anderson & McLeod, 2004).

8.6 Conclusion

The research findings of the content analysis and the interviews with online journalists and EPLO officers in both countries have revealed a series of problems that co-exist at the communication and organization level of the EP and hinder its visibility in the news websites in both countries.

These problems relate to a set of factors that have been identified in the above analysis: (1) the lack of collective representation or voice for the EP in the media, and to the co-existence of different news management policies and targets between the EP as an institution and the MEPs themselves (thus between the different voices of the EP), (2) the institutional and not newsworthy language and nature of the EP communication, (3) the limited role of the EPLOs to adequately customize the information they receive from the EP Secretariat, to the interest of domestic audiences—and journalists, (4) the inadequate source strategy and the institutional understanding of the function of the communication which promotes a culture of impartiality, neutrality and not so much of an aggressive source strategy and the promotion of communication, (5) the fact that the communication strategy of the EPLOs is not so much in accordance with the media logic (especially concerning timing issues and busy work schedules of online journalists) of the news websites, (6) the limitations in the personnel in the press service of the EPLOs, (7) the difficulties of the EPLOs to assess the efficiency of certain media relations activities, (8) the lack of skills for the management of the EPLO's Internet and social media communication, and (9) the fact that a big part of the daily routine is related to monitoring and reporting back to the EP Secretariat with the use of different tools, and probably there is not so much space within this routine for more communication activities.

The aforementioned problems reveal to a great extent the seeming inability of the European Parliament to communicate with the media, and thus enhance its institutional communication deficit (Meyer, 1999; Habermas, 2012; Anderson & McLeod, 2004; Blondel et al., 1998; Bijsmans & Altides, 2007), which in turn leads to the EP social legitimacy deficit. Potential solutions for the EP in order to overcome these problems and communicate more effectively in Greece and the UK are going to be identified in the following chapter (Chap. 9).

References

Anderson, P. J., & McLeod, A. (2004). The great non-communicator? The mass communicator deficit of the European Parliament and its Press Directorate. *Journal of Common Market Studies, 42*(5), 897–917.
Anderson, P. J., & Weymouth, T. (1999). *Insulting the public? The British Press and the European Union*. Longman.
Bijsmans, P., & Altides, C. (2007). Bridging the gap between EU politics and citizens? The European Commission, national media and EU affairs in the public sphere. *Journal of European Integration, 29*(3), 323–340.
Blondel, J., Sinnott, R., & Svensson, P. (1998). *People and parliament in the European Union: Participation, democracy, and legitimacy*. Oxford University Press.
Habermas, J. (2012). *The crisis of the European Union: A response*. Polity.
Meyer, C. (1999). Political legitimacy and the invisibility of politics: Exploring the European Union's communication deficit. *Journal of Common Market Studies, 37*(4), 617–639.
Morgan, D. (1995). British News and European Union News. The Brussels news beat and its problems. *European Journal of Communication, 10*(3), 321–343.
Raeymaeckers, K., Cosijn, L., & Deprez, A. (2007). Reporting the European Union: An analysis of the Brussels press corps and the mechanisms influencing the news flow. *Journalism Practice, 1*(1), 102–119.

Trenz, H. J. (2004). Media coverage on European governance: Exploring the European Public sphere in national quality newspapers. *European Journal of Communication, 19*(3), 291–319.

Valentini, C. (2008). EU Communication in the member states: Comparative analysis of Finnish and Italian communication strategies. *International Journal of Strategic Communication, 2*(4), 216–243.

Valentini, C. (2013). Political public relations in the European Union: EU reputation and relationship management under scrutiny. *The Public Relations Journal, 7*(4), 1–22.

Valentini, C., & Laursen, B. (2012). The mass media: A privileged channel for the EU's political communication. In L. Morganti & L. Bekemans (Eds.), *The European Public Sphere – From critical thinking to responsible action* (pp. 129–146). P.I.E.-Peter Lang.

Chapter 9
Identification of Potential Ways of Communicating the EP more Effectively in Greece and in the UK

This chapter presents the potential solutions for overcoming the problems of low visibility of the EP institutional powers and output. The identification of the proposed solutions has been based on: (a) the research findings of the content analysis, (b) the working routines of the online journalists along with what the online journalists have said that they actually would want from the EPLOs, and (c) the working routines of the EPLO officers in the UK and Greece.

9.1 Greece

In order to identify potential ways for communicating the EP more effectively in Greece—which would increase the visibility of the EP's powers and its output, the positive coverage of the EP and its impact, and the amount of additional Internet facilitated information provided in the coverage of the EP (hyperlinks, videos, etc.)—one should consider the findings emerging from (a) the interviews with the journalists and (b) the content analysis of the selected news websites. In particular one should consider that: (1) the basic news selection criterion for the writing of EP news stories is the domesticity of the story, (2) the EPLO website is among the main sources of the online journalists in Greece when writing EP news stories, (3) social media are part of online journalists' news gathering practices and are used in general to initiate news stories, (4) NGOs or specialized think tanks and domestic MEPs are used by the significant majority of the online journalists in Greece as sources when writing about the impact of the EP, (5) online journalists in the selected Greek websites are considered as important evaluators of the EP or the MEPs, and (6) (a) the basic selection criteria for online journalists for choosing hyperlinks to the EP/Europarl TV or to relevant EP documents are the extent to which the links add to the story, or lead to material that could be easily understood by the readers, or to material with domestic interest and (b) the basic selection criteria for online journalists for choosing the videos for EP news stories are the extent to which the video is interesting according to the journalistic news selection criteria, or the extent to which the videos are provided in the Greek language (or subtitled), or are ready-edited (in technical terms)—by the EP press service.

Concerning each one of the aforementioned conditions, that have been taken into consideration for the identification of potential ways of communicating the EP more effectively in Greece, the following apply:

1. As seen in Chaps. 7 and 8, the basic news selection criteria for writing EP news stories by the online journalists in Greece, are the domesticity of the news. In addition, journalists want to have the element of EP output in the information material they receive from the EP, since it would help them very much in their job and would make their news story more attractive.

   However, as it emerges from the interviews with the EPLO officers in Greece, the EP information and communication materials are mainly produced in the EP Secretariat in Brussels and thus are not, adequately, customized for the Greek audience. In addition, as shown by the research findings, the EPLO officers do not have the flexibility to change and customize the text provided by the EP Secretariat, as seen in Chap. 8, but they can only be involved in a minor editorial work where they select and promote certain aspects that they think could be more related to the Greek audience.

   Given these limitations of the EPLO in the customization of the information and communication material coming from the EP Secretariat, some potential remedial actions for increasing the visibility of the EP's powers and output could include the following:

   The information material concerning the activities undertaken by the local EPLO (for example, events regarding the EP's "Sakharov Prize for Freedom of Thought", regional conferences organized by the EPLO, press seminars, visits by MEPs or EP Committees, etc.) is produced by the local EPLO officers and meets the basic news selection criteria of domesticity (either in national or regional level). The EPLO officers could take advantage of that and could relate, when producing the specific information material, these events to the EP's institutional powers (for example, a regional conference might be held in the framework of a directive for environmental protection, or in the framework of a legislative proposal for the increase of investments) and to potential positive output on the citizens. In this way, they could publicize the EP's activities and impact and relate it to the domestic audience.

   In addition, since the EPLO officers can only be involved in minor editorial work by customizing the material provided by the EP Secretariat, it would be useful for them to receive further relevant training and enhance—as research has shown (Foster, 2008; Wilcox & Cameron, 2014; Singleton, 2014)—their editing and writing skills.

2. According to the findings of the research, the EPLO website is among the main sources of the online journalists in Greece when writing EP news stories.

However, the EPLO website, as seen in Chap. 7, does not cover journalists' needs since it has been found to use bureaucratic language, the information is given in a non-journalistic way, while some journalists have also characterized it as not technologically upgraded in terms of speed (for example, it is too slow when accessed, by a mobile phone). In addition, journalists have difficulty sometimes in navigating through the EPLO site and find, for instance, information on the ongoing discussions in the committees or in the plenary sessions. Online journalists in Greece have also stressed the need for improving the EPLO website by suggesting that it should get a more journalistic perspective and become more like a news agency providing every type of news material (news, events, agenda, photos, videos, multimedia, etc.) in the Greek language and in a non-stop flow of news.

Taking into consideration the limitations that the EPLO officers face in terms of making changes in the text of the information material they receive, and thus the content of the EPLO website, a potential remedial action could be for the EPLO website to get a different, more journalistic structure. The EPLO could develop a specific section in its website that could function as an online newsroom that would include the material needed by the journalists (photos, videos, news releases, feature stories, contact details, news, events, multimedia; everything provided in the Greek language and without journalists needing to go to the main EP website). This online newsroom policy has been also suggested by certain scholars while many organizations have already developed relevant initiatives (Holtz, 2002; Foster, 2008; Wilcox & Cameron, 2014; Scott, 2015).

Based on the aforementioned, the EPLO website could, partially, adopt a more media relations-oriented perspective since in its current form, the EPLO website is targeting simultaneously citizens, journalists, and other stakeholders. The customization of the structure of the website is possible, taking into consideration the fact that different EPLOs in different member states have slightly different website structures.

3. According to the findings from the interviews with online journalists, social media are part of online journalists' news gathering practices in Greece and are used in general to help them initiate news stories.

However, several journalists in Greece, as seen in Chap. 7, assess the relevant social media content as institutional (reflecting the way that the EPLO operates) and not newsworthy in comparison, for example, to the social media accounts of the MEPs, since the social media policy is more targeted towards the notification of the EPLO's activities, events, etc. Most of the journalists interviewed have never been contacted through social media by the EPLO (e.g., tags, messages), while for some journalists the EPLO social media accounts are useful in terms of finding quickly videos to upload in their news stories, or in terms of being informed of events that the EPLO is holding.

The EPLO officers, on their side, are interested in mapping the specific landscape of social and online media. They want to know the actors who speak for the EP (networks and opinion leaders) and subsequently provide them with relevant information material. One of the main target groups of the EPLO social media accounts are the online journalists. The EPLO Twitter account operates mainly from the EP Secretariat (Brussels) where a Greek journalist manages it, while the EPLO Facebook account is managed by the EPLO officers who upload mainly posts regarding forthcoming events and material coming from Brussels that they think (again making an editorial decision here) are interesting and might catch the attention of the followers and journalists. Last but not least, the EPLO officers identify the need for training and skills development regarding Internet and social media communication.

Taking into consideration the aforementioned findings and the lack of adequate skills for the management and the development of the EPLO's Internet and social media communication, as a problem identified by the EPLO officers themselves, a remedial action for more effective EP communication in this area would be a more personalized social media policy provided by the EPLO officers, specifically through their FB account. This policy would use more personalized techniques (such as personal messages, tags, etc.) in order to build relationships with online journalists. Besides, these personalized techniques in social media are really effective techniques for building relationships and engaging with the target audiences (in our case, journalists) as relevant research shows (Scott, 2015; Sweeney & Craig, 2011; Singleton, 2014). This more personalized FB approach could be used for journalists who already have a kind of interaction with the EPLO (e.g. they have already contacted on their own the EPLO, or they have participated in a journalistic mission, or a press seminar and they are in a relevant database), since this tactic is more efficient when it is applied to journalists that already know the organization (in our case the EPLO) (Romo, 2012; Wilcox & Cameron, 2014).

Regarding the training of the EPLO officers in Internet and social media communication, it seems necessary that they (EPLO officers) should develop their skills in areas of social media communication such as integrated storytelling, content creation, visual content creation, use of social media data and analytics (Bhurji, 2012) so that they could handle future challenges and enhance the visibility of the EP.

4. In line with the research findings from the interviews with online journalists in the selected Greek news websites, NGOs, specialized think tanks, and other stakeholders (along with domestic MEPs) are used by online journalists in Greece as sources when writing about the impact of the EP.

The EPLO officers in Athens, on their side, and regarding the process of dissemination of the EP information material, publish the institutional communication coming from the EP Secretariat and send the relevant material automatically to every contact (without applying any selection criteria) included in the contact database, through mail. The contact database includes a large number of stakeholders who receive the relevant information material.

However, it could be argued that problems identified in Chap. 8, such as the inadequate personnel in the press service of the EPLO, the great pressure to cope with the daily routine, and the difficulties in updating and maintaining the contact details of stakeholders and journalists (for journalists it is even more difficult

9.1 Greece

Table 9.1 Who is evaluating the EP and the MEPs in the selected Greek news websites?

Who is evaluating the EP or the MEPs	Number of news items
Domestic political party evaluating negatively domestic MEP	2
Journalist has negative stance towards the EP	2
Journalist has a negative stance towards a non-domestic MEP	1
Journalist has a negative stance towards a domestic MEP	6
Non-domestic MEP has a negative stance for the EP	1
Domestic MEP has a negative stance for other domestic MEP	1
Other media (foreign media) has negative stance for domestic MEP	1
Journalist has a positive stance towards a non-domestic MEP	1
Journalist evaluating positively a domestic MEP	1

because of the mobility in the industry) in the database, decrease the extent and the number of stakeholders that the EPLO's material can reach.

As a first step, a potential remedial action for the enhancement of the communication efficiency of EPLO would be to further identify specific NGOS, think tanks, or other stakeholders that are visible in the media. Then, instead of sending information material to every contact included in its database (without any selection criteria) it could adopt a more targeted media relations policy towards these specific stakeholders by trying to engage with them and build relationships either through social media, as seen before, or on a more personal level. Another remedial action would be for the EPLO to suggest to journalists (probably during the press seminars that it organizes) specific stakeholders that could be used as additional sources when writing EP news stories.

5. Table 9.1 presents the research findings from the content analysis of the selected news websites relating to the news items with an evaluative stance towards the EP. Based on these findings, online journalists in the selected Greek news websites are emerging as main evaluators of the EP or the MEPs.

Thus, a potential way of increasing the positive coverage of the EP would be for the EPLO officers to push online journalists (who are emerging as evaluators of the EP) to publish EP news stories with a positive stance.

However, an interesting and contradictory issue is that the EPLO's officers in Greece do not exercise spin doctoring practices in order to push journalists to publish stories with positive stance about the EP since they believe that in this way the EP will lose its credibility as a source and as a provider of factual and accurate information. The EPLO officers are interested predominantly in maintaining (securing) the credibility and the prestige of the institution that they represent and in building long-term relationships with the journalists.

One potential remedial activity for increasing the visibility of the positive coverage of the EP and the EP's output/impact in Greece, taking into consideration the limitations in the personnel of the press service of the EPLO, the great pressure to cope with the daily routine, and the fact that the EPLO officers do not practice spin doctoring, would be for the EPLO Officers to identify the journalists and the media that have a negative evaluative stance towards the EP and in the

cases where this negative stance is based on untrue facts about the EP, to explain to the specific journalists what the correct facts are.
6. Findings suggest that the basic selection criteria used by the online journalists interviewed in Greece for choosing hyperlinks to material provided by the EP are the extent to which the links add to the story, lead to material that could be easily understood by the readers, and to material with domestic interest. In addition, the basic selection criteria for online journalists for choosing the videos for EP news stories are the extent to which the video is interesting according to their journalistic news selection criteria, is provided in the Greek language (or subtitled), and is ready-edited (in technical terms)—from the EP press service.

The EPLO officers in Greece, acknowledge that such kind of online elements are important and useful for online journalists and they try to provide such material—as much as they can. However, the main production of such online elements is done again at a central level (whether we talk about videos produced by the EP, or about the material that the hyperlinks lead to). Yet, the need of the Greek online journalists for more material (both in quantitative and qualitative terms) customized for online media, such as hyperlinks and multimedia, is not met.

A potential way of increasing the online elements (hyperlinks to EP material and multimedia provided by the EP) in the relevant news items would be for the EPLO to provide to other stakeholders, and specifically to those who are used as additional sources by journalists in the EP news stories, the relevant material. The hope would be that the journalists would pick up the links from these stakeholders and that there would be an increase in the amount of the relevant online material.

In addition, taking into consideration that most of the videos in the EP news stories in the selected news websites originated from affiliated TV channels (e.g., Mega Channel, ANT1), a remedial activity for the enhancement of the visibility of the videos (provided by the EP) would be for the EPLO officials to develop simultaneously their media relations with the relevant journalists or editors on TV channels.

At the same time, the EPLOs, through their press seminars, could also train and assist online journalists in producing their own video features that could be later embedded in the relevant news stories.

9.2 UK

With the aim of identifying potential ways for communicating the EP more effectively in the UK the following key factors that have been revealed by (a) the interviews with the journalists and (b) the content analysis of the selected news websites should be taken into consideration: (1) the domesticity of the story (relevance to the UK) is the main selection criteria for online journalists when choosing to write a EP news story, (2) domestic analysts are also used as sources when they write EP news stories, (3) social media are part of the online journalists' news gathering practices, (4) domestic analysts are also used by the majority of the journalists as sources when they write about the EP's impact, (5) online journalists in the UK websites under examination are important evaluators of the EP or the MEPs, and (6) (a) the basic criteria for the selection of hyperlinks in online journalists' EP news stories are the extent to which the hyperlinks lead to material with added value for the reader, to official sources, or to material with simpler and concise language and (b) the basic criteria for the selection of a video in an EP news story are the language of the video and the extent to which the video is tailored in a media friendly form.

Drawing on the aforementioned conditions that have to be taken into consideration for the identification of potential ways of communicating the EP more effectively in the UK, the following suggestions can be made:

1. Domesticity of the story is the main selection criteria for online journalists in the UK when choosing to write an EP news story. Thus, it seems necessary that the information and communication material provided by the EPLO in the UK should be as much as possible customized and relevant to the UK and the UK audience.

    However, as emerged from the interviews with the EPLO officer in the UK, the EP information and communication materials are mainly produced in the EP Secretariat in Brussels and the EPLO sends them automatically to their contacts through mail. As it is in the case of Greece, the EPLO faces limitations as far as the customization of the message coming from the EP Secretariat is concerned. The flexibility of manoeuvre rests on the selection by the EPLO of topics that are going to be communicated or not in the UK, since there are not specific media strategies and guidelines for the UK as such, as there are not indeed for any other member state. Since the EPLO in the UK has limited power to customize the information and communication material coming from the EP Secretariat, potential ways of increasing the visibility of the EP through the customization of information would be, similar to the case of Greece, the following:

    The information material regarding the activities undertaken by the local EPLO would be produced by the EPLO officers and meet, by default, the basic news selection criteria of domesticity (either in national or regional level). The EPLO officers could take advantage of that and could relate, when producing the specific information material, these events to the EP's institutional powers (for example, a regional conference might be held in the framework of a directive for environmental protection, or in the framework of a legislative proposal for the increase of investments) and to their potential impact on the citizens. In this way, they would publicize the EP's activities and impact and relate them to the domestic audience (whether at a national or regional level).

    In addition, since—as it is the case in Greece—the EPLO officers do not have the flexibility to change, to a large extent, the information material provided by the EP Secretariat, in order to at least customize it for the domestic audience, it would be useful for them to receive further relevant training in editing techniques. Through this, the EPLO officers could develop and enhance their skills in editing or even in writing attractive—for journalists—headlines (Foster, 2008; Wilcox & Cameron, 2014; Singleton, 2014).

2. According to the relevant findings, domestic analysts are used by the online journalists in the UK as sources when they write EP news stories.

   The EPLO in the UK publishes the institutional communication material coming from the EP Secretariat and sends it automatically through mail to all of their contacts, without any particular selection criteria. The contacts database according to the interviews with the EPLO officer includes a large number of stakeholders who receive the relevant information material.

   As a first step, a potential action for the enhancement of the EP's communication efficiency would be for the EPLO in the UK to identify the domestic analysts who are visible in the media. Then instead of sending information material to every contact included in its database (without having any selection criteria) it could adopt a more targeted media relations policy towards these specific analysts by trying to engage and build relationships with them.

   Another remedial action would be for the EPLO to suggest to journalists (probably during its press seminars) specific analysts that could be used as additional sources when writing EP news stories. The aforementioned tactics become even more necessary if we consider that a key problem of the UK EPLO is that it is really difficult to get the interest of the media themselves.

3. According to the findings from the interviews with the online journalists in the UK, social media are part of the UK online journalists' news gathering practices.

   The EPLO officers in the UK acknowledge the importance of social media as a media relations tool that has an added value, especially for the case of UK where the majority of journalists are online. Thus, the social media are considered as an important channel for the UK EPLO for information and communication purposes. For instance, there is a Twitter account which is operating from the EPLO in the UK, and it is used a lot by the EPLO press officer to chat with journalists or invite them to an EPLO event (especially in the case of the web journalists at a local and regional level who are difficult to approach in other ways).

   On the other hand, as seen in Chap. 7, some of the journalists interviewed in the UK who use social media as news gathering tools, say that they have never been contacted by the EPLO through social media, while they also assess the language in the social media content as apolitical.

   A remedial action for more effective EP communication in this area would be a more personalized social media policy by the EPLO officers (for example, conversation via Twitter) towards more journalists. This policy would use more personalized techniques (such as personal messages, conversation, etc.) in order to build relationships with online journalists; it should be mentioned here that these personalized techniques in social media are really effective techniques for building relationships and engaging with the target audiences (in our case, journalists) (Scott, 2015; Sweeney & Craig, 2011; Singleton, 2014).

4. According to the Table 9.2, which contains research findings from the content analysis of the selected UK news websites related to the news items with an evaluative stance towards the EP, UK online journalists in the websites under

9.2 UK

Table 9.2 Who is evaluating the EP and the MEPs in the selected UK news websites?

Who is evaluating the EP or the MEPs	Number of news items
Non-domestic politician has negative stance towards the EP	1
Journalist has negative stance towards the EP	5
Journalist has a negative stance towards a domestic MEP	8
Non-domestic MEP has a negative stance towards other MEPs	1
Domestic MEP has a negative stance towards other domestic MEP	3
Journalist has a positive stance towards a non-domestic MEP	1
Domestic MEP has a negative stance towards the EP	2
Domestic MEP has a positive stance towards the EP	1
Domestic politician has a negative stance towards the EP	3
Domestic politician has a negative stance towards domestic MEP	2
Other actor in the news item has a negative stance towards domestic MEP	1
Other actor in the news item has a positive stance towards the EP	1
Other actor in the news item has a negative stance towards the EP	2
Domestic MEPs have positive stance towards domestic MEPs	1
Journalist has a positive stance towards a domestic MEP	1

examination are considered as important evaluators of the EP or the MEPs. In addition, campaigners (environmental organizations, broadband network campaigners, agricultural campaigners, fishing groups, etc.) are also emerging actors with an evaluative stance towards the EP or the MEPs.

The EPLO officers in the UK are interested in simply publicizing the EP (and not in promoting it aggressively or via spin) by providing adequate communication material and the available resources for the journalists, who wish to use them. They characterize themselves in this case, as informers and publicists of what the EP does.

However, taking into consideration the fact that (a) online journalists are emerging as important evaluators of the EP, (b) online journalists have assessed as inadequate the source strategy followed by the EPLO, and (c) online journalists have expressed their need for a more aggressive source strategy, it seems that the EPLO should employ a more aggressive and source—promoting strategy.

As it is the case for Greece, one potential remedial activity for increasing the visibility of the positive coverage of the EP and the EP output/impact in the UK, would be for the EPLO Officers to identify the journalists and the media that have a negative evaluative stance towards the EP. Then, in the cases where this negative stance is based on incorrect facts about the EP, to explain to the relevant journalists what the correct facts are. In addition, the EPLO in the UK could further identify specific campaigners that are visible in the media and could adopt a more targeted media relations policy by trying to engage with them and build relationships either through social media or on a more personal level. Similar to the case of Greece, another remedial action would be for the EPLO to suggest to

journalists (probably during its press seminars) specific campaign groups that could be used as additional sources when writing EP news stories.
5. According to the findings of the conducted interviews, basic criteria for the inclusion of hyperlinks (leading to EP material) in UK journalists' EP news stories are the extent to which the hyperlinks lead to material with added value for the reader, to official sources, or material with simpler and concise language. In addition, an important criterion for the inclusion of a video in an EP news story is the language of the video, which has to be in English, also taking into account whether the video is tailored in a media friendly form.

The EPLO officers send website friendly packages to online journalists which include hyperlinks to more material and codes for embedding videos or live coverage of sessions and meetings. However, there is not any pressure from the EPLO towards the online journalists to use the online elements in their stories. In addition, the main production of such online elements is done again at a central level in Brussels (whether we talk about videos produced by the EP or about the material where hyperlinks that accompany information material lead) with not much space for customization.

Thus, taking into consideration the limitation in the customization and changes that the EPLO can make to the information provided by the Brussels Secretariat, a potential way of increasing the number of online elements (hyperlinks to EP material and multimedia provided by the EP) in the relevant news items would be for the EPLO to provide to other stakeholders, and specifically to those who are used as additional sources by journalists in the EP news stories, the relevant material. Again, similar to the case in Greece, the hope would be that journalists would pick up the links from these sources. At the same time the EPLOs, through their press seminars, could also train and assist online journalists in producing their own video features that could be later embedded in the relevant news stories.

9.3 Conclusions Concerning the Identification of Potential Ways of Communicating the EP more Effectively in Greece and in the UK

Based on the aforementioned, a set of potential solutions—remedial activities that could be proposed for the enhancement of the communication performance of the EP in the news websites in the UK and Greece, includes the following:

9.3.1 In the Case of Greece

- The EPLO officers could use the information material they provide regarding the activities undertaken by the local EPLO in order to relate to the EP's institutional

9.3 Conclusions Concerning the Identification of Potential Ways of...

powers and impact. They could also show in more detail how EP actions impact locally. This information material, which by default meets the news selection criteria of domesticity, is more likely to be published or used by journalists.
- Relevant training for the development of effective writing and editing skills should be delivered to the EPLO officers.
- The EPLO could get a different website structure with a specific dedicated section in its website that could function as an online newsroom and could include photos, videos, news releases, feature stories, contact details, news, events, and multimedia in Greek.
- A more personalized social media policy (through, for example, personal messages, tags, etc.) provided by the EPLO officers towards online journalists specifically through the FB account seems also necessary.
- Relevant training of the EPLO officers in Internet and social media communication is also needed.
- Further identification of specific NGOS, think tanks, or other stakeholders that are visible in the news websites in Greece is needed by the EPLO officers, followed by a more targeted media relations policy towards them.
- The EPLO could also propose to journalists (probably during its press seminars) specific stakeholders that could be used as additional sources when writing EP news stories.
- The EPLO could identify the journalists and the media that have a negative evaluative stance towards the EP and in the cases where this negative stance is based on incorrect facts about the EP, try to explain the actual/correct facts.
- The EPLO officers could also provide to other stakeholders, and specifically to those who are used as additional sources by journalists in EP news stories, more relevant online material (hyperlinks to EP material, videos, etc.) so that they could also forward it to journalists.
- The EPLO officers could enhance simultaneously their media relations with relevant TV journalists or editors, since most of the videos in the selected news websites are coming from affiliated TV channels.
- The EPLO officers, through their press seminars, could also train and assist online journalists in producing their own videos that could be later embedded in relevant news stories.

9.3.2 In the Case of the UK

- The EPLO officers could use the information material they provide regarding the activities undertaken by the local EPLO in order to relate them to the EP's institutional powers and impact. They could also show in more detail what is the local impact of the EP actions. As it is in the case of Greece, this information material, which by default meets the news selection criteria of domesticity, is more likely to be published or used by journalists.

- The UK EPLO officers should be offered training programmes for the development of effective writing and editing skills.
- The EPLO in the UK could identify the domestic analysts who are visible in the media and then it could adopt a more targeted media relations policy towards them by trying to engage and build relationships.
- The EPLO in the UK could suggest to journalists (probably during the press seminars that it organizes) specific analysts that could be used as additional sources when they write EP news stories.
- A more personalized social media policy provided by the EPLO officers (for example, conversation via Twitter) towards more journalists seems also necessary.
- The EPLO Officers could identify the journalists and the media that have a negative evaluative stance towards the EP and in the cases where this negative stance is based on incorrect facts about the EP, try to explain to the relevant journalists what the correct facts are.
- The UK EPLO could further identify specific campaigners that are visible in the media and could adopt a more targeted media relations policy by trying to engage with them and build relationships either through social media or in a more personal level.
- The EPLO could suggest to journalists (probably during its press seminars) specific campaign groups that could be used as additional sources when writing EP news stories.
- The EPLO could provide to other stakeholders, and specifically to those who are used as additional sources by journalists in EP news stories, more relevant online material (such as hyperlinks to EP material, videos, etc.) so that they could also forward it to journalists.
- The EPLO officers, through their press seminars, could also train and assist online journalists in producing their own video features that could be later embedded in relevant news stories.

A consideration in greater detail of the practical problems that might arise in the effort to implement the remedial actions identified here, together with a critical analysis of their likelihood of being realized, given the political realities and limitation within the Parliament and the EU will be provided in Chap. 10.

References

Bhurji, D. (2012). Skilling up for the future. In S. Waddington (Ed.), *Share this: The social media handbook for PR professionals* (pp. 177–192). John Wiley & Sons.
Foster, J. (2008). *Effective writing skills for public relations* (4th ed.). Kogan Page.
Holtz, S. (2002). *Public relations on the net: Winning strategies to inform and influence the media, the investment community, the government, the public and more* (2nd ed.). AMACOM.
Romo, J. (2012). Pitching using social media. In S. Waddington (Ed.), *Share this: The social media handbook for PR professionals* (pp. 137–144). John Wiley & Sons.

Scott, D. M. (2015). *The new rules of marketing and PR: How to use social media, online video, mobile applications, blogs, news releases, and viral marketing to reach buyers directly* (5th ed.). Wiley.

Singleton, A. (2014). *The PR masterclass – How to develop a public relations strategy that works.* Wiley.

Sweeney, S., & Craig, R. (2011). *Social media for business. 101 ways to grow your business without wasting your time.* Maximum Press.

Wilcox, L. D., & Cameron, G. T. (2014). *Public relations- strategies and tactics* (10th ed.). Pearson Education MUA.

Chapter 10
Critical Analysis of the Potential Ways of Communicating the EP More Efficiently

This chapter aims at identifying potential practical problems that might arise in the implementation of the proposed remedial actions, and at providing an evaluation of their likelihood of being realized, given the political realities within the European Parliament and the EU. The first section of the chapter describes a picture of an EP which is a much more effective communicator with the selected news sites—and which achieves a much higher degree of visibility within them. In the second section, there is an analysis of the barriers which stand in the way of the EP for being an effective communicator. In the last section, there is a critical analysis of the various possibilities for reform, along with the examination of which of them come out at the end as still having potential for working in the "real" as opposed to the "ideal" world.

10.1 The EP as a More Effective Communicator

Based on the findings of the interviews with the online journalists in Greece and in the UK, the EP would be a much more effective communicator with the selected news websites and would achieve a much higher visibility within them, if the following conditions are met:

10.1.1 An Institution with a Communication Strategy Customized for News Websites

Journalists, according to the findings of the semi-structured interviews, have expressed their need for more material coming from the EPLOs and specifically material that fits the news websites' media logic (e.g. hyperlinks, videos, and infographics). In addition, journalists would like to receive material from the

EPLOs on a regular basis, at a faster pace and with a better fit with the media logic of the news websites. Journalists would also prefer to have the most updated information possible from the EPLOs, especially when things change at the last moment (e.g. the programme, the agenda of a plenary session, or a press conference); it is really crucial for online journalists who work under heavy pressure and want to be in real time.

Last but not least, online journalists also want the EPLOs to customize their communication approach within an online news mentality, by providing for example fast and not necessarily complete information, since news websites often want something fast which they can add to and fill out later. Thus, they would like to have a provision of material by their side that could fit the 24/7 news cycle that news websites follow.

10.1.2 An Institution that Applies (Via the EPLOs) a More Aggressive Source Strategy towards Online Journalists

Journalists in both countries, according to the findings of their interviews, would like to be approached, more frequently, by the EPLO and be notified, in a more personal way (e.g. by receiving a call), for EP news or for forthcoming EPLO events.

10.1.3 An Institution that Does More to Facilitate Contacts Between Online Journalists and MEPs or High-Profile EP Executives

Journalists would also like the EPLO to enhance its facilitation and mediation role in the arrangement, for example, of interviews with high-profile executives, without journalists needing to arrange (and thus contacting their office) these interviews by themselves. In the same vein, journalists also want the EPLOs to invite more often senior officials and other key people from the EP to their states in order to create direct contacts with them, develop their networks, and have discussions that could initiate EP news stories.

10.1.4 An Institution that Provides Information Customized for Domestic Audiences

Since the basic news selection criterion for journalists when writing EP stories, as seen in Chap. 8, is the degree of domesticity of the story, the EP would be a more effective communicator if it could provide material adequately customized in order to be relevant and more attractive to the domestic audience in the countries under examination. The EP information could be customized not only at a country level but at a regional level as well, so that it could have greater relevance with the citizens of the specific region.

10.1.5 An Institution with the EPLO Website Structured in an Online Newsroom Format

Online journalists, in their interviews, have also stressed the need for improving the EPLOs' website, by suggesting that it should get a more journalistic perspective and become more like a news agency providing every type of material (news, events, agenda, photos, videos, multimedia, etc.) in the relevant domestic language and in a non-stop flow of news.

10.1.6 Conclusion

According to the aforementioned, the EP ideally would be a much more effective communicator with the selected news websites and would achieve a much higher visibility within them, if it had a communication strategy specifically customized for news websites.

Through this online communication strategy, the EP would provide on a regular basis and at a faster pace material that fits the news websites' media logic (e.g. hyperlinks, videos, and infographics). The basic characteristic of this strategy would be an online news mentality according to which the EP would provide fast and not necessarily complete information, since news websites often want to be the first to break initial details of stories and then build them up as more information becomes available. This online communication strategy would necessitate the EPLOs (e.g. in the case of Greece) to create a different structure for their websites, for instance, an online newsroom structure providing different types of material (news, events, agenda, photos, videos, multimedia, etc.) in the relevant domestic language and provided in a non-stop flow.

In addition, the EP ideally would be a much more effective communicator with the selected news websites and would achieve a much higher visibility within them, if it could exercise a more aggressive source strategy towards online journalists, since journalists would like to be approached and notified, in a more personal way (e.g. receiving a call), in order to be informed about EP news or about forthcoming EPLO events. This aggressive source strategy could also be exercised through social media, which are used as news gathering tools by the interviewed online journalists.

Another characteristic that would make the EP ideally a much more effective communicator with the selected news websites and would achieve a much higher visibility within them would be the provision of information customized for domestic audiences in order to be attractive to them, since the basic news selection criterion for the interviewed journalists is domesticity.

Last but not least, the EP would become a much more effective communicator if the EPLOs would take on a more active role in order to facilitate contacts between journalists and MEPs and were also making more of an effort to invite EP senior officials to the relevant states.

10.2 Barriers in the Way of the EP Becoming a More Effective Communicator

However, the findings of the interviews have revealed certain barriers and limitations that stand in the way of the EP becoming a much more effective communicator with the selected news websites and achieving a much higher visibility within them. These barriers are discussed in the following sections.

10.2.1 Institutional Mind-Sets

Despite the fact that journalists would like a more aggressive source strategy, the EPLO's officers in both countries do not implement such strategies because they consider it as spin doctoring. They argue that they have to maintain (secure) the credibility of the EP as an institution and they believe that if they always ask for journalists' attention, the EP will lose its credibility as a source.

Thus, it could be argued that this institutional understanding of the function of EP news communication, which promotes a culture of impartiality and neutrality—and which has also been identified by other scholars (Valentini, 2013; Statham, 2010), is still part of the institutional mind-set of the EPLO officers and still stands in the way of implementing more aggressive source strategies that could enhance the visibility of the EP in the news websites. In the same vein, it could also be argued that this specific institutional understanding of the function of news communication could be blamed for the lack of any communication strategy specifically for news websites, as it has been seen in Chap. 8 (a strategy that would take into consideration specific online journalists' needs).

Last but not least, the blocking of innovative ideas, concerning the communication and media relations performance of the EP, from within the parliament's internal decision-making machinery that has been identified by scholars such as Anderson and McLeod (2004) is another fact indicative of the institutional mind-sets in the EP.

10.2.2 Barriers Deriving from Institutional Characteristics

Barriers that do not allow the EU institutions to become more effective communicators also exist at the organizational and strategic level. More specifically, and as identified by Valentini (2008a), at an organizational level there is a tendency for the EU to propose ideas, but not concrete actions with an explanation of what has to be done in detail to implement the ideas. At a strategic level, despite the fact that relevant EU documents emphasize diversity and the need for tailored communication strategies for publics in different member states, EU institutions try to address these needs in a similar and homogenous way, without taking into consideration the different historical, cultural, political, and social backgrounds in the various member states (Valentini, 2008a). Thus, the fact that the communication strategies of the EU institutions (thus of the EP as well) are not sufficiently tailored to the individual communication needs of the member states also hinders the communication performance of the EP (Valentini, 2008a).

In addition, the EP is an institution with a highly bureaucratic organization, which is also a barrier into its communication efficiency. This problem has been identified by online journalists in the semi-structured interviews, as it was seen in Chap. 7. This bureaucratic organization is a blockage in the way of the identification of political impacts and political angles which will make news stories more attractive and newsworthy and that is a key reason why the EP often fails in its attempts to be used as a source in EU news stories. Furthermore, in this bureaucratic organization, there are different Directorates (DGs) with rivalries among them and different news management policies, a barrier that also hinders the institutional communication efficiency of the EP as a whole (Morgan, 1995; Trenz, 2004; Anderson & McLeod, 2004). As in the case of other EU institutions (Balcytiene et al., 2007), there is probably considerable influence on the exact content and the final wording of EP information and communication material by other specialized staff in other DGs, different to the Communication DG of the EP, which also has an effect in shaping the non-attractive language and nature of EP news communication material.

The centralization of the EP's communication activities, specifically regarding the production of the EP's communication and information material, which does not allow flexibility for the EPLO offices to customize their strategy to local needs, is another institutional barrier in the way of the EP becoming a more effective communicator.

This tendency for EP information to be centrally produced and for the material to be so bland and largely "uninteresting" for journalists is also due to the need of the EP to avoid various types of cultural offences (when the information material is translated across all member states), that could easily occur where the stories are not carefully worded.

10.2.3 Resource Limitations

The limited EP's resources also pose important barriers in the way of the EP becoming a more effective communicator. The resource limitations exist both at the EP level centrally and at the level of the EPLOs, since in many cases the EPLOs are not adequately staffed, given the requirements of the posts and the work that needs to be done. In the case of the European Parliament's Information Office in London, the problems of under-resourcing have long been identified (Anderson & Weymouth, 1999; Anderson & McLeod, 2004), while Valentini (2008b) also pointed out that there are only a few EU press officers in the member states.

In the case of the EPLO in Athens, limitations as regards the personnel have also been identified. The EPLO officers argue that these limitations do not allow them to face adequately the pressures of the daily routine and be as effective as they would like to.

10.2.4 The Competition from Non-Media-Related Tasks in the Daily Routine of EPLO Officials

Another important issue that has been acknowledged in the interviews with the EPLO's communication officers is that a large part of their daily routine is related to monitoring and reporting back to the EP Secretariat, and that reduces the space for news communication activities.

The same problem has also been identified by Valentini (2008b), who noted that the EU press officers in the member states are often engaged in activities not directly linked to media relations since much of their time is spent on monitoring and reporting on national media coverage back to Brussels-based communication personnel. At the same time, she also pointed out that the EU press officers too often spend much of their energy in translating general EU news material into material for national journalists without considering the national media logics and national news values relating to the issues presented.

10.2.5 Insufficient Media and Public Relations Training of the EPLO Officers

Another factor that hinders the effort of the EP to become a much more effective communicator (with the selected news websites) and to achieve a much higher visibility is related to the insufficient media and public relations training of EPLO officers, who acknowledge themselves that they do not have adequate skills for the management of the EPLO's Internet and social media accounts, in order to properly develop their communication potential.

The insufficient media and public relations training of the majority of the officials in DG-COMM (Directorate General for Communication) in the European Parliament has also been raised as an issue in the past by scholars such as Anderson and McLeod (2004).

10.2.6 Barriers Deriving from the Political Nature of the European Parliament

The European Parliament has a unique political nature since it is a multinational assembly, with many languages used that make the debates far from spectacular and attractive due to the inevitable complexity of the translation issues (Baisnée, 2003: 79; Corbett et al., 2011).

The technicality of the issues discussed in the EP in most cases and the way by which the political debates unfold and votes are timed (Corbett et al., 2011; Baisnée, 2003) are factors that do not fit well with the usual criteria of newsworthiness, and thus hinder the visibility of the EP's powers and impact in the media. In addition, the complex cooperation and co-decision procedures followed in the EP have been identified as a major obstacle, as they cannot be understood by the citizens and ordinary voters in the EU (Anderson & Weymouth, 1999). In the same vein, Raeymaeckers et al. (2007) support the view that the EP's lack of a right of initiative (although it can ask the Commission to initiate a proposal) is also a structural factor which impedes the efficient flow of information from the EP to the news media.

The EP does not also fit well with the traditional political "right" and "left" struggle in national terms (Baisnée, 2003). In the same vein, it has been argued that the EP is not a "sexy" parliament in media terms, since—compared to national parliaments—it lacks the cut and thrust of debate between the government and the opposition because the spirit of compromise in the policymaking process of the European Parliament makes it harder to sell to the general public (Corbett et al., 2011).

Last but not least, the political attitude of the MEPs could also be considered as a barrier that does not help the enhancement of the EP's institutional visibility. In many cases, the MEPs are not interested in relating themselves to the EP on a truly European level, but rather prefer to deal with domestic issues, since they are primarily interested in making political careers in their countries.

10.3 Filtering the Various Possibilities for Reform

In both countries (Greece and the UK), it was suggested that the EPLO officers could use the information material they provide regarding the activities undertaken by the local EPLO in order to relate them to the EP's institutional powers and impact. They could also show in more detail how actions of the EP have local impacts. This information material, which by default meets the news selection criterion of domesticity (at a national or regional level), is more likely to be published or used by journalists. This specific remedial activity seems that it could be realized relatively easily, since it does not necessitate a great amount of additional resources, and since the publicizing and promotion of local events is already a task included in the daily routine of the EPLO officers.

Relevant training for the development of more effective news release writing and editing skills of EPLO officers has also been proposed as a remedial action in both countries, while relevant training of the EPLO officers in Athens in the Internet and social media communication has been suggested. In order for these remedial actions to be realized, the EP needs to overcome some existing financial limitations (with regard to the willingness of the EP to fund training costs) and overcome the barrier of its institutional and overly narrow understanding of the function of communication. The scale of the necessary changes in mind-sets, as demonstrated most particularly through the interviews with EP officials, shows that there is only a slight possibility of these specific remedial activities to be realized.

A different website structure was also suggested as a remedial action for improving the visibility of the EP. This new website could support a specific section that would function as an online newsroom and include photos, videos, news releases, feature stories, contact details, news, events, and multimedia without any need for journalists to go to the main website of the EP. Despite the fact that some of the EPLOs in the different member states have slightly different website structures, it should be noted that at the moment there seems to be a general centralized guidance concerning the EPLO websites' structure, which could restrict the ability of specific EPLOs to make changes in their websites. This limitation seems to derive directly from what the interviews have pointed out as a firmly fixed mind-set concerning how information should be presented and the dangers of spin and news promotion.

A more personalized social media policy to be devised and provided by the EPLO officers (e.g. through personal messages and tags) in both countries was also suggested for the building and enhancement of relationships with online journalists. The realization of this specific proposal requires considerable effort and time and would be hindered partially by the institutional mind-sets in the EP and probably by the heavy daily routine of the EPLO officers with regard to non-media-related tasks. A re-prioritization of the tasks that have to be accomplished during the daily routine of the EPLO officers, which would place more emphasis on media-related tasks, could help in realizing this remedial action. The institutional mind-set, however, could not be considered a complete barrier here, at least at a local level, since in both

10.3 Filtering the Various Possibilities for Reform

countries, the EPLO officers already communicate, even on a minor scale, with online journalists.

Another remedial activity that was proposed was related to the identification by the EPLOs of specific NGOS, think tanks, campaign groups, and analysts that are visible in the news websites in Greece and the UK and to whom the EP is directly relevant in a positive sense, followed by a more targeted media relations policy towards them by trying to engage and build relationships either through social media or on a more personal level. The EPLO officers could also provide to the aforementioned stakeholders more relevant online material (hyperlinks to EP material, videos, etc.) so that they could, on their side, also forward it to journalists, thus increasing further the chances of the EP being covered in online news sites. Barriers that may stand in the way of this proposal relate again to the EP's institutional mind-set that promotes a "non-aggressive" strategy of providing information on the parliament's activities and output and the probable continuing reluctance of MEPs to alleviate the resource limitations constraining the EP's communication activities. This reluctance has been evidenced in every EP budget settlement during recent years.

A more feasible solution, which does not necessitate any extra effort, would be for the EPLOs in both countries to propose to journalists (probably during the EP press seminars) specific stakeholders, campaign groups, and analysts that could be used by those journalists as additional sources when writing EP news stories. In both countries, the EPLO could identify the journalists and the media that have a negative evaluative stance towards the EP and in the cases where this negative stance is based on untrue facts about the EP, try to explain, and develop the real facts. It is highly unlikely that such a strategy would change the attitude towards the EP of online news providers such as the UK's Daily Telegraph, but it might at least kill negative stories based entirely on falsehoods, given the claims of such news providers to be accurate in their presentation of "facts". This proposal has the potential to be realized, since it is not in conflict with the non-spinning attitude of the EPLO officers.

Last but not least, a more feasible solution would be for suitably skilled EPLO officers to train and assist those online journalists who lack the necessary skills in producing their own videos about the EP so that they could create and embed "self-made" videos in EP news stories.

Based on the aforementioned, the remedial activities that are more feasible and likely to be realized are (a) the customization of the information material provided by the local EPLOs so that this material would also include more detailed data concerning the EP's powers and impact at a local level, (b) the use of press seminars by EPLO officers for the proposal of specific stakeholders, campaign groups, and analysts to journalists so that they could use them in their stories, and (c) the training—through the press seminars—of journalists in making videos that they could potentially be embedded in an EP story. The strengthening of the EPLOs' ability to defend the EP when news stories are based on untrue facts also seems to be feasible. Besides, Commission representations in member states already do this to some extent, but they are of course approaching the task from within their own institutional framework with primarily Commission-related interests in mind.

Of course, it has to be clarified that this is a modest list of remedies that are actually feasible and that this modesty is a testimony to the power of the well-evidenced mind-sets that journalists see as holding the EP back.

References

Anderson, P. J., & McLeod, A. (2004). The great non-communicator? The mass communication deficit of the European Parliament and its press directorate. *Journal of Common Market Studies, 42*(5), 897–917.
Anderson, P. J., & Weymouth, T. (1999). *Insulting the public? The British press and the European Union*. Longman.
Baisnée, O. (2003). The (non) coverage of the European Parliament. In M. Bond (Ed.), *Europe, parliaments and the media* (pp. 77–104). The Federal Trust for Education and Research.
Balcytiene, A., Raeymaeckers, K., De Bens, E., Vincuniene, A., & Schroder, R. (2007). Understanding the complexity of EU communication: The spokespersons' perspective. In AIM Research Consortium (Ed.), *Understanding the logic of EU reporting from Brussels: Analysis of the interviews with EU correspondents and spokespersons. Adequate information management in Europe-working papers* (Vol. 2, pp. 151–162). Project Verlag.
Corbett, R., Jacobs, F., & Shackleton, M. (2011). *The European Parliament* (8th ed.). John Harper Publishing.
Morgan, D. (1995). British news and European Union news. The Brussels news beat and its problems. *European Journal of Communication, 10*(3), 321–343.
Raeymaeckers, K., Cosijn, L., & Deprez, A. (2007). Reporting the European Union: An analysis of the Brussels press corps and the mechanisms influencing the news flow. *Journalism Practice, 1*(1), 102–119.
Statham, P. (2010). Media performance and Europe's communication deficit: A study of journalists' perceptions. In C. Bee & E. Bozzini (Eds.), *Mapping the European public sphere. Institutions, media and civil society* (pp. 117–139). Ashgate.
Trenz, H. J. (2004). Media coverage on European governance: Exploring the European public sphere in national quality newspapers. *European Journal of Communication, 19*(3), 291–319.
Valentini, C. (2008a). EU communication in the member states: Comparative analysis of Finnish and Italian communication strategies. *International Journal of Strategic Communication, 2*(4), 216–243.
Valentini, C. (2008b). *Promoting the European Union. Comparative analysis of EU communication strategies in Finland and in Italy*. Jyvaskyla University Printing House.
Valentini, C. (2013). Political public relations in the European Union: EU reputation and relationship management under scrutiny. *The Public Relations Journal, 7*(4), 1–22.

Chapter 11
Overall Conclusion

The book aimed to address the challenges of the social legitimacy deficit of the European Parliament in the UK and Greece, by considering it, partially, as a communication deficit. In this respect, a key goal was to identify the relevant inadequacies of the EPs' communication and media relations performance. To this end, the analysis has pointed out and critically discussed the problems that the EP is facing in communicating itself to selected news websites in the UK and Greece and suggested a set of solutions that could be applied with some potential for success.

In particular, the book has examined: (1) issues of legitimacy of the EP in the UK and Greece, with a focus on social legitimacy, (2) issues of media coverage of the EP institutional powers and output in selected news websites in the UK and Greece, (3) issues of the communication and media relation activities of the EP towards news websites journalists in the UK and Greece, and (4) issues regarding the role of the EPLOs in the EP communication activities in the specific states.

In order to address these issues, the empirical investigation tried to answer the following key questions:

RQ1: What is the coverage of the European Parliament's institutional powers and their output in selected news websites in the UK and Greece?
RQ2: What are the problems that the EP faces in communicating its institutional powers and their output to the selected news websites in the UK and Greece?
RQ3: What solutions could be proposed to the EP to enhance its communication performance in relation to the news websites of the UK and Greece and which of these solutions could be applied with some potential for success?

In methodological terms, an examination (both in quantitative and qualitative terms) of the coverage of the EP's institutional powers and output in selected news websites in Greece and in the UK for a routine (non-EP elections period) 2-year period (2011–2013) was conducted by the use of content analysis as a research methodology. In total, 1051 news items relating to the European Parliament were collected from 2 news websites from each country and were analysed, for the 2-year routine period under examination. In addition, an assessment of the EPLO's media relations performance was made, via in-depth semi-structured interviews with online journalists in Greece and in the UK, as well as relevant EPLO officials with direct knowledge of EP communication strategy.

The examination of the EP's online media coverage in the selected news websites in Greece and the UK revealed that the EP is not gaining adequate visibility for its institutional powers and for its output, in the sampled Greek and UK news websites in the period under examination. However, when it gains a degree of visibility, the EP is rather successful in both countries in securing online media coverage with no evaluative stance in the selected news sites, while in the cases where there is an evaluative stance the tone is mainly negative towards MEPs, but positive towards the output of the EP. Besides, the very limited information that is provided in news stories about the EP via online elements such as external hyperlinks to EP material or multimedia is an indicator, inter alia, of the poor relationship between the news websites, or the journalists themselves, and the EP as a content provider.

In the same vein, despite the fact that the facilitation role of both the EPLOs in Greece and the UK has been generally assessed as successful by the online journalists, it seems that the EP is not very effective in specific elements of its media relations with online journalists. The information material it provides (both in written and oral form) does not meet journalists' needs and expectations. Furthermore, the EPLO's source strategy seems to be inadequate, while the EPLO's media relations activities do not always take into consideration the particular journalistic practices of the online journalists in both countries.

The low coverage that the EP has been getting in the selected Greek and British news websites, along with the problems in the media relations performance of the EPLOs in both countries, is due to a series of weaknesses that have been identified and are linked to: (1) the lack of a collective representation or voice for the EP to speak to the media, (2) the institutional and not newsworthy language and nature of EP communication, (3) the limited role of the EPLOs in customizing the information they receive from the EP Secretariat in order to make it adequately interesting for domestic audiences and journalists, (4) the inadequate source strategy and institutional understanding of the EPs' communication function, which promotes a culture of impartiality and neutrality at the expense of a more aggressive source strategy, (5) the fact that the communication strategy of the EPLOs is not greatly in accordance with the media logic of the news websites, (6) the limitations in the personnel in the press service of the EPLOs, (7) the difficulties that the EPLOs is facing in trying to assess the efficiency of some of their media relations activities, (8) the lack of skills for the management of the EPLO's Internet and social media communication, (9) the fact that many tasks of the EPLO's daily routine are related to monitoring and reporting back to the EP Secretariat, instead of developing vital communication activities.

Taking into consideration the aforementioned problems in the EP's communication and media relations performance, potential solutions—remedial activities have been identified for the enhancement of the communication performance of the EP with regard to the news websites in the UK and Greece, such as the customization of the information material provided by the local EPLOs, the training of the staff as regards the Internet and social media communication skills, the development of new methods of communicating EP's information material to domestic online journalists (also by providing greater flexibility to the journalists), the initiation of a more aggressive and targeted—when needed—source strategy, and, overall, the development of a coherent communication and media relations strategy for news websites.

However, the EP has to overcome certain weaknesses and deficiencies that have been analysed on the basis of the substantial and cumulative evidence provided by the interviews with EP officials. A major weakness that has been pointed out is the existence of a deeply ingrained bureaucratic mindset in the EP, which hinders the effectiveness of the EPs' communication strategy and limits its ability to have an impact on the online news media. In addition, other barriers that do not allow the EP to become a more effective communicator derive from the institutional characteristics and the political nature of the EP along with relevant resource limitations.

Notwithstanding the limitations and the factors that may stand in the way of implementing these remedial proposals, some of them seem more feasible in practical terms, namely: the customization of the information material provided by the local EPLOs in order to include more detailed data concerning the EP's powers and impact at a local level, the change in the prioritization of tasks during the daily routine of the EPLO officers with more emphasis on media-related tasks, the use of press seminars by EPLO officers for the suggestion of specific influential stakeholders to journalists so that they could use them in their stories, and the training of journalists in making videos that could be embedded in an EP story.

Overall, this book has provided a targeted assessment of the problems that the EP faces in its communication and media relations performance in two of the most difficult states as far as the communication of its messages is concerned and tried to form a foundation upon which others can build similar comparisons.

Its focus on a small number of prominent, carefully selected websites has been shown to be particularly potent—given, for example, in the case of the UK, the largely pro-EU stance of the Guardian online and the requirement that the BBC's online reporting should be impartial across the range of its coverage—and failures of the EP to secure adequate levels of visibility on such relatively "benign" sites automatically signify serious basic weaknesses in its communication strategy and little else can be tackled until these are dealt with. One of the most important contributions of this study has been to identify those weaknesses, their causes and the likelihood of their being resolved.

Future research may also link these findings to broader developments and critical milestones that followed the period under study, such as the conclusion of the 8-year economic adjustment programme of Greece and, most importantly, the events that have led to the Brexit. In this respect, the findings of the book provide an explanatory framework that could relate the dissatisfaction and scepticism towards the EU institutions to fallacies of their communication strategy that, in turn, might negatively affect some aspects of the EU legitimacy on the long run.

Appendix A

Questions Asked in the Semi-Structured Interviews with Online Journalists in the UK and Greece

Assessment of the information provided to journalists (in written form):

- What kind of information (provided by the EP/EPLO) do you usually use? (e.g. press releases and statements)
- Where do you find the EP information?
- Does the available EP information match your needs as a journalist? Is it newsworthy? (Is it clear, technical, bureaucratic, informational, available, factual, etc.?)
- How do you assess the website of the EP? How do you assess the website of the EPLO in Athens?
- Is there any information provided to you with additional elements for use in an online journalism environment (e.g. hyperlinks, video elements, and infographics)?
- If there is, how do you assess the hyperlinks or multimedia or infographics or any other online element provided?
- Any problems or inadequacies concerning the material provided by the EP?
- What about the period of plenary sessions? Is there a different approach in the material provided by the EP/EPLO?
- What about the information material concerning the EP institutional powers? How would you characterize that?
- What about the information concerning the EP output? How would you characterize that as well? Is there any output reference in the EP material?

Assessment of the oral communication between the EPLO/EP officers and journalists:

- How do you characterize the oral information provided by the EPLO or the EP press officers in press briefings, in conferences, or in other activities, events?
- Do they provide more newsworthy information in their oral communication?
- Do you prefer oral information in comparison to the written one?
- Any problems or inadequacies in this issue?
- What about the period of plenary sessions? Is there a different approach by the EP/EPLO?
- What about the oral information concerning the EP institutional powers? How would you characterize that?
- What about the information concerning the EP output? How would you characterize that as well? Is there any output reference in the EP oral communication?

Assessing the EP/EPLO's support of the journalists' work:

- Have you ever asked for EPLO support when doing your job?
- When do you usually ask for their support?
- Does the EPLO or the EP press service support you when you are doing your job?
- Are they willing to help you?
- Do they provide you with the knowledge, the contacts, and the sources to help you whenever you ask it, in doing your job?
- Any problems or inadequacies in this issue?
- What about the period of plenary sessions? Is there a different approach in the support given by the EP/EPLO? Are they more supportive?
- Are they supportive in helping you write about the EP institutional powers?
- Are they supportive in helping you write for the EP output?

Assessing the EP's "source strategies" performance:

- What is the frequency with which you are contacted by the EPLO when it wants to get its message across and supply you with press statements, or other similar material?
- How this kind of contact is being made?
- How do you evaluate the credibility of the EPLO or the EP press service as a source?
- Is the EPLO a benchmark for you (e.g. your first point of contact) when you want to find something concerning the EP?
- Any problems or inadequacies in this issue?
- What about the period of plenary sessions? Is there a different approach in the "source strategy" developed by the EP/EPLO? (e.g. more intense?)
- Is there a different approach in the "source strategy" developed by the EP/EPLO when writing about the EP institutional powers?
- Is there a different approach in the "source strategy" developed by the EP/EPLO when writing for the EP output?

Assessing the extent to which the media relations between journalists and the EPLO have been created, established, and maintained:

- How do you evaluate your relationship with the EPLO officers or EP communication officers in Brussels?
- Does the EP/EPLO try to create links and relationship with your media outlet?
- What, in your opinion, do you consider a successful EP media relations strategy/policy?
- Any problems or inadequacies in this issue?

Assessing the extent to which the EP takes into consideration overall the characteristics and the working routines in the online journalism:

Does the EP/EPLO overall take into consideration, in its media relations activities, dimensions of the online journalism, such as:

- Modifications in the editorial workflow? (e.g. increased workload and pressure to work and create content for different media platforms)
- Alterations in news gathering practices (e.g. use of Internet as a news gathering tool, social media in the daily practice of the online journalists for gathering information, initiating a story, finding sources)
- Acceleration of temporal patterns of the content production (e.g. increased pressure for online journalists to immediately upload their stories and the "publish-first-and-update-later" routines of the online journalists)
- Any other dimensions that you think the EP media relations should take into consideration specifically for online journalists?

Problems you might face in your media relations with the EP/EPLO:

- What kind of problems do you face with the media relations activities of the EP?
- How do you think that the EP could improve its media relations performance?
- How do you think EP could create better relationships with the online journalists?
- Any changes that you propose?
- Any specific problems concerning the plenary sessions?
- Any specific problems concerning the news stories for the EP institutional powers and output?

EP news production by online journalists—Working routines of journalists
Writing the story

- What are your selection criteria when deciding to write a news story for the EP?
- How do you make your story more attractive and newsworthy?
- What is the framing you give when writing the EP news story?
- Any limitations you face in writing/publishing the EP news story? (e.g. deadlines, space, and media organization)
- What about the period of plenary sessions? Is it more possible to write a story in that period? A different approach in selection criteria of the EP news stories?
- Do you have a different approach when you write about the EP institutional powers or the EP output? (in selecting, writing, making more newsworthy, or framing the story)

Gathering news practices of online journalists

- What are usually your sources when you are writing an EP news story?
- Have you ever used the social media accounts of the European Parliament or of the EPLO as a source or in order to initiate a news story?
- Have you been contacted/or have you ever contacted through social media the EPLO or EP for asking information for a story?
- Is the EPLO a first contact for you when searching for more information?
- How do you evaluate the credibility of the EPLO as a source?
- What about the period of plenary sessions? Do you differentiate your news gathering practices?
- Do you have a different news gathering approach when you write about the EP institutional powers or the EP output? (e.g. sources)
- What kind of sources you use when you write about the output of the EP institutional powers?

Online journalism characteristics

Modifications in the editorial workflow? (e.g. increased workload and pressure to work and create content for different media platforms)

- Do you adapt your story specifically for being published online? If yes, what kind of adaptations you do?
- What is your website policy in hyperlinking practices, use of multimedia, videos, etc.?
- How do you make your hyperlinking and multimedia decisions in an EP news story? (selection criteria)
- Do you take multimedia from the EP/EPLO? How do you evaluate them?
- Why in some cases there might not be any hyperlink or multimedia element in an EP story? What are the factors that stop hyperlinking and multimedia in the EP news stories?
- What about the period of plenary sessions? Do you try more to have such online elements to your story?

Alterations in news gathering practices

- Do you use more the Internet as a news gathering tool?
- Have you ever used the social media accounts of the European Parliament or of the EPLO as a source or in order to initiate a news story?
- Have you been contacted/or have you ever contacted through social media the EPLO or EP for asking information for a story?

Acceleration of temporal patterns of the content production

- Was there ever a "publish-first-and-update-later" logic in an EP news story?
- What was your interaction (if any) with the EP/EPLO at that time?
- What about the period of plenary sessions?
- Is there a different approach when you write about the EP powers or the EP impact? (in the publish-first-and-update later strategy)

Appendix B

Questions for Semi-Structured Interviews with Officers in EPLO's

Assessment of the European Parliament's (EP) coverage in news websites

- What is your communication strategy/policy concerning the EP's coverage in news websites during a routine period? Both in quantitative terms (e.g. amount of news items and patterns of visibility) and qualitative terms (e.g. tone of the coverage and evaluative stances)
- What is the aim of your communication strategy regarding specifically the coverage (e.g. amount of news items, patterns of visibility, and tone) of the European Parliament's powers (legislative powers, budgetary powers, supervisory and scrutiny powers, and system development powers) in news websites?
- What is the aim of your communication strategy regarding the coverage of the European Parliament's powers effectiveness and output, in the news websites?
- Are there any written guidelines or working staff documents specifically for the case of Greece or the UK concerning the EP news websites coverage?
- Is the communication strategy concerning the news websites different, to any extent, from the strategy you have for other media? (e.g. perhaps because of the different format and technological features that news websites provide)
- Do you consider important the fact that there could be additional information provided for the EP in the news websites (e.g. hyperlinks, audiovisual material, and files)
- What kind of techniques or tools you use in order to affect the EP visibility (both in quantitative and qualitative terms) in the news websites?

Assessment of the media relations activities of the EP with journalists in news websites (online journalists)

- Is there a clear EP media relations strategy/policy? What is that? What are the aims of this policy?
- Is there a clear EP media relations strategy for news websites and online journalists?
- What do you consider, from your side, a successful media relations performance? In what cases you consider yourself successful in media relations terms? In what elements of the media relations practice?
- What kind of communication material do you use in order to communicate the European Parliament to the online journalists? Do you have any tools specifically targeted for journalists in the news websites?
- How do you create, maintain, and develop relations with the online journalists?
- Could you describe me the full dissemination process of a message from the EPLO to the news websites (e.g. press release, timing dimension, editing, and proofreading)?
- How do you assess the information material (written or oral) that is available for online journalists?

Difficulties regarding the coverage of the EP in the news websites and the media relations activities for the news websites

- What kind of difficulties (if any) you face in promoting EP coverage in news websites in Greece/UK?
- What kind of difficulties (if any) you face in your media relations activities with journalists in news websites in Greece/UK?

CPSIA information can be obtained
at www.ICGtesting.com
Printed in the USA
BVHW061935240223
659177BV00004B/71